HIGHER EDUCATION:
Who Pays?   Who Gains?

OTHER INTERSTATE BOOKS BY DR. CHAMBERS:

The Campus and the People

Organization, support, and control of higher education in the United States in the 1960's. (82 pp., card covered)

Chance and Choice in Higher Education

A discussion of what should be done to meet the problem of the mushrooming population of college-age young people and how we can go about it. (119 pp., card covered)

The Colleges and the Courts, 1962-1966

An examination of the principal court decisions during these years affecting higher education in the United States. (ix + 326 pp., cloth bound)

M. M. CHAMBERS

School of Education
Indiana University

HIGHER EDUCATION
Who Pays? Who Gains?

FINANCING EDUCATION BEYOND THE HIGH SCHOOL

THE INTERSTATE
Printers & Publishers, Inc.

Danville, Illinois

Copyright © 1968 by
M. M. CHAMBERS

AG69051

Library of Congress
Catalog Card Number: 68-56277

Printed and Published by
THE INTERSTATE
Printers & Publishers, Inc.

Printed in U.S.A.

There are few earthly things more splendid than a University. In these days of broken frontiers and collapsing values—when every future looks somewhat grim, and every ancient foothold has become something of a quagmire, wherever a University stands, it stands and shines; wherever it exists, the free minds of men, urged on to full and fair inquiry, may still bring wisdom into human affairs.

—John Masefield

PREFACE

ONE OF THE MARKS of advancing civilization is the gradual lengthening of the "period of nurture" of the young of the human species.

In primitive societies boys and girls are often put through more or less elaborate pubertal rites which mark their entrance into adulthood in the early teens.

In any "economy of scarcity" it seems necessary for the young to become self-supporting at the earliest possible moment, and to become producers for the family or the tribe, whether it be from the chase or from tending livestock or cultivating and harvesting crops.

As recently as the eighteenth century and even later in Britain and America young boys were commonly apprenticed to tradesmen or shop-keepers at the ages of 12 to 14 and went to live in the household of the master, where they received subsistence in return for their labor. Young girls were similarly employed as domestic servants and in certain trades deemed "women's work." In agricultural work, by which a majority of the population subsisted, small children contributed some help, and boys and girls began to do the work of adults while in early adolescence.

Mere ability to read and write was far from universal. Public schools were almost unknown except in New England. Such elementary schools as were available depended upon private fees and charity. For the great majority of people the outlook was for a life of drudgery, and it was thought the "hewers of wood and drawers of water" needed little or no education and were incapable of benefiting from it in any event.

A tiny élite group, separated from the common herd by economic privilege and social caste, could get elementary education from private tutors, and might pursue secondary and higher education in a few private establishments where fees were high and snobbery rampant. University careers were completed at about the age of 20 or earlier, and boys of the aristocracy often assumed army or navy commissions before the age of majority, or entered political careers and sat in legislative bodies during their twenties.

During the nineteenth century the idea of universal free public elementary education available to all became firmly established in the United States and in Britain and most of the countries of northern and western Europe. In most of our states elementary schooling became an eight-year undertaking extending to about age 14; and hard on its heels came the four-year public high schools to occupy the pupil up to about age 18. Universal secondary education is now almost achieved. Compulsory education statutes in four states[1] have for some years required school attendance to age 18 or until high school graduation.

Into the scene has come the two-year college, for youth aged about 19 and 20 and for adults, already enrolling more than a million students in addition to the estimated 3 million in the first two years of four-year colleges and universities.

The Educational Policies Commission, a respected and respectable voluntary deliberative body with nationwide representation, publicly recommended in 1964 that *at least two years of education beyond high school, with emphasis on intellectual growth, should be made accessible to all high school graduates, tuition-free.*

Meantime the immemorial "economy of scarcity" has become for the United States the "economy of abundance." Mechanization of agriculture has reduced the proportion of farmers and farm workers to 7 per cent of the total labor force, while production of food and fiber continues to exceed all records. Automation in factories and offices has speeded production while abolishing the places of unskilled workers, apprentices, and young persons of deficient education. Apprenticeship has indeed almost vanished, partly on account of restrictive practices of craft labor unions, but mainly because there are few places for untrained or partly-trained craftsmen.

In commerce and the distributive industries, which once provided employment for hordes of cash boys, delivery boys, messenger boys, stock boys, office boys, and other boys, there are no longer jobs for adolescents. The ubiquitous supermarkets, filling stations, and chain stores are organized and automated to the extent that their employees must be adults, of high school education or beyond. The same is true of financial institutions, insurance companies, and the numerous and varied service industries such as automobile repair, appliance repair, cosmetology, and scores of others.

---

[1] Ohio, Oklahoma, Oregon, Utah.

All this adds up to an unprecedented opportunity to elevate the levels of decency, dignity, and humanity in our civilization. The young can be in school up to the age of 20 and beyond, with opportunity to acquire learning hitherto inaccessible to any but a favored few. Adults, largely relieved of age-old drudgery and with a constantly shortening work day and work week, have time to upgrade their education to fit the new conditions of today and tomorrow.

Dismiss any doubt that these changes mean a higher quality of citizenship, a speeded rate of progress in technological and social advance, and a promise of ever greater control by man over his environment and himself.

Education beyond high school has become the concern of every family, of every man and woman. Therefore, the mundane questions of how it is afforded, how it is organized and supported, who pays for it, and who ought to pay for it, are questions of universal concern. This discourse is addressed not especially to economists or to educators, but to all men and women of intelligence and good will who recognize higher education as the great "growth industry" of our time.

M. M. Chambers

Bloomington, Indiana
September, 1968

TABLE OF CONTENTS

LIST OF TABLES

PART ONE

Chapter 1

THE MOVING PANORAMA:
THE PLURALISTIC SYSTEM

"HIGHER EDUCATION" is any formal schooling beyond the high school. Thus it includes "adult education" for persons who are already high school graduates, without regard to their ages or levels of attainment.

The core and heart of the enterprise in the United States consists of some 2,200 institutions called colleges, universities, professional schools, technological institutions, community or junior colleges, and technical or vocational institutes. Some 800 of these are primarily "independent" four-year colleges of liberal arts (and this was the type of establishment that heavily predominated in American higher education until less than a century ago). About 700 are two-year "junior colleges" or "community colleges," four-fifths of which are tax-supported in considerable part by states and their local taxing subdivisions. This type, with comparatively few exceptions, has come into existence within the last half-century, and is currently increasing in number at the rate of 30 or more new institutions each year.

Something more than 200 establishments have, in addition to undergraduate colleges, graduate schools in which doctoral degrees are offered, though not on a large scale in every instance. Generally

3

these also operate several professional and graduate-professional schools, for instruction and research in law, medicine, theology, education, engineering, agriculture, business, dentistry, pharmacy, nursing, medical technology, forestry, veterinary science, home economics, public health, music, fine arts, or others; and thus fully merit the style of "university," definable in one sense as an institution having a college of liberal arts, a graduate school of arts and sciences granting doctoral degrees, and several professional schools. Such an institution is sometimes called a "cosmopolitan university."

The number is increasing too, in large part because some 200 state institutions which originated during the latter half of the nineteenth century as "normal schools" for the education of "common school" teachers have long since evolved into four-year degree-granting "teachers colleges," then into "state colleges" as they added master's degree programs and undergraduate liberal arts departments, thereby becoming "multipurpose" and eventually offering baccalaureate degrees in arts and sciences and, often, in business or agriculture or home economics or technology. Many of the leading establishments of this type have already been properly redesignated "state universities," and several of them are in the early stages of expanding doctoral programs.

Having accounted for three main classes of institutions aggregating about 1,700 in number (with at least one class mounting in numbers rapidly), we can note that the additional 500 include considerable numbers of independent technological and professional schools unconnected with other institutions: three-year Bible schools, two-year independent technical institutes, and occasional other types.

The main impressions to be gained are that in the whole system there is enormous diversity, so that it is impossible to find any two institutions exactly or even nearly identical; that the whole system is expanding at a rapid rate, in numbers of institutions and in total numbers of persons involved (this we shall come to in more detail presently); and that within it there is also a rapid *upgrading* process in which gradually greater proportions of those students who enter at the bottom continue further up the educational ladder, to and beyond the level of the bachelor's degree and into and through the graduate and graduate-professional programs. Thus the most rapid rate of growth, proportionally, is coming to occur at the top levels.

A "still picture" of American higher education today will be badly out of date and inaccurate next year. It can only be conceived as a very complex moving panorama in which the action is swirling. Only in this way can higher education serve its purposes in our time.

An effort to see higher education as it is today will be greatly aided at the outset by observing the numbers of persons involved as students, and getting a few glimpses into the past as well as some reasonably reliable projections into the future. A few simple ratios will be useful: (1) the number of students in relation to the total population at a given time; (2) the number of students in relation to the total population of *college age* (hitherto usually defined as the four-year span, 18-21 inclusive); and (3) the number of students entering college or some further education in relation to the annual crop of high school graduates.

A century ago the total number of college students in the United States was about 50,000, in a total national population of 40 million. One person out of 800 was in college. In 1900 there were 275,000 college students in a population of 76 million. One person out of 250 was in college. In 1966, with roughly 200 million people, we had 6 million in college. One person out of 33 was in college.

This means that the percentage of the total population in college rose from ⅛ of 1 per cent in 1868 to ⅓ of 1 per cent in 1900 to 3 per cent in 1966. Out of 1,000 people of all ages, one was in college a century ago, 4 were in college in 1900, and 30 are in college today.

In terms of the population of *college age*, about 1¼ per cent of those people were in college in 1868; 4 per cent in 1900; and 40 per cent in 1966. In one century the ratio has moved from one in a hundred of college age, to 40 in a hundred.

This is unprecedented anywhere in all human history.

As of 1966, about two-thirds of the some 6 million students above high school level in the United States were in public educational institutions and about one-third in private establishments. This distinction is fundamental, and not a mere "legalism"; and though some well-meaning educators have spoken or written of it as "becoming blurred," it is in fact perfectly sharp, and without comprehending it one would find it difficult to think accurately about the financing of higher education.

A public institution is one whose physical property is owned by the state or other governmental unit, such as a city, county, or other local taxing subdivision. In nearly all cases the governing board of such an institution is itself a public corporation charged with the duty of managing the institution and its property, but controls it in trust for the state; and the state is the owner of the real beneficial interest.

A private institution is one whose physical property is owned by a private corporation, or a partnership or an individual entrepreneur. Nearly all reputable private universities and colleges are now owned and managed by nonprofit charitable corporations, chartered under statutes of their respective states which strictly prohibit any accrual of profits or distribution of assets to any private person or persons. All the states also permit the operation of schools as a business for the private profit of the proprietors, and such schools are properly called proprietary. Less than a century ago many medical schools, law schools, and other independent professional schools were of this type; but the schools at these professional levels have virtually disappeared, though many other proprietary schools continue to operate at the immediate post-high-school level, offering instruction in such specialized fields as clerical and secretarial occupations, mechanical, electrical, and electronic technology, cosmetology, and a variety of others.

With the financing of proprietary institutions this discourse has no concern. To own and operate a school as a private profit-seeking enterprise is neither *ipso facto* unlawful or necessarily reprehensible, and many such schools do indeed supply unfulfilled instructional needs, else they could not exist; but all should understand unmistakably that, in general, students in these schools are expected to pay, and do pay, the full cost of all the instruction or other services they receive, plus an added margin of profit to the proprietors.

In contrast, the students in the nonprofit charitable college or university generally pay somewhat more than half the annual operating costs of the institution in the form of tuition fees and fees for closely related services. In some institutions the proportion is a little less than half, and in some it is much more than half, approaching full cost in cases where the institution is financially weak and has almost no other sources of income.

In the public institutions the students who are residents of the state or local governmental subdivision which owns the physical plant of the school generally pay in the form of tuition and incidental fees only about from 15 to 20 per cent of total annual operating costs. In some important instances, as in the large multi-campus City University of New York, regular full-time undergraduate students are and always have been admitted tuition-free. In California's vast system of public higher education, including the multi-campus University of California, 18 state colleges, and some 75 local public junior colleges, there are no tuition fees, though at the university level "incidental" fees have mounted up to more than $200 per year for residents of the state. A similar situation exists in half a dozen other states whose constitutions or statutes prohibit "tuition fees," but whose state university and college authorities have countenanced the subterfuge of charging modest sums under the guise of "registration fees" or some other equally innocuous name.

A great deal more needs to be said about student fees, and this will be the subject of Chapters 11, 12, and 13. It is briefly mentioned here only for the purpose of giving some clarity to the distinctions between public, private nonprofit, and proprietary institutions of higher education, in their practical financial relations with their respective clienteles. It may appear that the general outline of those relations has bearings on the fact that two-thirds of all students were in public institutions in 1967, and that the trend toward more rapid growth of the public sector than the private sector was continuing apace.

To put it more bluntly, the doctrine that the student should pay half or more of the cost of operating his college or university was past the point of challenge and was already in full retreat except for a minority. It could not be expected to be practicable except for a minority, in view of the widespread commitment to education beyond high school for nearly all high school graduates—as a prerequisite and stimulus to the productivity of industry, to the economic growth of the states and the nation, to the elevation of thought and culture, and to the fulfillment of the quite legitimate and achievable aspirations of free men and women in an open society.

"Diminishing minority" of students is not, however, an absolute term, but only a proportional and comparative one. In the context of 1966 the private colleges and universities had not only more students, but also more money and more property than they had ever had.

Behind them were two decades of unprecedented growth. Currently their enrollments appeared to be increasing at roughly the rate of about 50 per cent every 10 years—while those of the public establishments grew by something like 100 per cent over the same period of time.

Thus within about 20 years the *proportion* of students in private institutions decreased from about 50 per cent to about 34 per cent, but in *absolute numbers* it was doubled. The "swing of the pendulum" toward the public colleges and universities bade fair to continue, but this did not necessarily portend any absolute decline in the nationwide enrollments in the private colleges. This fact is reason for rejoicing. No one would want to sacrifice the pluralism and diversity of American higher education. A monolithic public monopoly in the field is not only unwanted but is impossible under our Federal and state constitutions. Wide freedom to choose one's way of earning a livelihood and to make one's educational and vocational choices is fundamental among the liberties we cherish.

Those who prefer a college lawfully authorized to provide instruction in sectarian religion, and to have its atmosphere and activities permeated with a particular denominational tone, can find what they desire in a private college of their own choice. Affluent families able and willing to pay high fees for the distinctive privileges that go with attendance at the great private universities of national and international renown may do so if they wish. There are, no doubt, a thousand other preferences and prejudices that will maintain a demand for private higher education as far as can be seen into the future.

Limited numbers of prospective students of high academic promise but from economically underprivileged families will be enabled to attend the private colleges of their choice by means of scholarships and other student aids. Private colleges are fully within their rights in granting free tuition and other aids to selected applicants, with preference, for example, to aspirants to the ministry of a particular denomination or to children of pastors of that denomination, if a college is church-supported. Other preferences might be to children of the schools' own alumni, or even to children of their own faculty members. This latter has from one viewpoint the appearance of a very practical and reasonable "fringe benefit" to attract good teachers;

but from another standpoint it has the astounding semblance of making higher education a hereditary privilege.

Enough has been said to illustrate that reputable private colleges can lawfully do many things for their clientele that public colleges and universities can not do. A good private college, to a degree greater than a good public one, is a distinctive clan or club bound by ties of sentiment which guarantee its perpetuation except in the rarest and most untoward circumstances. The "dual system" of higher education is here to stay. Its proportions are changing, but this is no cause for alarm.

The distinctions between public and private educational corporations are simple and clear, and ought not to be befogged, as they often are. The source of their operating funds has little to do with it. The fact that a private corporation receives large subsidies from tax funds does not make it public. The fact that a state university receives large private gifts does not make it private.

The University of Miami is no less private because it receives $4,500 a year from the state of Florida for the education of each of its medical students who is a resident of Florida. Nor does the composition of the governing board have much to do with the public or private character of a college or university. Temple University and the University of Pittsburgh are no less private corporations because one-third of the membership of their respective boards of trustees were appointees of the governor and legislature of Pennsylvania in 1967. Pennsylvania State University is no less a public institution and a state university for all practical purposes, because a majority of its board have long been elected by its alumni and by representatives of local nonpublic agricultural and engineering societies.

The fact that some 20 to 30 of the nation's leading private universities have rapidly come to the point where large fractions of their annual operating income (in some instances half or more) are currently derived from federal tax funds in the form of grants and contracts does not destroy or even modify their character as private corporations. It would be well to avoid speaking of "blurring" of differences, which can only be derived from a superficial view. This is not to say the Federal involvement is without problems and dangers. Some of these are discussed in Chapter 29.

Chapter 2

SOME MACRO-STATISTICS OF HIGHER EDUCATION

HAVING OBSERVED THE OUTLINES of the dual system of higher education, it is now possible to consider some of the quantitative aspects of the total scene with a minimum of confusion.

Of more than 6 million students in 1966, approximately 4 million were in the public sector and about 2 million in the private sector. The total of annual educational and general operating expenses of all the institutions of all types was estimated at about $11 billion.[1] It follows that the grand average annual operating expenditure per student was substantially less than $2,000—perhaps about $1,775.[2] The range, however, was wide. The average per student was as high as $5,000 to $6,000 in medical schools, and as low as $500 in some of the weaker undergraduate colleges and junior colleges.

---

[1] This does not include "auxiliary enterprises," therefore it is smaller than some other widely circulated estimates.

[2] From figures appearing in *Projections of Educational Statistics to 1975-76* (Washington: Government Printing Office, 1966, 113 pp.), it is possible to compute educational and general expenditures per student for 1966-67 as estimated at $1,750, and for 1967-68 at $1,804.

In cases of individual students, the portion of the institutional operating expense for a single advanced doctoral aspirant in the physical or biological sciences or engineering may have in some instances exceeded $10,000 a year, while for a freshman in liberal arts in the same institution it may have been as little as $500.

Perhaps it is also well to introduce at this early point the phenomenon that whenever a college, or a department of instruction, has insufficient students to keep its teaching personnel and its physical facilities maximally occupied, it can induct a marginal number of additional students without incurring any additional institutional operating expense on their behalf; and in such limited number of instances any fees these students pay are "velvet" for the college.

This concept must be reflected upon carefully, however, because the line between underenrollment and overcrowding may not be easy to determine precisely; and the quality and worth of the whole operation can be adversely affected by pushing enrollment to a point where teachers are overloaded and physical facilities in use at highly inconvenient times for students, thus subtly undermining morale.

"Efficiency" in higher education is the subject of Chapter 9, and the whole matter of operating costs per student per year and other "unit costs" of instruction receives attention.

To cling to the macro-figures, observe the fact that of the total of $11 billion of annual operating expenses, parts roughly in proportion respectively to their aggregate student enrollments are attributable to the public and private sectors (more than $7 billion for the former; less than $4 billion for the latter).

The scene is not static, but forever moving. Some concept of the direction and extent of change during the decade prior to 1967 is essential. During that decade the dollar figures were more than tripled, while the student enrollment figures were only slightly more than doubled. It follows that annual operating costs per student-year were increased by approximately half. This is evidence that the "economy of scale" has only limited applications in higher education during a period of simultaneous expansion, upgrading, and additional diversification.

There are ample reasons why operating costs rose faster than student enrollments, and convincing justifications for the continuing rise in operating costs per student-year. These will be examined in more detail in Chapter 24. At this point it is desirable to notice that these trends have been proceeding as indicated. There is no apparent reason to believe that they are about to cease suddenly. That they will go on beyond 1967 seems certain. Their speed may or may not be somewhat decelerated within the ensuing 10 years, but not on any massive scale.

With slightly more than half of each annual crop of high school graduates going on to college or some type of further formal education in 1967, it appears that we are only a little beyond the mid-point in progress toward universal higher education.

Lest this be hastily dismissed as a visionary concept, observe that in California, with 19 million people—nearly one tenth of the nation's population—, more than 80 per cent of each year's high school graduates were going on in 1965. Prophetic was the clarion pronouncement of the Educational Policies Commission in January 1964 that opportunity for at least two years of formal education above high school, with emphasis on intellectual growth, should be accessible to every high school graduate, tuition-free. This is not only possible, but wholly desirable and inevitable.

Statistics of births during the 20 years preceding 1967 made it possible to predict with considerable accuracy an unprecedented level of enrollments in higher education in the late-middle Sixties. Up to at least 18 years ahead, it is not necessary to project birth rates—an enterprise that is full of hazard. The children who will be aged 18 and ready for college in 1977 had been born in 1959 and were aged 8 and enrolled in the third grade of elementary schools in 1967. They were already "present and accounted for." They had been weighed, measured, tested, and counted. Their numbers would be diminished only slightly by 1977.

The major variable is the percentage of these youth who go beyond high school each year. Indications are overwhelming that the percentage will approach 75, 80, perhaps more, nationwide, as it had already done in California and a few other states by 1967.

This will mean the decade 1967-77 will witness another doubling or near-doubling of students above high school; a tripling or more of total annual operating costs of the aggregate higher educational enterprise; and a probable rise of more than 50 per cent in annual operating costs per student-year.

This might be an overexpansive prospect for a static or declining national economy. But there is every reason to suppose that
our national economy will continue to grow—that the productivity
of our manpower will increase, and that the gross national product as
measured in reasonably stable dollars will be larger each year than ever
before. It was $760 billion at the beginning of 1967, and credible
predictions foretold that it would probably reach $1,000 billion by
1975.

This affords opportunity to look at the ratio between aggregate
annual operating expenses of higher education and the gross national
product. For decades prior to the early Sixties this ratio hovered
around 1 per cent, so that when, for example, the one was $5 billion
the other was $500 billion. In the Sixties the ratio began to rise, so
that in 1967 it could be said to be close to 1½ per cent. By 1975 it
will reach 2½ per cent, the ratio between roughly $25 billion and
$1,000 billion. (The $25 billion will represent somewhat more than a
tripling of aggregate operating costs of about $7½ billion for 1965.

Thus over a period of a dozen years or so, the percentage of the
gross national product devoted to the operation of higher education
will have gone up from the long-accustomed 1 per cent to 2½ per
cent. These dozen years from 1963 to 1975 cover a period of rapid
technological development, of great economic growth, of vast increase
in the relevance of higher education, and of huge expansion of the
availability of this education. It is no cause for wonder that in this
unusual period higher education's claim on the gross national product
should go up to a modest 2½ per cent. It is probably the best
possible investment of resources.

Thus far the discourse has been on annual operating expenses,
and not upon capital outlays. A notion of proportion may be gained
by noting that expenditures for the acquisition of land, buildings, and
equipment for institutions of higher education in the aggregate for
any one year usually equal about one-fifth to one-fourth of the annual
operating expenses. This ratio varies greatly from year to year in
individual institutions, and in the nationwide picture it may be somewhat higher during years of rapid physical expansion than at other
times.

The financing of capital improvements is the subject of Chapters
4 and 5.

Chapter 3

HIGHLIGHTS IN THE HISTORY
OF COLLEGE FINANCE

THE GIFT OF JOHN HARVARD'S LIBRARY was a major event in the early days of Harvard College. Later when 13 clergymen were called together to plan the founding of Yale College, it was agreed that each would bring one volume to be donated to the college library.

These incidents indicated two thoughts: (1) recognition that the library was "the heart of the college," and (2) belief that the material support of the college would come, at least in part, from the generosity of private donors.

All the pre-Revolutionary colleges were private foundations. At that time no one had conceived of the tax-supported state or municipal college or university in this country. No one supposed that a college could properly be anything other than a private charitable corporation.

However, there was no hesitancy in granting tax support on a more or less intermittent basis. Through its first two centuries Harvard frequently received appropriations from the Colony and from several of the towns, and from the Commonwealth of Massachusetts. To this day Harvard is recognized with commendation and encouragement in the Constitution of the Commonwealth, though it no longer receives any tax support from the state or its subdivisions, and no material aid other than the privilege of property-tax exemption, dating from its Charter of 1650.

All the Colonial colleges that have survived continue to be private corporations, with two exceptions: the College of William and Mary became in the early twentieth century a public institution of the Commonwealth of Virginia; and Queen's College (now Rutgers, the State University of New Jersey) became in the mid-twentieth century, after a transition period of several decades, a state university.

The other seven—Harvard, Yale, Princeton, Brown, Dartmouth, Columbia, and Pennsylvania—are ancient private corporations under charters predating the Revolution. Near the end of the eighteenth century and the beginning of the nineteenth, short-lived gestures were made toward transforming King's College in New York (now Columbia University) and the University of Pennsylvania into public institutions of the respective states; but both proved abortive and both reverted quickly to their private character.

All the seven (plus the upstart Cornell, a private corporation founded as a late-comer in the 1860's) constitute the "Ivy League"—the Northeastern élite among the private universities of today. Although they vary considerably in size and wealth, all are relatively heavily endowed, possessed of large and valuable physical plants, and capable of attracting a continuing flow of private benefactions in large volume. They charge student fees higher than those of any other universities in the world. These fees for tuition alone are now in the vicinity of $2,000 for an academic year. Even with such fees, however, probably the average Ivy League students are paying not much more than half the cost of what their universities provide for them—for their facilities are superior (vast and diverse libraries and laboratories) and their faculty salaries are at the top of the pyramid nationally.

All these are "national institutions" in the sense that they are not particularly devoted to serving the people of their respective states, but take care to attract and admit students from every one of the 50 states and from many foreign lands. A few other private universities of roughly equal size and repute have come upon the scene during the fourth quarter of the nineteenth century—Johns Hopkins, Chicago, and Stanford, for example. New York University, after following somewhat ambivalent if not erratic policies for nearly a century and a half, seems recently to have decided definitely to forego the Gallatin idea of service to large numbers of the moderate and low-income families of its urban environment and instead to concentrate upon moving toward the ideal of a rigorously high-quality, high-fee institution having nationwide drawing-power.

There are numerous other private universities rather close to the Ivy League model, but somewhat more recent in their establishment, somewhat smaller in size and wealth, and perhaps predominantly regional in appeal though aiming at nationwide service and repute. Some of these are Rochester, Western Reserve, Duke, Tulane, Vanderbilt, and Washington University, which are nonsectarian, though some of them may have originally had a church connection. We have not mentioned the large private universities which retain some semblance of church-relatedness, though generally to a gradually attenuated degree. Among these are (related to the Methodist Church) Boston University, Syracuse, Northwestern, and University of Southern California. There are several large Roman Catholic universities: Fordham, St. John's, Detroit, Notre Dame, Loyola (one in Chicago, one in New Orleans), St. Louis, Georgetown, and Boston College.

We have also omitted thus far the large private urban universities which have become state institutions in recent years: Buffalo, Houston, Kansas City, and more recently, Chattanooga. Temple University in Philadelphia and the University of Pittsburgh have not become state institutions, but they have received substantial state tax-fund appropriations for many years (Pennsylvania is the only state which directly subsidizes nonsectarian private institutions on a large scale); and beginning in 1965 and 1966 they are the beneficiaries of nearly $10 million each in "tuition-supplement appropriations" specifically to enable them to reduce their student fees to levels approximating those of state universities. Though private corporations, they are newly designated "state-related universities" and, together with the Pennsylvania State University, compose the "Commonwealth Universities Segment" of higher education in Pennsylvania.[1]

The recent failures of several large private urban universities

---

[1] For some of the earlier history of state aid to private colleges in Pennsylvania, see *Collins* v. *Kephart*, 271 Pa. 428, 117 Atl. 440 (1921).

to finance themselves without tax subsidy, when they really undertake
to serve their local urban populations on an adequate scale, constitute
one type of evidence that the bulk of higher educational expansion
from now on will continue to be at the expense of the public, though
benefactions from the private sector of the economy will continue
to be important.

If we pass over the few great private technological institutions
such as M.I.T., Caltech, Carnegie Tech, and Rice University, the
next appropriate grouping is that of roughly 800 "independent"
liberal arts colleges, mostly four-year institutions granting only the
baccalaureate degree, plus only an occasional handful of masters'
degrees. This is the type of institution that was the backbone of
American higher education during most of the nineteenth century.
The regiment is now headed by a dozen or more well-endowed and
prestigious schools such as Oberlin, Carleton, Reed, Swarthmore,
Williams, Hamilton, Bowdoin, Union, Whittier, Knox, Cornell (Iowa),
Beloit, and Antioch, with a long train of others close on their heels,
and with the lengthy procession eventually dwindling down to a
few hundred at the end which are without significant endowment, without much evidence of distinction among their alumni or their faculties,
and leading somewhat precarious lives both financially and academically
(accreditation-wise).

The comparatively well-endowed and academically impeccable
"Seven Sisters" or "Heavenly Seven" colleges for women (now nearly
all coeducational to some extent) must not be overlooked: Barnard,
Bryn Mawr, Mount Holyoke, Radcliffe, Smith, Vassar, and Wellesley.
These are in a sense counterparts of the eight Ivy League universities, which were originally all exclusively for men, but are now in
one way or another coeducational to some degree. Like the Ivy League,
the Heavenly Seven also have their more or less close relatives elsewhere, such as Simmons in Boston, Pembroke in Providence, Goucher
in Baltimore, Mills in California, and Sophie Newcomb at Tulane,
to name only a few.

All the independent liberal arts colleges, though generally growing and flourishing, are finding that they no longer practically preempt
the field as they did in the early and middle nineteenth century.
All the state universities now have large undergraduate colleges of
arts and sciences, sometimes under distinctive and prideful names such

as the University of Michigan's famed "College of Literature, Science, and the Arts."

Lastly, in the private sector there are perhaps 200 private two-year colleges, some of strong denominational orientation, some vocationally oriented, and some of various other types.

In the public sector the history is somewhat shorter, for although the University of Georgia was on paper in 1785 and the University of North Carolina and the University of Vermont both have plausible claims to having been founded in 1791, very little was accomplished until after the turn of the century, and even then the concept of the state university was everywhere embryonic and largely unformed except perhaps at the University of Virginia (1819) and the University of Alabama (1833), until after the Civil War. Ohio University at Athens (1804), Miami University (1809), the University of Michigan (1817), and Indiana University (1820) had all been founded as state institutions, but none received any substantial or regular and dependable state tax appropriations for operating expenses until about 1865. Like the private colleges of the time, they were left largely to shift for themselves and to subsist on student fees, private gifts, and the sacrifices of their ill-paid faculty members. Occasionally the "state universities" received intermittent small appropriations for specific purposes (even to pay debts), and occasionally they might be authorized by statute to resort to the expedient of conducting a lottery to raise funds; but the idea of regular tax support had not yet taken root, and even the lawyers and judges of the day groped unsuccessfully to find clear distinctions between private colleges and public colleges. Speaking of all types, an accurate and amusing historian of higher education has written that the faculties, by teaching for a pittance, were a very large factor in the financing of nineteenth-century colleges and universities.

This continues to be true of the considerable numbers of Roman Catholic colleges operated by the various religious orders, wherein much of the teaching and administrative work is done by priests and sisters—sworn to vows of poverty—, who receive only a modest subsistence. (Many such colleges, however, have added numerous lay teachers in recent years.) It also will continue to be true to some extent for practically all colleges and universities until professional salaries reach a level of parity with those of the other learned professions.

Once the concept of regular tax support became firm (during the last third of the nineteenth century), its volume increased rapidly with the growth of the state universities and colleges. Meantime the enactment by Congress of the Morrill Land-Grant Act of 1862 had started the train of events which led eventually to the existence of 69 land-grant colleges in 48 states, two territories, and Puerto Rico.

Encouraging the founding of "at least one college" in every state, "where, without excluding other classical and scientific studies, and including military training, the leading object shall be" to teach the elements of agriculture and mechanics and prepare "for the ordinary pursuits and professions in life," the Morrill Act was the answer to the dissatisfaction that had already manifested itself against the narrow and rigid classical curriculum and methods of the liberal arts colleges; and while it placed emphasis on practical pursuits, it expressly did not exclude "other classical and scientific studies." This is the prophetic justification of the fact that in nearly half of the states the existing state university (or one founded in the 1860's or 1870's) was designated as the land-grant college, and that each of these is now a comprehensive cosmopolitan state university. In half a dozen of the older states which had no state universities (Pennsylvania and the New England states, except Vermont), the land-grant college became a separate state agricultural college and functioned as such on a rather small scale for half a century or more before it blossomed into a comprehensive state university. In 20 states, each of which already had or subsequently developed a "principal state university," the land-grant college was established as a separate institution located at a distance. Every one of these "separate land-grant colleges" has now become a comprehensive university in its own right, has been given the name of "university" and in some instances, as in Oregon, Montana, and South Dakota, has long been slightly larger and better supported financially than the "separate state university" (in the same state, not a beneficiary of the Morrill Act).

The largest "separate land-grant university" is now Michigan State University at East Lansing. Its enrollment is currently larger, but its tax support somewhat less, than that of the University of

Michigan at Ann Arbor, because the latter has a preponderance of students at the graduate, graduate-professional, and upper-division levels. Michigan State is inaugurating a two-year medical school and is the only "separate land-grant university" having a school of human medicine. Other leading institutions of this type include Purdue University in Indiana, Iowa State University at Ames, Washington State University at Pullman, Oregon State University at Corvallis, Oklahoma State University at Stillwater, Kansas State University at Manhattan, Texas A & M University, and Auburn University in Alabama.

The existence of 69 land-grant colleges in only 51 jurisdictions can be accounted for by the fact that Massachusetts divides the designation between Massachusetts Institute of Technology (a private institution receiving one-third of the proceeds) and the University of Massachusetts (receiving two-thirds); and that 17 states of the Southeast each established a separate land-grant college for Negroes. One of these (West Virginia) has withdrawn the designation from West Virginia State College, so the actual national total of Morrill Land-Grant institutions is now 68.

For the most part the separate land-grant institutions for Negroes are not large by modern standards, nor especially well-financed. Currently the leading ones are Florida Agricultural and Mechanical University at Tallahassee, Southern University in Louisiana, and Virginia State College. There is variation in the extent of racial desegregation accomplished at present.

A method of partial but dependable state tax support of the state colleges and universities, popular and widespread in the late nineteenth century and early twentieth century, was that of the allocated or "earmarked" property tax, or "millage tax" as it was commonly called. By mid-century this type of tax support had disappeared in all but a few states. Most of the states have ceased to use the property tax for any state purposes, leaving its entire proceeds to the local subdivisions; and the cities, counties, and school districts now need in addition substantial state-collected tax funds from the newer types of taxes (sales taxes, income taxes, and others) to enable them to maintain and improve their necessary services.

The more recent history of the roles of state tax support and of Federal contributions is discussed in Chapters 22 through 27 and 29.

PART TWO

Chapter 4

FINANCING CAPITAL IMPROVEMENTS: ACADEMIC FACILITIES

COLLEGES OR UNIVERSITIES require land, buildings, furniture, and equipment for many purposes. In the language of accountants these are called capital assets, and expenditures to purchase or lease them are designated capital outlays.

These matters are sharply distinguished from *operating* expenses.

Land is necessary for the campus, even if the physical facilities of the institution are wholly enclosed in a single multistoried skyscraper.[1] In many instances land is needed and used for esthetic purposes, for practice and experimentation in agriculture and horticulture, and for various purposes related to other types of instruction and research. We do not include farms or urban real estate not used for educational purposes, but acquired and held as a form of investment for endowment funds.

Buildings for educational purposes are of two distinct classes from the viewpoint of their financing and uses: (1) academic or nonresidential buildings (which do not produce any regular income

---

[1] This does not apply if the college property consists only in "air rights," a specified distance above ground possessed by another owner.

from rentals) and (2) non-academic buildings in which a large part of the space is regularly leased to rent-paying tenants, lodgers, or other users.

These latter include dormitories, dining halls, housing for married students and for faculty members, and student-service buildings housing a great variety of facilities such as meeting rooms, dining rooms, snack bars, barbershops, newsstands, lounges, bookstores, and bowling alleys, billiard rooms, handicraft rooms, reading rooms, and other facilities for indoor recreation, and lodging rooms for transient visitors.

In reflecting upon the two classes of uses thus distinguished, one may be excused for recalling that there are factors, some old and some new, tending to break down the distinction or to make its applicability somewhat less than universal. The early pioneer college sometimes possessed only one large building, in which all instruction (except perhaps bird-walks and other field work) took place, and which housed the library and the laboratories (such as they were), and also served as a dormitory for students of both sexes and as a residence for the president and some members of the faculty and their families.

Then there is the relatively recent tendency at some large universities, in the effort to improve the academic atmosphere of large-scale student housing, to construct huge dormitories in which more than a negligible amount of the space is designed for non-income-producing academic purposes, such as a few classrooms and seminar rooms, perhaps a lecture-hall, a small library, a simple demonstration laboratory, and offices as well as living-quarters for a small number of faculty members who, by the mutual preferences of the students and themselves, choose to live and work in that milieu. The "bedroom city" thus acquires some resemblance to several small residential colleges, in which it is hoped the students may have the advantages inherent in the small college as well as those to be had nowhere except in the large university.

These developments may seem to add complexity and difficulty to the accounting, but this certainly is no obstacle if they prove to be educationally superior; and the main distinction between income-producing residential buildings and non-income-producing academic buildings continues to be useful in the domain of financing.

Structures to house classes, seminars, laboratories, libraries, lecture halls, and faculty or administrative offices carry with them no expectation of income from their operation and therefore can not be self-liquidating. Financing their cost is therefore a one-way operation from which the institution expects no return. It must obtain the necessary funds from gifts, legislative appropriations, student fees, or some form of borrowing.

Private colleges or universities often mount fund-raising campaigns to finance the construction of one or several academic buildings rather generally designated. Sometimes, either during such a campaign or unrelated to it, they receive a large gift from a wealthy donor to finance a particular academic building in which he or his representative is to have a hand in the design. Better yet, they sometimes receive such a gift for an academic building with "no strings" on its design, or even a wholly unrestricted gift for whatever academic facilities the institution's board of trustees deems most needful.[2]

The same kinds of windfalls may drop in the lap of a state college or university. For example, a decade ago it was said that nearly half of the entire academic plant of the University of Michigan at Ann Arbor had come from private sources. The incomparable Law Library Building and other law school facilities, the magnificent building housing the Rackham School of Graduate Studies, and the huge Hill Auditorium were a few among the structures thus acquired.

Such benefactions, however, have thus far fallen chiefly upon only a few of the older and more renowned state universities; and it remains to be seen whether the smaller and less known state universities and colleges will eventually receive such a volume of capital giving.

Financing academic buildings from tax sources, in the form of state appropriations (pay-as-you-go) or general obligation state bond issues, has been traditionally the principal method for state institutions. Private institutions do not participate in this type of financing, on

---

[2] The unrestricted gift is preferable because it does not interfere with the institution's own physical plant planning. Proffers of restricted gifts have sometimes been so out of harmony with the programs and plans of the college that they had to be rejected.

account of state constitutional inhibitions, except in a very few states such as Maryland, where there is a long history of intermittent (and usually small) state grants to private colleges for capital purposes. Johns Hopkins University, St. Johns College, and several denominational colleges have been beneficiaries of these state grants in Maryland.

It is fresh in mind however, that the Maryland Court of Appeals in late 1966 held that such grants to one Methodist and two Roman Catholic colleges were void as in violation of the "establishment of religion" clause of the First Amendment to the U.S. Constitution. The same opinion declared that a similar grant to a fourth institution— Hood College—was unaffected, because the facts showed that this college, though nominally connected with a Protestant denomination, was in such a tenuous relationship and so little dominated by the church that it could not be adjudged an establishment of religion. Each such case, thought the court, should be determined on its own particular merits.[3]

Although both adversaries appealed to the Supreme Court of the United States, that tribunal declined to review the decision, and it currently stands as the law in Maryland but has not been declared the law of the United States. What the courts of other states may decide if the issue arises, and whether such a decision may eventually be accepted for review by the highest court of the land, is not now known.

For most state colleges and universities, this outright state appropriation of capital funds was once the principal reliance for additions to the academic plant; but "pay-as-you-go" was always a rather distasteful pill for state legislatures, and in recent years it apparently had to be heavily supplemented by other methods of financing.

The next logical step was toward state bond issues of the "general obligation" variety (pledging the "full faith, credit, and taxing power of the sovereign State") and creating no obligation against the university or college as such. Many of the states, unfortunately, are hampered in this day and age by antiquated limits on state indebtedness imbedded in their constitutions. These close

---

[3] *Horace Mann Society* v. *Board of Public Works of Maryland* (Maryland Court of Appeals, June 2, 1966). *Certiorari* denied by U. S. Supreme Court, 35 *U.S. Law Week* 3174 (November 15, 1966).

limitations have been difficult if not impossible to change and have forced the development of other methods of financing the academic buildings required in these decades of great expansion.

One alternative method is that of creating a "State Building Authority" or special species of public service corporation by some similar name, which is authorized to borrow money without reference to the constitutional limit on state indebtedness, use the proceeds to construct and equip buildings on the state university and college campuses, and allow the institutions to use them for annual rentals sufficient to amortize their cost over a period of years.

The large and populous state of Illinois has recently adopted this device, and the state supreme court has declared the process outlined is constitutional and otherwise lawful.[4] Somewhat similar schemes have been in operation in other states, particularly New York and Georgia, for several years.

A further means of financing non-income-producing academic buildings is by permitting the institution itself, as a public corporation, to borrow by issuing bonds of its own, pledging some specified part of its own future income, and expressly negating any liability of the taxpayers of the state. The part of the institution's future income thus hypothecated is the receipts from student fees for tuition, registration, or incidentals, sometimes including a special fee for the amortization of the cost of one or more buildings. (These fees are distinguished from the charges paid by students for room, board, and related services provided in dormitories, dining halls, and student service buildings which are operated as self-liquidating auxiliary enterprises, with their operating costs as well as the amortizing of their construction costs paid by the students. These are income-producing nonacademic buildings, not here under discussion, but to be noticed soon.)

Financing academic buildings by pledging future student fees to the retirement of institutional bonds is in essence a device to shift the cost of academic plants from the taxpayers of the state (meaning the whole population of the state) to the students—on the

———————
[4] *Electrical Contractors' Association of City of Chicago* v. *Illinois Building Authority*, 33 Ill. 2d 587, 213 N.E. 2d 761 (1966).

seemingly plausible theory that the buildings should be paid for by those who use them.

This theory is not at all in harmony with modern concepts of the utility and indispensability to society of the expansion of higher educational facilities and opportunities. It is not solely the students, but the entire state that is benefited by the expansion of its universities and colleges; and the whole public should pay for the academic plants, through a productive and equitable system of taxation.

Pledging student fees is also unwise and undesirable for many reasons:

1. It hamstrings the growth of student enrollments by tending to exclude able but impecunious prospective applicants who are unable to pay the fees, and runs directly counter to the principle that the simplest and best way to expand opportunities is to make instruction available at low fees or tuition-free in public institutions.

2. It makes any downward revision of fee policies unlikely or impossible for a long period of time (the period of the life of the bonds), the only possibility's being a "refunding" of the indebtedness such as by substituting general obligation bonds of the state, bearing the same rates of interest.

An illustration of how the nervousness of private lending agencies may place obstacles in the path of proposed public policies was provided by events of early September 1967 in New York State. When Anthony J. Travia, president of the Constitutional Convention then in session, advocated, with strong support among the delegates, a clause mandating free tuition for all units of the State University of New York, it appeared that this might become the declared policy of the state. The State University of New York had had in progress for some four years an extensive building program involving some $700 million over a decade, financed by securities issued by the New York Housing Finance Agency and pledging student fees. When on September 7 that agency placed on the market, in accord with its recent practice, a $47 million issue of "State University construction notes," all investment bankers and bond houses dramatically refused to bid. A week later the agency was able to sell a portion of the issue ($27 million) which was the amount necessary to meet its immediately maturing debts. If free tuition becomes the state's policy, the state will, of course, have to provide new funding for the outstanding obligations, as well as for new securities issued to finance the continuing State University building program. Many persons were inclined to believe the private financiers were in collusion to create a panicky impression that the building program would be wrecked, with half-finished structures standing uncompleted, if the free tuition policy were adopted.

3. Perhaps most important of all is the fact that in the bond market, bonds backed only by future student fees are salable only when bearing rates of interest substantially higher than the rates carried by general obligation state bonds. The difference may be as much as ½ of 1 per cent; and on a large bond issue running for 40 years, even a difference of a single decimal may mean what amounts to a loss of millions of dollars of public money.

Among the states now practicing this method, at least in substantial part, for financing academic buildings are Kentucky, West Virginia,[5] South Carolina,[6] and Arizona.

Kentucky is apparently not inhibited by a constitutional limitation on state indebtedness, but has long been obsessed with the idea that the voters of the commonwealth will not approve state bond issues for university buildings. A possible harbinger of change was the overwhelming approval in November 1966 of a state bond issue of $176 million, chiefly for highways, but of which $17 million was earmarked for university construction.

Arizona, frustrated by a very restrictive constitutional limitation, placed a constitutional amendment on the ballot a few years ago, only to see it rejected by popular vote. Without attempting the "State Building Authority" route, the state authorized the Board of Regents of State Universities (governing three institutions) to sell $25 million of tuition fee bonds in late 1966, bearing interest at a rate

---

[5] State ex rel. Board of Governors of West Virginia University v. O'Brien, Secretary of State, 112 W.Va. 88, 94 S.E. 2d 446 (1956).

[6] Arthur v. Byrnes, 224 S.C. 51, 77 S.E. 2d 311 (1953).

only a fine line less than 5 per cent. It should be said for Arizona, however, that the 1967 session of the legislature supplemented the state universities' capital resources substantially by appropriating to them some $12 million for pay-as-you-go capital outlays.

Pay-as-you-go appropriations have much to commend them, as is well-known. They avoid any future interest-bearing obligations against the institutions or the state. They do not conflict with any constitutional limitations on state indebtedness. They do not necessitate payment of "rentals" on the buildings to any state borrowing authority. It is true that there may be some semblance of logic in the assertion that academic buildings usually have a useful life of half a century or more, and that the taxpayers of our day need not be expected to pay in full for facilities that will be used by future generations yet unborn. But this consideration is countervailed by several others:

1. With today's rapid technological and architectural advances, buildings will become obsolete and require extensive remodeling or total replacement more quickly than ever before.

2. Needs for the housing of new academic programs now undefined and uncomprehended will arise in swift sucession. Expansion of the sheer size of the higher educational enterprise will continue for another generation.

3. Even when fully backed by the credit of the state and bearing the lowest possible rates of interest, long-term bonds virtually require "paying twice" for the facilities they are used to finance—that is, amortization of principal and interest over a period of years costs nearly or actually twice the proceeds obtained at the beginning of the period. In its worst light, this enriches the bondholders at the expense of the public— though this bold statement is subject to many qualifications.

It is also true that if inflation of prices continues throughout the period, then the facilities may cost the public no more than they would have cost if construction had been delayed until it had become possible to pay-as-you-go.

All these musings about the comparative merits of borrowing and pay-as-you-go are, however, at least in part based on an unspoken assumption that the state's resources are not sufficient to carry its capital outlay needs on a pay-as-you-go basis. This is a holdover from the "economy of scarcity," now out of place in the "economy of abundance."

It is not to be overlooked that in recent years both private and public colleges and universities have had accessible to them under appropriate circumstances both outright grants and low-interest loans from agencies of the Federal government, covering at least part of the cost of specified types of academic facilities.

Not only are these provided for under the Higher Education Facilities Act of 1963 and in its extension in the Higher Education Act of 1965; they are also found in contemporaneous acts relating especially to facilities for education in the medical and paramedical professions. And in the several other acts of recent years authorizing and funding programs of contracts and grants for university and college research projects and related enterprises, available from more than half a dozen major Federal agencies, a substantial but apparently not precisely ascertainable fraction of the total of Federal funds is lawfully used for necessary new physical facilities. The types of partnership here only hinted at will undoubtedly be continued and expanded.[7]

---

[7] For a somewhat more detailed description and critique of Federal participation in the financing of college plants, see Chapter 29.

Chapter 5

FINANCING INCOME-PRODUCING "NONACADEMIC" BUILDINGS

IN CONTRAST with the plant facilities used wholly for instruction and research, the types of buildings used for residential housing of students and staff members, to house recurrent athletic contests or other public events to which substantial charges are made for admission, and to house the considerable variety of service enterprises often found in a college union building may be "self-liquidating" in the sense that they eventually "pay for themselves." Thus they may be financed merely by borrowing against their own future receipts, without necessitating any invasion of the other resources of the institution, and without the use of gift money or tax money, except perhaps in the form of moderate-interest loans from a governmental agency such as the Community Facilities Administration of the Federal Housing and Home Finance Agency.

Half a century ago college buildings of these types, such as they were, were usually financed in the first instance by the same methods as used for academic buildings; i.e., gift or tax moneys. In the state institutions the charges to student lodgers were kept quite low, and there are at least a few instances where students living in a designated building were granted free lodging.

Dormitory housing of students who came from a distance and did not find lodgings in fraternity houses or other private rooming-houses was early regarded as an inescapable function of a college. Dormitories and dining halls are now universally seen to be as much a part of the educational plant as are classroom buildings. They are exempt from property taxes, though there are even yet a few last-ditch litigated controversies as to whether this privilege should be permitted or denied in the case of housing for married students and their families, or for members of the faculty and staff.

Efforts of operators of private rooming and boarding houses to prevent colleges from requiring all students, or designated classes of them, such as freshmen or women, to live in college-owned housing have been made intermittently in the courts.[1] This is of considerable importance to all institutions maintaining dormitories and dining halls, especially since "self-liquidating" financing has become nearly universal among public institutions as well as private ones. Obviously, the best-laid plans to amortize the cost of a large facility of this kind from its own future income may "gang agley" if for one reason or another the students can desert it at will and leave it half-empty. This is the mundane and practical reason why the college may require its students to reside in college-owned dormitories; and it is power-fully reinforced by educational considerations stemming from the belief that living and dining in safe, sanitary, and well-supervised facilities in the immediate control of the college constitute an essential part of the educational experience of all students except a few in exceptional circumstances, such as those having family homes within commuting distance.

The vast growth of urban universities and of two-year local junior colleges and university branch institutions has already greatly increased the proportion of daily commuters among students and faculty, and this change is undoubtedly a permanent and progressive one. This can not, however, alter the history of the past half-century, nor does it reduce the magnitude of the responsibility for student housing on the part of all institutions, large and small, public and

---

[1] *Pyeatte* v. *Board of Regents of University of Oklahoma* (U.S.D.C.), 102 F.Supp. 407 (1952); *affirmed* in 342 U.S. 936, 72 S.Ct. 567, 96 L.Ed. 696 (1952).

private, that attract varying proportions of their students from beyond the commuting area.

There are many unsettled issues regarding the cost, design, quality,
and optimum operation of student housing at various types of institutions. Some heavily-endowed and prestigious private universities have
received enormous gifts from private benefactors to finance the construction of student living quarters intended to be ideal from many
standpoints, without too much regard for the expense involved. Such
are the Harvard "Houses" and the "Colleges" at Yale—beautiful and
superbly-appointed structures of not too enormous size, having private
rooms for each student and an adjacent "common room" for each
group of three students; as well as ample quarters for one or more
faculty residents known as "fellows" or "masters," and dining rooms,
libraries, and every facility for a small "community of scholarly gentlemen," carrying forward the best of the tradition of the residential
colleges at Oxford and Cambridge.

At the opposite extreme are the ideas of some persons who believe
a college dormitory need be only a bare barracks-type structure
cheaply constructed to enclose the maximum of space at minimum cost,
designed for two or more students in the same small room, or four to
eight students in each small "suite," with communal toilet facilities
on each floor, and withal lacking the amenities such as a degree of
privacy, suppression of noise by carpeting in rooms and corridors,
and esthetic touches such as suitably decorated walls. Buildings of this
type, especially when of vast size, as they are on some large university
campuses, with echoing corridors running in straight lines for hundreds of yards and with identical rooms side by side and piled vertically, unmistakably have some of the aura of a prison cell block or a
"tenement" of the nineteenth century, rather than the atmosphere of a
residence for scholarly persons pursuing serious studies in a thoughtful
manner in a suitable environment.

With the foregoing contrast fresh in mind, the financial implications must be noted. "De luxe" student quarters cost a great deal more
to construct than the barracks-type, and they involve higher operating
costs, and higher charges to the occupants, unless perchance these
quarters are maintained and operated on the income of an endowment.
"Cell-block" dormitories are erected and operated at much less cost
per occupant-capacity, and can afford much lower charges to the stu-

dent-occupants, unless they are designedly managed to produce a margin of profit to be turned into the educational and general funds of the college.

This question of operation aimed toward an annual surplus, as well as the question of the quality of the living quarters, depends in part upon the nature of the college's clientele, now and over the ensuing half-century. Well-endowed and prestigious institutions can survive without squeezing profits out of their student housing; but on the other hand a majority of their students are from affluent families who are accustomed to and expect superior amenities, and who are very little concerned, if at all, as to whether the charges exceed somewhat the cost of the services provided.

But many other private colleges, smaller and in various degrees of financial precariousness, may come to feel that an annual surplus from the operation of the residence and dining facilities is an indispensable source of income, and feel obliged to make the charges "all the market will bear" and the amenities as minimal as can be decently tolerated. What relationship this "pinch" bears to the proverbial student complaints about dormitory food, let us not undertake to say!

Among the state institutions (which also have their share of student discontent) the theory and practice are now practically universal that the residence halls and dining halls, carefully segregated in all accounts as "auxiliary enterprises," are properly managed as "breakeven" operations, so that over the years they are self-supporting—no more, no less. Any small surplus or deficit in one year is expected to be counterbalanced in the next year or some near future. The doctrine is that the charges to students for room and board are kept at levels such that they pay the cost of what they receive, and no more.

This doctrine is derived from the very widespread conviction that the state universities and colleges are for all the people—the deprived as well as the affluent, and that there are more of the former than of the latter. They are also for those in the great middle strata of family incomes, who, depending upon the number of children in the family and many other factors, may be in various degrees of private financial stringency. It seems simple and just that none— not even the wealthy—should pay more than the cost of such housing and feeding services as the institution affords. The university or college is not in the competitive hotel and restaurant business for dollar profits. The enterprise is, indeed, profitable to all concerned in an *educational* sense, not measurable in decimal points.

Some state institutions are able to differentiate slightly their room and board charges according to the quality of the facilities offered—room rents being slightly higher in newer and more modern dormitories than in older and less attractive ones; but in general the differences are not large and are not stressed, because ordinarily any emphasis upon distinctions of economic class is not popular.

An instance of perhaps unique interest may be recalled. The Ohio State University at Columbus during the early Twenties erected a vast "Horseshoe Stadium," financed by popular subscription. Literally acres of space were protected from the weather under the vast sloping banks for stadium seating, which ran from ground-level upward to 50 feet or more in height at the outer curve, where they were supported by a series of quadrangular pillars alternating with narrow open spaces topped with arches, in a sort of neo-Roman effect. All that remained to enclose completely the vast protected area was merely to eliminate the open spaces between the pillars. Nothing was done for several years, and the huge space was virtually unused.

Then in the Depression of the Thirties the expansion of enrollment created an acute need for dormitory space which could be made available to students at low charges. Such space would not need to be of the highest esthetic quality—it would only need to be simple and adequate shelter for students—and it dawned upon the university authorities that by doing some construction work under the vast stadium, they could convert all or selected parts of the unused space into usable housing at minimum cost. This was done at first on a comparatively small scale, and the dormitory was christened "Stadium Towers." Through ensuing years it was enlarged many times to help accommodate successive waves of students at modest charges, and today it could be said the enormous horseshoe is perhaps as much dormitory as stadium, and thousands of students of modest financial resources have been housed within its heavy steel-and-concrete mass.

It is true that state institutions, especially the leading state universities, have many students from affluent families. For those whose tastes demand living quarters and dining facilities superior to those afforded by the university, there are at many such institutions, conveniently adjacent to the campus, one or more luxury residence halls erected and managed for profit by private entrepreneurs. These are supervised in a manner conforming to the current university rules regarding student housing and provide more expensive facilities (such, for example, as swimming pools) and more privacy than are afforded in university-owned dormitories, at charges substantially higher than those made for university-owned housing.

The presence of these "de luxe" accommodations, and especially the models supplied by the very superior English-college-type quarters for students at Harvard, Yale, and other élite private universities, provides an answer to a question often raised by present-day thoughtful observers of the gigantic residential buildings burgeoning everywhere on university and college campuses: Is there any danger of overbuilding? When we reach a stage where enrollments will no longer be increasing at unprecedented rates, will some of these vast structures stand empty?

The answer is no, for at least three compelling reasons which come readily to mind:

1. These buildings are now crowded to what would be at least twice their capacity if we upgraded our standards of college housing to approach those now in practice at Harvard, Yale, and the high-quality private dormitories at many places. By those standards, these buildings are now grossly insufficient, even if no further overall increase in occupancy ever occurred. And in an affluent society—an "economy of abundance"— there is scarcely room for doubt that the adoption of higher standards will be *educationally* profitable and will take place.

2. In the ensuing decade college enrollments will continue to expand at a rapid rate; after that the rate of increase will be somewhat less, but increase will probably go on at least until the end of the century. By that time the newest building of 1967 will be 33 years old, and possibly far advanced in obsolescence, considering the different standards of that day. This will necessitate extensive remodeling or total replacement in many cases.

3. Disregarding for the moment the probability that greatly increasing numbers of young students who have completed two-year courses in home-town junior colleges will swell the influx

into the four-year colleges and universities, by the end of the century the advance of technological change will have so far reduced the daily and yearly hours of work for the bulk of all workers that millions of adults will seek sojourns of greater or lesser duration at colleges and universities, both for cultural refreshment and to keep abreast of the very technological advances that have reduced their former drudgery, but threaten to outdate their present skills.

Half a century ago and earlier the desire for a certain apartness in living and dining quarters on the part of students of upper economic class and the socially élite (and those who imagined themselves as such or overweeningly aspired to become such) was satisfied on many campuses by national fraternity and sorority chapter houses or analogous exclusive local clubhouses. At first the residences were often merely leased, but this was succeeded by an era of building large and ornate houses financed by the organized alumni of the chapter, and this in turn gradually became a practice of constructing dormitory-type houses of still larger size, capable of housing 40, 60, 75, or perhaps 100 students (twice to five times the size of the earlier fraternity chapters), and resembling nothing so much as a small dormitory.

At the same time that the fraternity houses have come to resemble physically the dormitories, the artificial social distinctions between aristocratic "frat men" and plebeian "barbs" have declined, and fraternity membership is no longer anywhere near the status symbol it formerly was. Also, fraternity life has become markedly less rugged (the tortures, endurance tests, and hazardous pranks of "Hell Week" are gone), and at the same time less austere. (The author has seen a member solemnly and tearfully expelled from his chapter for a violation of a house rule such as a ban on alcoholic liquors of any kind within the premises or a ban on the presence of any female above the first floor of the house. It seems that in most houses on most campuses, expulsion of a member by his fraternity for such offenses has long been unheard of and undreamed of.)

Fraternity and sorority houses have more and more tended to be built on university land and sometimes with the aid of loans from the university, and to be occupied at the sufferance of the university. For these reasons, they approach the character of a more or less indistinguishable segment of the university housing system, and even come near to being owned by the university.[2] This trend has occurred partly because of an assumed need for closer university supervision of fraternity life and partly because, in almost all states, chapter houses owned by their own alumni corporations have not been able to obtain the privilege of exemption from property taxes. Nearly always the courts have insisted that a college fraternity is primarily a *social* organization for the convenience and pleasure of its members and have taken a dim view of its pleas that it is in good part for *educational* purposes, or that it is *charitable* by virtue of occasionally absorbing the bills of an impecunious member or of distributing Christmas baskets to the poor.

One large university business officer once blurted that "Taxes are killing fraternities" (something of an exaggeration); and there are indeed signs that this is one of the influences, among many others, that tend to make a fraternity just another unit of university housing, at the expense of its former character as an independent private club.

Concurrently with the expansion of dormitories and fraternity houses came the growth of student personnel services as an administrative function of the college or university. Each residence hall came to have its own counselors (often part-time graduate students or junior faculty members); each fraternity and sorority its housemother and its faculty advisor. The mellow dean of men and the racious dean of women were succeeded by a dean of students or vice president for student affairs who topped a hierarchy of middle-level administrators responsible for such functions as admissions, registration and records, student health service, student financial aids, student activities, and individual counseling services, to say nothing of discipline and social chaperonage.

The dean of students on a large campus indeed has a job at least as demanding and difficult as that of mayor of a sizable city.

---

[2] This was the case in *Alford* v. *Emory University*, 216 Ga. 391, 116 S.E. 2d 596 (1960), where tax exemption was sustained; but to the contrary is *Cornell University* v. *Board of Assessors*, 24 A.D. 2d 526, 250 N.Y.S. 2d 697 (1965).

Chapter 6

FINANCING ANNUAL OPERATIONS

THIS CHAPTER does not deal primarily with the sources of operating income. It is concerned chiefly with aspects of the management and the strategies by which institutions keep their annual operations on a "solvent" basis while expanding them both vertically and horizontally. By "vertically" we mean raising both the level and the quality of instruction and related services. By "horizontally" we mean enlarging the clientele at any particular level or at all levels.

In our money-oriented society, no great discrepancy between annual operating income and annual operating expenses can be tolerated long. The annual operation of a college is expected to be generally an approximately "break-even" enterprise. Large successive annual surpluses (rare almost to the point of nonexistence) can, of course, be plowed back into financing new and better facilities and higher salaries; but even in this event there is a legitimate question as to whether the institution is actually departing from the mode of operation defined by its charter as a charitable corporation.

This question may undercut its entitlement to the privilege of tax-exemption and, in states where the doctrine of "charitable immunity" prevails, may weaken its defenses against liability for torts. Besides, if it possesses an endowment fund to which many donors have contributed,

there is the question of whether operation producing consecutive annual surpluses is not a breach of trust with those who donated to a
charitable corporation in the expectation that their gifts would help
assure that many generations of worthy but needy students would be
assisted in obtaining education at less than its actual cost.

The charitable character of a private college is not destroyed by
the fact that it charges substantial fees for tuition; but if its annual
operation habitually produces large surpluses, it seems to be practically
self-evident that the students are paying for more than is necessary
for their own education, and thus being compelled to contribute financially toward the future enlargement or improvement of the institution
—an unconscionable concept.

Annual operating deficits, especially if substantial and repeated,
spell ruin. Many wealthy and well-disposed prospective donors are
understandably appalled by the idea of making current gifts to pay
institutional debts; and the existence of debt stemming from annual
operating deficits is universally taken to be evidence of "bad management" and tends to repel these donors.

There are two distinct strategies in annual or longer-term budgeting: (1) the counsel of hidebound caution, in which probable income
is estimated with astringent conservatism, and program plans are
shaped accordingly, even if so parsimoniously that this means a stand-
still or a decline in the size or quality of the college; and (2) the counsel
of risk-taking, in which the first consideration is mapping a suitable
program and the probable cost thereof, then followed by a commitment to that program even if its cost exceeds current optimistic estimates of probable income.

The risk of incurring deficits is obvious; but there is a certain
stimulus to fund-raisers, trustees, alumni, current faculty and students,
and all friends of the college, derived from this situation: "We are em-
barked on an excellent program, which represents progress. Now
we *must* get the necessary financial support." This requires courage on
the part of the president and trustees but it is sure to have a certain
appeal for donors if the desirability of the projected program is persuas-
ively presented to them, and becomes a matter of local public knowledge and enthusiasm.

Members of the board of trustees of a private college or university
are generally expected themselves to be large donors, and to attract

other gifts from their affluent friends and associates; hence the importance of their participation in the formulation and final approval of the future program to which the college commits itself not without an element of risk. A good trustee is bold as well as generous.

Members of the governing board of a state institution are not ordinarily expected to make large gifts nor to attract large private donations, though a deserved reputation for integrity and wisdom may have that effect without aggressive effort. More often the board member may be a respected public figure who is influential with the governor and members of the legislature, and thus able to wield influence in favor of adequate annual or biennial operating appropriations of state tax funds.

Unfortunately there has been in the past among educators and politicians in many state capitals a tendency to accept dictation from the incumbent governor as to the maximum sum available for operating expenses of higher education during the next fiscal period, and then "cut the pie" accordingly. That is, under an oversimplified and really inverted concept of the process of determining the distribution of public expenditures, the governor's estimate of the total amount available is the first consideration and is adhered to religiously.

Instead, the prime element should be the formulated needs of the institutions, verified and substantiated in their budget askings (whether separate or "unified"); and if the needs as justified in the budget askings are accepted and credited by the governor, and their total exceeds the sum he estimates will become available, it should then become his duty to recommend additional sources of revenue and actively advocate their enactment by the legislature. In recent years some governors have done this with courage and success.

Others, however, have continued to handcuff themselves by promising "no new taxes" in their election campaigns. There is at least one instance, nevertheless, wherein a prominent governor had the good sense to repudiate his pledge of "no new taxes," in order to provide necessary support for a rapidly developing system of public higher education and other essential functions of his state government.

At this point we do not labor the fact that the decades from 1950 through 1980 are a period of manifold expansion for public higher education, such that the total contribution of the 50 states to the annual operating expenses of this enterprise will inevitably be increased many times over (between 1959 and 1967 they were approximately tripled).

Nor do we dwell here upon the fact that the portion of the gross national product going for the operating support of all higher education, which fluctuated about 1 per cent in former years, will now inevitably go up to 2 or 2½ per cent by 1975, when an estimated $20 to $25 billion [1] will go to that purpose out of an estimated gross annual product of $1,000 billion or more. These matters receive attention in other chapters, especially Chapters 24 and 25.

---

[1] This amount is for "educational and general" annual operating expenses, not including capital outlays and not including "auxiliary enterprises."

Chapter 7

A PRIMER OF COLLEGE ACCOUNTING

RECORDING THE INCOME AND OUTGO of dollars and showing "where the money goes" and what value is obtained for the dollars expended, is one concept of accounting and financial reporting. Kept current and summarized at the end of designated fiscal periods, the records serve many purposes.

In private competitive business where (despite protestations to the contrary) the central aim is profits, accounting is an important instrument of *control* of the enterprise, indicating graphically which divisions or departments are gaining and which declining profit-wise, and furnishing at least *prima facie* evidence as to which might profitably be enlarged and which reduced or eliminated, and, by implication, what new enterprises show most promise of success. Thus the chief finance officer is always a prominent member of the top management team and often becomes the chief executive officer.

In a university or college, either public or private nonprofit, this function of *control* is greatly de-emphasized, on account of the nature and purposes of the enterprise. Normally it is expected that there will never be any dollar profits from the educational and general operation of the institution, or from any of its instructional, research, or service departments. To be sure, great gains accrue to the state, the nation, and the whole society in the form of the input of educated citizens who are larger producers and better consumers than they would otherwise have been; in the form of discoveries that contribute to the hastening of technological advance, the improvement of the public health, and the elevation of the level of well-being of all citizens—relieving drudgery, conquering disease, and diminishing ignorance, superstition, bigotry, and prejudice.

But these great values are hardly measurable precisely in dollars, over a specified fiscal period. They are priceless imponderables. For this reason public support of higher education is in good part an article of faith, but one which has justified itself overwhelmingly again and again and again over centuries—and especially so within the most recent one hundred years.

Some industrious and competent economists have made efforts to quantify in dollars the contribution of higher education to the nation's economic growth in recent decades.[1] This is so nearly an impossible task as to be dismissed by practical men as an "academic" exercise, but the attempt may serve a great public purpose if it succeeds only in drawing more public attention to the crux of the matter, hitherto very largely neglected: the long-existing tendency to emphasize investment in the production of material goods in private industry and to treat as an unloved stepchild public investment in enterprises producing nonmaterial goods such as education, health, recreation, and the arts. As has been convincingly argued by John Kenneth Galbraith, a large shift in this emphasis is now overdue.

Rather than digress further into the economics of higher education, note merely that the accounting of a college or university is not the dominant part of the enterprise. It is distinctly outranked by the imponderable factors. Yet lucid accounting of the dollars is equally indispensable, though not always the heaviest element in *control*. Comprehension of this difference is indubitably growing. An archaic form of college organization has all but disappeared—the type in which the board of trustees had *two* executive officers reporting to it directly: the president and the business manager, the latter often called

---

[1]Example: Theodore W. Schultz, *The Economic Value of Education.* New York: Columbia University Press, 1963, 92 pp. See also William G. Bowen, *Economic Aspects of Education.* Princeton University, 1964, 126 pp.

comptroller. The business officer ran the institution in all its aspects and had the confidence of the board, while the president made the speeches and conducted the chapel exercises, and was regarded as a respected but naïve figurehead, not to be entrusted with financial affairs. The best of university business officers, and indeed virtually all university and college business officers, now report only to and through the president and regard their whole function as distinctly accessory and facilitative of the educational purposes of the institution, not as a means of *control* of the entire enterprise. An academic vice president or dean is usually at least coordinate and sometimes senior in rank to the business officer; and in large institutions there are other vice presidents for student affairs and for public relations and for research and graduate studies, and one or more assistants to the president, who are all members of the top administrative team headed by the president and having the chief business officer as a valued member.

Thus the function of managing business and financial affairs is not an entirely separate domain. Instead it is a realm which should maintain constant *liaison* and cooperation with the other administrative areas (academic affairs, student affairs, college or university relations, advanced studies and research, and sometimes others), not to dominate them but to serve with them as a partner in advancing the purposes of the whole enterprise, and all under the leadership of the president and the governing board. In many institutions it has become customary for the heads of these several administrative functions to confer *en banc* with the president once a week or oftener. Thus, to a limited degree, the central administrative head tends to become a collegial body.

Accounting is an exacting profession. Mastery of its technicalities requires years of study and practice. College and university accounting is a specialized branch, or might perhaps better be called a separate profession. This is because the main body of accounting knowledge and techniques has been developed for use in private business wherein the dollar profits or losses usually quickly determine the fate of the enterprise; whereas in higher education nearly all the institutions are either public or private nonprofit corporations, in whose operation monetary gains to private individuals are interdicted.

The operating funds of colleges or universities are not expended in the hope of private dollar profits, but in the expectation of imponderable gains for the whole society, including the students as well as all other persons. Such expenditures are not properly regarded as unrecoverable costs, but as *investments* in the improvement of human resources for society's well-being and advancement. As such, it has come to be the consensus of economists that they are very productive investments.

Without laboring further at this point, the differences between profit-seeking and nonprofit public or charitable undertakings, it may be noted that in the operation of colleges and universities neither annual deficits nor annual surpluses are normally expected, except perhaps occasionally as a result of fortuitous circumstances; but large parts of the annual operating income normally come from sources such as tax support, private philanthropy, and endowment income, so that the student is in good part the beneficiary of an opportunity provided him by the state for its own good, or by private benefactors through charitable motives.

Accurate and meaningful accounting of funds is no less desirable in a public or charitable establishment than in a private business, though the differences in the mode and spirit of the two types of operations are marked.

Accounting is probably thought of by most laymen as primarily a matter of mathematics, involving the manipulation of numerals, decimals, and dollar symbols. This it is; but it becomes apparent on cursory acquaintance that it is even more a science of *definitions* and *classifications* without which the numerical symbols would be merely confusing or deceptive.

A simple and meaningful groundwork for college and university accounting has been in the process of development on a nation-wide scale for nearly half a century, in an effort spearheaded by certain leading university business officers, such as the late Lloyd Morey of the University of Illinois, William T. Middlebrook of the University of Minnesota, and others. One of the early products was a manual of college and university business management published by the American Council on Education in 1935. Later from the same source appeared the two-volume *College and University Business Administration* in 1952 and 1955. More recently a revision and updating of that landmark work has been in progress.

Eighty per cent of the total operating picture, viewed nationally, consists of "Educational and General Income and Expense." Two other smaller categories are treated separately for the following reasons:

(1) "Auxiliary enterprises" embrace chiefly the operation of dormitories, dining halls, and student union buildings. While indispensable as adjuncts to the educational enterprise, these facilities are generally operated on a business basis with the aim of "breaking even" so as to provide the facilities at reasonable charges to students but without depleting or augmenting the institution's educational operating funds. The category also includes athletic enterprises and a variety of others, such as bookstores. (2) "Student aids" of all kinds are properly treated in a distinct second category because many of them are restricted gifts or revolving funds requiring separate accounting, and they should not be allowed to augment or deplete the general operating funds of the institution.

So far as they can or ought to become fixed in a rapidly changing scene, the basic essentials have thus been made quite clear after long study and agreement by competent and thoughtful practitioners.

The fundamental but simple questions are: "Where does the money come from?" and "Where does the money go?"

Operating Income

On the income side, the largest single source is tax funds, coming from three levels of government—state, Federal, and local, in the order named.

In 1967 the states provided some $3.5 billion, the Federal government some $2 billion (roughly estimated), and the various local subdivisions perhaps $0.5 billion, making a total governmental contribution in the amount of approximately $6 billion—more than half of the aggregate total of annual operating incomes.

Next in magnitude were student fees, estimated at about $2 million. Private gifts were estimated at about $1.5 billion, endowment income at about $0.5 billion, and all other sources at about $1 billion.

State tax fund appropriations were almost wholly for state institutions, save in Pennsylvania, where three large private universities (Temple University, the University of Pittsburgh, and the University of Pennsylvania) received tax subsidies of $20 million, $20 million, and $9 million, respectively, and smaller subsidies went to Drexel Institute of Technology, Lincoln University, and several independent private medical schools. A few other states, including Vermont, Maryland, Alabama, and Florida, appropriated comparatively negligible sums for operating expenses of one or more private institutions.

The Federal contributions, by way of contracts and grants for research, appear to be about equally divided between public and private universities, and quite largely concentrated in some 60 institutions. This means that about 30 of the leading private universities are receiving major fractions of their total operating income from the Federal government—in a few cases more than half. Considerably smaller in volume are the Federal appropriations to the 68 land-grant institutions —only 2 of which are private. There are many other channels of Federal support, including the funding and partial funding of various student aids and capital improvements. Justice can be done to these only in a subsequent separate chapter on the Federal role.

The tax contributions of local governmental units include those for a few municipal universities (principally the City University of New York, and such others as Cincinnati, Akron, Toledo,[2] Louisville, and Topeka), though in all such cases the institutions are also substantially state-aided; and for greater or lesser numbers of local public junior colleges located in more than 30 states. In 23 states these latter also receive appropriations of state tax funds in aid of their operating expenses. Often the state's share is about one-third of the total, as it is in New York State. A third source of local tax funds for higher education is the tax contributions of the counties toward the support of the Federal-state cooperative agricultural extension service, which maintains offices and small staffs at work in most counties.

Of the aggregate of $2 million in student fees, probably somewhat more than half goes to private universities and colleges. Though they have only about half as many students as the public sector, the private institutions maintain fees on the average more than twice as high.

The private colleges are said to receive about 85 per cent of the total of $1.5 million annually of gifts from private sources; and their share of the total of endowment income also amounts to the bulk of it, since only relatively few public universities have substantial endow-

---

[2] The Universities of Akron and Toledo, long municipal institutions, became state universities in 1967. The University of Cincinnati continues as a municipal university, but "state-related."

ment funds. Even within the private sector, however, endowment income is heavily concentrated in about 150 institutions having as much as $10 million or more each in permanent funds; and a majority of all private colleges have only relatively negligible endowments or none whatever (see Chapter 10).

Operating Expenditures

Stated briefly for our present purposes, around 75 per cent of the annual outflow of dollars for operating expenses goes for what accountants call *Educational and General Expense* (with variations according to the character and purposes of different institutions).

Smaller categories which may be pushed aside for our purposes include *Auxiliary Enterprises* (chiefly the operation of residence halls, dining halls, and student-service facilities), because their management usually resembles that of a break-even or limited-profit business undertaking, and they are "self-supporting"; and *Student Aid Funds*, because they are usually restricted gifts or grants or revolving funds that have to be separately accounted for.

Within Educational and General Expense the largest category is that of Instruction and Departmental Research, comprising usually half or more of the whole; and within this nearly all is expense for faculty and staff salaries, though in a chemistry department necessary purchases of expendable supplies may be substantial. Departmental Research is a small portion of instructional expense, allocated for modest research efforts closely related to the teaching activities of individual faculty members, to cover in part minor items such as limited clerical assistance or small supplies. Though comparatively of negligible magnitude, such grants are regarded as important incentives to improved teaching and scholarly productivity.

Libraries, embracing salaries of library staff and purchase of current books and periodicals, are put by college accountants into a separate category using approximately 5 per cent of total Educational and General Expense.

Maintenance and Operation of the physical plant, including heating, lighting, air-conditioning, cleaning, painting, and routine small repairs (not remodeling, which is a capital outlay), comprise a category which is perhaps more constant than any other, usually taking around 16 per cent of Educational and General Expense.

The most elastic of these major categories is called by accountants Administration and General Expense—showing much variation among different sizes and types of institutions because of practical considerations dictating different allocations of items to General Expense. For example, in a very small college all telephone service may be charged to Administration and General Expense, while in a large university this expense will certainly be allocated to the numerous schools, divisions, and departments. In a small college the dean of students and a staff of assistants and counselors may be charged as Administration, while in a large university they will certainly go into General Institutional Expense or perhaps into an entirely separate category as Student Services.

Thus in some small colleges Administration and General Expense have been known to embrace as much as 28 or 30 per cent of Educational and General Expense, and some large universities as little as 2 to 3 per cent; and these figures are useless for purposes of any meaningful comparison.

Two other rubrics that are very erratic, but existing in only a minority of institutions—mostly large universities—, are Extension and Public Services and Organized Research.

Almost all colleges do something in the nature of providing public speakers, consultants, conferences and workshops, extension classes, and the like, but in many instances these activities are "self-supporting" from their own fees. Many larger institutions, however, find it necessary to budget Educational and General funds to statewide networks of extension classes, and in some instances to half a dozen or more branch institutions known as "extension centers" or "university centers" or "regional campuses." These branch outposts often develop and mature rapidly, so that the problem of maintaining a proper place for them in the university accounting picture is a fluid and changing one. (The Cooperative Agricultural Extension Service in the Morrill Act land-grant colleges is usually budgeted separately.)

Organized Research includes major research projects funded by contracts or grants from outside agencies such as departments of the Federal government or private industrial firms or philanthropic foundations. (This should not be confused with the Departmental Research mentioned previously.)

Organized Research is significant in only a small minority of institutions, mostly large universities; but in some of these it involves as much as one-third to one-half or more of the total operating budget. Obviously if this is counted within Educational and General Expense, the percentage norms for the traditional subcategories can be greatly distorted and lose their usefulness as norms.

Another classification that can not be avoided in many large universities is that of Organized Activities in Conjunction with Instructional Departments. These include such things as farms, orchards, gardens, dairy and meat-processing plants and food-preservation plants operated by colleges of agriculture and home economics (not to be confused with agricultural experiment stations); laboratory schools, practice-schools, or demonstration schools operated by colleges of education; and teaching hospitals and clinics operated by medical colleges.

Even among teaching hospitals alone, there are scores of distinctly different financial arrangements that make accurate comparisons extremely difficult. Sometimes the university itself owns and operates the hospital for teaching and research purposes primarily. In many other instances the university has cooperative agreements with one or several public or private hospitals under which it uses their facilities for instruction and research. Sometimes a very large state hospital is operated by the university, largely for instruction and research but partly for the care of indigent "welfare" patients from all parts of the state; and in such cases it is not easy to determine what portion of the hospital expense is properly allocable to the welfare functions of the state and what portion to the educational functions of the university. The scene is further complicated by various "inducement" arrangements permitting professors of medicine and surgery to receive and treat private fee-paying patients in the university facilities in lieu of higher salaries. Enough has been said to indicate that university medical centers often maintain their own financial and accounting procedures practically wholly separate from those of other units of the university, because comparisons with other units would be meaningless in a large degree.

Before paying respects to the notions of interdepartmental and interinstitutional comparability it is necessary to add that the fluidity of accounting classifications is an inescapable result of the flexibility and adaptability of university programs as well as of changing economic and social conditions. An example is the comparatively recent mushrooming of faculty "fringe benefits" and "staff benefits." These are so important that they are now coming to be placed in a separate major category under Educational and General Expense, apart from salaries and wages. Their magnitude in some instances amounts to as much as 20 per cent of salaries.

The foregoing changes and fluidities are sufficient to indicate that the norms of yesterday can not be relied upon as the norms of tomorrow, and that *absolute* numerical comparability among different institutions and departments is utterly impossible and undesirable as well. Only if the operations could be miraculously frozen stiff and encased in ice would it be possible to compute absolutely comparable figures, and probably not even then. Moreover, the diversity of higher education is so great, and its product so imponderable, that comparability in any exact sense is unattainable.

To be sure, excellent purposes are served by constant dedicated efforts of college and university business officers to communicate with each other in associations and conferences and to keep abreast of new developments in programs and procedures, all with the general aim of achieving an ongoing reasonable and practicable approach to comparability of accounting and reporting wherever feasible.

But to believe that this is actually the road toward rigid uniformity of college and university accounting, necessarily implying rigorously uniform college and university programs, would be the acme of näiveté; and the achievement of any such result would be disaster unthinkable. Any aspirations of that kind that actually survive today derive from sources such as a nineteenth century "business mentality" wholly unworthy of present-day businessmen and long since abandoned by most of them, combined with an appalling ignorance of the nature, purposes, functioning, and quality of institutions of higher education. Such notions also stem in part from decades of experience in certain states in which until relatively recently four, five, or more small and embryonic state normal schools or teachers colleges, rigidly single-purpose institutions, existed in presumed competition for state financial support. Few or none had any academic prestige; most were too small and meagerly supported to attract competent business officers; the local constituency of each demanded "equity" in the allocation of operating funds from state taxes—"equity" based on some notion of equal treatment with other similar institutions, and in total ignorance or disregard of the peculiar economic needs or natural resources of each institution's local region—; all were assumed to be alike in purpose and achievement; and "equity" was supposed to be achievable by some mechanical formula which would embrace narrowly fixed limits for faculty-student ratio, faculty salaries, and other expenses.

Now many of these same institutions are multipurpose universities having 3, 5, or 6 colleges within their scope, having 4, 5, 6, 8, 10, 12 thousand students, and all the growing pains of a continuing explosive expansion. The narrow and constrictive bonds of one and two generations ago have been burst by the inexorable logic of history. These institutions are now well on the way to becoming universities in fact (and many of them already have been so named). In today's context, their entitlement to state funds must no longer be based on any outmoded conceptions of "equity," but on the true functions of a multipurpose university—what it is doing and ought to do for its region, for its state, and for the nation. In short, their claim to public support is properly based on the flexible and adaptable and ever-developing *program* of each institution. No two will ever be alike, for no two regions and no two constituencies will ever present the same needs and demands.

This situation is an important part of the reason and the justification for two new developments of much current significance and promise: "program budgeting" in which the requests for dollar support are based as meaningfully as possible on what the institution plans to *accomplish* in its several subdivisions, rather than merely on how many employees it will need or how many multifarious items of hardware and software it will need to buy; and state budgeting based on needs as demonstrated, rather than primarily on the limitations of estimated state revenues. Both these matters will receive fuller attention in Chapter 23.

The purpose of the foregoing is only to provide a most rudimentary sketch of college expenditure accounting and to rein in somewhat the much overplayed idea of uniformity and rigid comparability.

The full story of the quality and productivity of a varied and vast congeries of institutions of higher education can never be told solely in terms of dollars and cents. Nor would any sensible citizen reduce the picture to uniformity even if it were possible, which fortunately it is not.

Chapter 8

ACCOUNTING AND MANAGEMENT

DESPITE THE FACT that public education is not an enterprise aimed at instant dollar profits, accounting is nevertheless an indispensible tool of administration. Although everywhere higher education is known to be productive of high returns, both tangible and intangible, literally no one is able to place a precise value on these returns, in the form of Arabic numerals preceded by dollar signs or followed by percentage symbols; yet it is not to be supposed that the operation can be managed without financial accounting and reporting. Despite the strictures against the fetishes of "comparability" and "equity" as among institutions and departments in the preceding chapter, the functions of accounting continue to be necessary to the operation and continue to be susceptible of improvement and refinement.

Educational accounting is not the profit-and-loss bookkeeping of private business. It is a different kind of accounting—so different that business officers, comptrollers, and auditors, accountants, and book-keepers concerned with the accounting of universities and colleges are to be regarded as members of a separate profession which has its own major principles established and developing, its own manuals and reference books, its own periodical literature, and its own professional associations—regional and national.

The vast and ever-changing complexity of a large university exceeds in diversity the operations of the largest international private business corporations. This fact is too little understood. It means that accounting procedures, if they are to serve their purpose of informing the top administration, the governing board, and the public, must be specially adapted and under flexible development.

In its ongoing informational function, accounting becomes financial reporting. It is evident that the rapidly developing automation of business machines and "computer science" will increase enormously the volume of data that can be analyzed and passed before the eyes of the top management as a basis for decision-making. Any notion, of course, that this will cause decision-making to be easier, or to become automatic, is erroneous and mischievous. The fruits of automated data-processing will be merely the marshaling of more abundant sets of facts upon which decisions can be based. In a sense, decision-making will be harder, for it will involve options that formerly may not have been revealed and were therefore not available. In a sense the augmented availability of data will tend to cause decisions to be wiser because they can be developed from broader factual foundations than ever before. It is this potential of improving the quality of decisions that is the chief promise of automation—not the chimerical hope that it will cause decision-making to be easier or to be automatic, or that by any chance any electronic mechanism can become a substitute for brains, or that any amassing of organized data can usurp the primacy of human discretion and judgment.[1]

Financial reporting to the top administration is not the same as financial reporting to the public—not that anything is to be concealed, but that in the nature of things the documents prepared for wide public distribution must be relatively brief and simple and more attractively reproduced and organized than print-outs from the computer.

This involves a whole complex set of professional skills of which accountants and business officers are hardly expected to be masters.

---

[1] See Francis E. Rourke and Glenn E. Brooks, *The Managerial Revolution in Higher Education*. Baltimore: The Johns Hopkins Press, 1966, 184 pp.

For this purpose their reports need the ministrations of scholarly and accurate newswriters familiar with the forms of presentation that attract, please, and hold the attention of the general reader, of whatever age, sex, or occupation.

Almost every college or university publishes, or at least prepares, an annual financial report. In some cases this is a colorless and dreary offset reproduction of a typed document filled with lengthy lists and tabulations, totally without illustrations of any kind, and perhaps with virtually no translation of the technical terms into language intelligible to the layman. Often it has been grumpily said that such reports "conceal more than they reveal"; and it may be that they have contributed somewhat to the most unfortunate air of suspicion so widely prevalent in the attitudes of legislators, politicians, and other citizens.

On the other hand, many institutions have already made good progress in the art of selecting the major essentials of the annual financial report, interpreting them briefly and clearly in simple and well-styled prose, interspersing them with graphic illustrations and with photographs of the activities to which they appertain, showing students at work in classroom, laboratory, or library. The end product can be, and often is, a not overlarge brochure printed in large format on high-quality paper, characterized by skillful layout, simple sequential organization, and altogether colorful and attractive, which will give almost any reader a sense of satisfaction and pleasure, and leave him with a feeling that he has learned some rudiments of the financing of the university which all citizens should know, and that the spirit of the institution appears to favor full disclosure upon reasonable inquiry.

Production of this result flows from constant and close cooperation between two of the institution's general staff divisions: those of financial affairs and of public relations (often called "university relations"), which fuse their respective professional skills in this project. Extensive circulation of such a document will build broad-based popular good will for the support of the institution.

There are scores of other specific techniques in different phases of the broad function of college accounting, financial reporting, and business management, by means of which that broad function can be kept abreast and ahead of its responsibilities as a major unit in the small galaxy of top-echelon administrative provinces. But the purpose here is not to construct a handbook of techniques. Instead we look for a few general principles. First among these is the maintenance of a progressing knowledge of the type of social institution the offices are serving, and of the major differences between it and other contemporary social agencies, public and private.

Equally important is keeping cognizant of current advances in the whole realm of administrative theory. James G. March and Herbert A. Simon published a discourse in 1958 in which the key concern was with the issue of *inducing contributions from members of the organization*[2] ("contributions" meaning not gifts of money, but "best efforts").

Both Rensis Likert and D. McGregor published separate works in 1960 in which the central interest was in organizational arrangements for *releasing the underutilizd energy of individual members.*[3] Chris Argyris, in a 1964 book, emphasized *the impact of the organization on individual development.*[4]

Manifestly the main thrusts of all these thinkers in administrative theory are similar in their focus on opportunity for each member of the organization to do his best, and to develop his capacities. This is not far from the true purpose of a university, as epitomized in the motto: "Let each become all he is capable of being."

To the extent, then, that leading contemporary management theoreticians are heeded and their precepts put into practice—in business and industrial organizations as well as in universities and colleges—, at least some of the disparities in problems of administration among these disparate types of organizations may tend to disappear. Management theory and practice are not static; they can and do achieve slow change, in business, in government, and in educational administration. This is not to say that the differences engendered by the proprietary profit motive on the one hand and the induce-

---

[2] James G. March, and Herbert A. Simon, *Organizations.* New York: John Wiley, 1958.

[3] Rensis Likert, *New Patterns of Management.* New York: McGraw-Hill, 1960. D. McGregor, *The Human Side of Enterprise.* New York: McGraw-Hill, 1960.

[4] Chris Argyris, *Integrating the Individual and the Organization.* New York: John Wiley, 1964.

ments that are effective in the nonprofit or public sectors on the other hand are about to vanish. But their respective influences can be gradually modified and refined; and this, it seems, is taking place before our eyes.

Thus when the differences between a proprietary business concern and a university or college are stressed, neither can be conceived of as frozen in its present form or habits of thought. The author has concurred in the theme sentence of John D. Millett's admirable little book,[5] wherein he said in effect that the currently accepted principles of business administration, such as they are, have very little application to universities or colleges. It may be added that improvement is occurring in both areas, and that some of the better innovations in thought and practice may be useful in both, so that perchance they may grow slightly to be a little more compatible. Some of the major roots of incompatibility will continue. The author still subscribes to Millett's statement and does not claim to add anything to Millett's thought, being confident that he would agree with the view just stated.

In sum, it behooves college financial administrators, college business managers, and college accountants to recognize that theirs are dynamic professions, requiring constant cognizance of innovations in general administrative theory and in higher educational administrative theory, as well as unending attention to techniques by which better ideas can be made effective. Having let fling with this hortatory homily, let me hasten to say that in my judgment these professions have always done very well, by and large, for American higher education; that today, by and large, they are doing better than ever before; and that the prospect is bright.

Another stimulating concept of the relation between accounting and management is well described by Leon E. Hay, professor of accounting at Indiana University: "In the last ten years it has become apparent that a sizable new breed of accountant has evolved from the cost accountants and budget officers of earlier years. These people answer to the name of management accountants." Their focus is on the future, he says, and the past is of importance only as a guide

---

[5] John D. Millett, *The Academic Community: An Essay on Organization.* New York: McGraw-Hill, 1962, 265 pp.

to the future. Developing this idea, he makes a number of pithy statements: "Information as to legal, political, and social conditions, as well as economic and business conditions (and expected changes in these conditions), is often more important than internal information. . . . Internal information as to employee attitudes and behavior must be considered as well as accounting and statistical information. . . . No more time or money should be spent in obtaining an item of information than the information is expected to worth."[6]

He concludes that the role of the accountant in the planning function "is to foresee the information needed by all levels of management in the planning process and to provide it."

This may be something of a large order for the accountant alone, but certainly it indicates the general direction his thought should pursue. Probably one should assume that the very term "management accounting" implies that persons so engaged will be in frequent conference with other management officers, and that they should be equipped to make a valuable continuing contribution to the sum-total of ongoing research, planning, and policy-making. This is a modern view of the profession of college accounting. It is no constricted view of the accountant as a drudging "bookkeeper" without thought of the larger implications of his work. Gone is that concept—gone as irrevocably as is the spectacle of rows of elderly men in green eyeshades, sitting on high stools, wielding quill pens.

---

[6] Quoted from pages 66 and 69 of *The State Budget Analyst: His Role in a Changing Environment*. (Donald H. Clark, Director, Third Annual NASBO Budget Institute, held at Indiana University, Bloomington, Indiana, August 26-31, 1966.) Chicago: Council of State Governments, 1966, 150 pp. mimeo.

Chapter 9

THE MEANING OF "EFFICIENCY" IN HIGHER EDUCATION

CITIZENS WHO REQUIRE EVIDENCE of economy and efficiency in the operation of colleges and universities demand to be met on their own ground. That is, they want to be shown that this or that institution is producing as much education per dollar expended as some other similar institution in similar circumstances.

In our day education has become sufficiently regimented and bureaucratized so that there are at hand various units ground out of the educational juggernaut which literal minds are content to match with dollars to produce "unit costs." Operating expenses per student per year would be perhaps the crudest of all possible units and be likely to produce obviously meaningless or misleading results unless applied in institutions markedly similar to each other in size, purposes, and methods; or perhaps in comparing whole statewide or nationwide systems so large and varied as to embrace all general types of instruction and research in all general types of institutions, in an approximately equivalent "mix."

The unit can be more refined in a sense, but it can never really be a measure of the actual worth of what goes on. It can, for example, be a "semester credit hour" or a "quarter credit hour." The literal-minded inquirer can be shown that a large university during a fiscal year has turned out some hundreds of thousands of semester credit hours, and that each of its many departments has "produced" an appropriate fraction of the total. The approximate cost of producing each such credit hour can be shown in dollars and cents.

It will usually appear that a credit hour in freshman English costs less than one in comparative literature, and that either costs less than one in biochemistry, while any of these costs substantially less than one in poultry nutrition or human medicine. To make a few more random generalizations: Classical languages are generally much more expensive than history, English, or modern languages, because even in a large university the number of students is so small as to make a very high teacher-student ratio practically unavoidable; in undergraduate liberal arts, the laboratory sciences are a half more costly than the humanities and social sciences, because they require more instructor-time per credit hour, as well as costly items of laboratory equipment, more space per student, and many expendable supplies; instruction in law schools is not especially costly even though the professors are among the highest paid of any, because most of the instruction is in large lecture classes and the faculty-student ratio is relatively low.

Medicine is the most costly of all major professional instruction, because the professors must be highly paid, the laboratories and clinical facilities are expensive to operate, and the accrediting authorities require that most of the instruction be in very small groups, so that the overall instructor-student ratio is very high.

Another sweeping generalization, usually valid and much more important than generally thought, is that the unit cost of instruction varies sharply with its *level*; that is, a credit hour for a freshman or a sophomore usually costs no more than half as much as one for a junior or senior. There are numerous reasons for this. Many institutions are quite "heavy at the bottom"—the freshman class is much larger than any other, and the reduced sophomore class is still much larger than the junior or senior classes. A graph of the enrollment is a broad-based truncated triangle. Even if there is substantial enrollment at the fifth-year and advanced graduate levels, much more than half of the total enrollment is in the freshman and sophomore classes. At that "lower division" level, instruction is generally much less costly for several reasons, depending in part on the type of institution and its organization.

Lower division students can be grouped in classes of any standard size and placed in large lecture sections whose size can be tailored to fit the capacity of the hall. In small colleges much of the teaching is likely to be done by young instructors or junior professors whose academic wings are not fully fledged and whose salaries are modest or skimpy. In large universities perhaps even more of it is by ill-paid half-time graduate assistants, carrying the additional burden of completion of their own advanced studies for doctoral degrees. There has been much acrimonious discussion of the relative advantages of small and large institutions, focused on this very point. Actually there is probably not much to choose between the two types. In either case little of the instruction is carried on by really distinguished senior professors; most of it is by younger people who are somewhere in mid-flight in their careers of graduate study—and this may be no calamity, for it is quite possible that such persons can establish better rapport with young students and accomplish more with instruction at that level. At the small institution some of these half-fledged academicians are likely to be a trifle older than their counterparts at the large university, and more of them have practically given up their ambitions toward becoming distinguished in their fields and decided to settle for careers as patient and pliable pedagogues. No one can say in a blanket statement whether this is good or bad. At the large universities both the young students and the young teachers have the advantage of access to enormous libraries and a large complement of well-equipped laboratories, the presence of distinguished professors on the campus (whom they may seldom see), and the general air of stimulation that is generated in a large and lively academic community with many of its students beyond the bachelor's level in graduate arts and sciences or graduate-professional schools. The "center of maturity" is higher than in the small college. No blanket settlement of these arguments is intended here. They are mentioned and given a little space because they serve to illustrate very well that problems of economy and efficiency in higher education arise from considerations that can not be traced wholly to the books of financial accounting, and that solutions of these problems will probably always be varied and diverse in different institutions.

Incidentally, the rising "center of maturity" occurring in nearly all colleges and universities (but most rapidly and prominently in the large universities), due to the fact that students are continuing longer in college than formerly, and that much larger percentages of them are in the graduate levels, helps to explain why total operating costs are rising considerably faster than student enrollments. This is inescapable because *unit costs* of instruction go up rapidly with the *levels* of instruction, as already noticed. There are other reasons to be observed later.

Upper division instruction (junior and senior years) generally costs about twice as much per credit hour as that in the lower division, because courses are more specialized, classes are generally considerably smaller, professors must be of a somewhat higher level of qualification, and library and laboratory requirements are more costly per student.

Fifth-year study is usually still more expensive per unit, even though it has lost much of its earlier character as graduate work involving a research thesis and become for a vast number of students merely "another year" which is a prerequisite to a teaching credential or to a higher slot in a school-district salary schedule. The unit costs at this level may vary quite widely according to conditions existing in the college or university in a given year and according to the field of study.

Generally in a department of instruction having few master's aspirants the unit costs will be higher, because much professorial time, library and laboratory accessions, and other facilitating factors beyond what the department has been accustomed to providing will come into the picture. This, by the way, is an illustration of the maxim familiar to all men of business, that "every new enterprise is an island of high cost."

On the other hand, a department which has increasing hordes of master's aspirants may, at the almost certain risk of debasing the level and quality of the work somewhat, hold unit costs down by herding them into auditorium-sized classes for much of their instruction and by dispensing with the thesis requirement. An institution may also permit or compel many fifth-year students to enroll in various courses labeled "for graduates and advanced undergraduates"

Table 1. Net state appropriations required at University A and University B, based on semester credit hours produced by class level, with the net cost to the state per semester credit hour at the respective class levels being the same in both institutions.

Class Levels	University A					University B				
	Semester Hours	Per Cent of Total	Net Cost to State			Semester Hours	Per Cent of Total	Net Cost to State		
			Per Hour	Total				Per Hour	Total	
(1)	(2)	(3)	(4)	(5)		(6)	(7)	(8)	(9)	
Freshman–Sophomore	225,593	29%	$ 21.71	$ 4,898,088		402,111	50%	$ 21.71	$ 8,736,343	
Junior–Senior	294,903	38	31.45	9,273,444		286,130	36	31.45	8,998,789	
Master's	94,054	12	53.68	5,048,464		97,944	12	53.68	5,257,634	
Doctoral	44,345	6	173.29	7,684,324		12,272	1.5	173.29	2,126,615	
Graduate–Professor	112,681	15	91.46	10,305,935		4,935	0.5	91.46	451,355	
	771,576	100%		$37,210,255		803,692	100%		$25,570,736	

Source: Adapted from Robert L. Williams, *The Preparation of Requests for Legislative Appropriations.* Chicago: Council of State Governments, 1966, p. 32, 41 pp.

which are in fact filled up to 90 per cent or more with undergraduates and are actually no more than undergraduate courses.

Robert L. Williams of the University of Michigan, in his 1966 study for the Council of State Governments, has illustrated clearly how in two hypothetical midwestern state universities a different "student mix" causes the one legitimately to require an annual state appropriation nearly 50 per cent larger than the other, although average unit costs of instruction at the different academic levels are exactly the same for each institution.

Observe that the key to this exhibit is in Columns 3 and 7—the differing percentages of the total work done at the different class levels. University A tends to be heavy at the top, with 21 per cent of its work on the doctoral and graduate-professional levels. University B is heavy at the bottom, with half of all its work at the freshman-sophomore level, 98 per cent in the undergraduate and masters' levels, and only 2 per cent doctoral and graduate-professional. This accounts for its request for state appropriations being nearly one-third less than that of University A.

Ideally, when a university is besieged with numbers of master's and doctoral aspirants, or can foresee that it is soon to be so besieged, it immediately presses hard for the provision of modern and high-quality facilities for fifth-year and advanced graduate instruction. This is not accomplished overnight. Recruiting of professors especially qualified for graduate-school teaching and research, accumulation of library and laboratory facilities worthy of a graduate department, obtaining funds for fellowships and assistantships which will enable graduate students to finance themselves in part, and gradually acquiring recognition by a regional accrediting association and by the societies of academicians or professionals in the department's discipline—all these require years of well-directed effort.

There are perhaps a hundred colleges and universities, mostly in the class of state institutions that have undergone the evolution from normal schools to teachers colleges to multipurpose state colleges—and in many instances have already been renamed regional state universities—where this prospect should be understood and these efforts begun, if they are not already under way. All these institutions already offer master's degrees in at least some departments. Several of them offer doctorates in a few departments.

It would probably be conservative to say that of the some 225 institutions of this class or related to it, 10 per cent now have doctoral programs, 45 per cent should be actively contemplating such development, and another 45 per cent are not yet within artillery-range of it. This would mean, within another decade or so, an additional 100 universities having doctoral programs, added to the roughly 200 now existing. Three hundred full-fledged universities will be none too many, none too soon.

Advanced graduate work at the doctoral level involves unit costs from 4 to 10 times average unit costs at the lower division level (freshman and sophomore years). This is a fact of life not to be deplored or shrunk from, but to be more widely understood. The fact that unit costs of instruction escalate geometrically with the *level* of instruction goes far to explain that during a decade when a developing university's student enrollment merely doubles, its total operating costs at least triple.

If a layman is dumbfounded that doubled volume does not bring a reduction of unit costs, he can reflect that if a maker of ordinary nuts and bolts doubles his volume he may expect lower unit costs if other factors are favorable; but if half of the added volume of nuts and bolts are to be *gold-plated*, then unit costs will rise. That is a rough illustration of the plight of developing universities in recent, current, and future years for a least a decade.

The national policy on the point of developing additional centers of advanced graduate study all over the nation has indeed been voiced by the President, if not explicitly by the Congress. The policy is to effect a dispersion and distribution of these facilities so that they will be located in several regions of every populous state, and in all other states in reasonable relation to population and resources. Each will develop specialties appropriate to the resources and needs of its own region, and each will be locally accessible to a population of from a quarter of a million to a million or more people. Thus will the nationwide academic and scientific strength be increased, and man's control of his environment advance. With modern transportation and communication, it is by no means necessary or desirable to concentrate advanced graduate programs and facilities in a few congested centers.

These are a few of the background facts which support the conclusion, already obvious on its face, that no matter how meticulously unit costs of instruction may be computed, they prove exactly nothing about either economy or efficiency in higher education.

Unit cost accounting has uses, however, as well as limitations. It affords evidence that the top administration has opportunity to scan the annual operation and inspect its financial aspect in detail. It affords means of satisfying—at least partially—inquirers prompted by legitimate curiosity or harboring unfounded suspicions that the college is haphazardly operated with a loose financial rein which opens the door for extravagance and waste. The data of unit cost accounting do no harm if they are not used in disregard of the logical limits of their application.

Not for a moment can it be forgotten that nothing is proved about the efficiency and economy of a restaurant when in one restaurant we buy a sirloin dinner at $3.50, in another a dinner similarly named on the menu at $4.50, and in a third a ground beef dinner at $2.00. Only if we know with precision about each case, the quantity, taste, flavor, tenderness and digestibility of the meat, the sanitation in the kitchen where it is prepared, and the relative comfort and beauty of the surroundings in which it is served, can we hazard any estimate of the relative merits of any of the restaurants. Ordinarily we can not know these things with exactitude; but we sense them, take imponderable factors into account, make judgments about them, and act accordingly. The same sensible sequence must often be followed in college administration. There is danger that incautious emphasis on cost accounting may encourage a thrust toward uniformity—that bane of the human spirit and enemy of advanced learning. If the college has no more than half a dozen students studying classical Greek, and the cost of a credit hour is 10 times that of a credit hour in modern Spanish, we do not hastily conclude that classical Greek must be dropped from the curriculum. It may well be worth all it costs. There may be a possibility, if the study of classical Greek seems to be in permanent decline, of finding a professor who can do justice to the half-dozen students of Greek while at the same time teaching courses in classical Latin or ancient Hebrew, or both; but unit costs of instruction in all ancient languages will probably continue unavoidably high.

The same is almost sure to be true of a continuing procession of more or less esoteric new specialties, particularly in the sciences and technologies, in view of the literal "explosion of knowledge" in our generation. In the black book of educational administrative sins, next to a stunned dedication to wooden uniformity should be written "Zombie-like imperviousness to innovation; letting the world leave you behind." If used with imperfect understanding of their severe limitations, such procedures as those of unit cost accounting may exert a powerful adverse tendency against any new undertakings. If only a handful of students want a course in intergovernmental relations in the United States, or a seminar on the latest significant developments in urbanism, the unit cost may seem astronomical at first, but the wishes of the students had better be reasonably fulfilled. This may be contrary to the bull-in-the-China-shop advice of the late Beardsley Ruml, who urged in essence that the number of available courses in the undergraduate college should be kept down to a few staple standard offerings, class-size doubled, faculty-student ratio halved, and faculty salaries doubled without the necessity of any additional operating income. The recent experiences of some colleges that have more or less faithfully followed or paralleled that counsel seem to demonstrate what might have been suspected: Doubling faculty salaries in a substandard institution may not necessarily improve faculty quality, partly because scholars and teachers will not go to such an institution at any price, except an occasional exceptional one who goes out of motives of charity; doubling the size of classes and halving the teacher-student ratio can hardly do less than severely depress the quality of instruction; and a *modus operandi* too much dominated by crass considerations of "cutting the corners" financially can only lead to academic decline.

Hundreds of "studies" and "paired experiments" have been made by respected psychologists, pseudo-psychologists, amateur psychologists, and plain psychoquacks, obsessed with the idea that progress in college and *ergo* the worth of a college, can be minutely measured "objectively" by "achievement tests" akin to quiz-bowl technique, in futile efforts to prove the real effect of size of class upon learning. The vast mass of useless results, spotty and inconclusive to date, can only be summarized by the negative conclusion that there is little or no evidence (from this source) that small classes necessarily result in superior learning. This conclusion would be obvious to any intelligent layman after a moment's thought. The same layman would understand that there is no method of measuring the quality of higher education except in the most partial or fragmentary way; and his common sense would tell him that the quality and competency of the instructor are all-important (not his ability as a rote drill-master), and that it stands to reason that a small class affords generally a better opportunity for intellectual communication and consequent reflection and study and learning than a large one. This is why we do not have in our elementary and secondary schools the Lancastrian system, under which one teacher taught 1,000 pupils simultaneously with the aid of student monitors. The teacher-student ratio was 1 to 1,000. What a bonanza for a really thoughtless economizer!

PART THREE

Chapter 10

ENDOWMENT FUNDS AND ENDOWMENT INCOME

A FUND held by a charitable corporation under the stipulation that the principal is to be held intact and inviolate, and only the income is to be expendable for the corporate purposes, is "endowment." It is sometimes spoken of more loosely as a "permanent fund" or as a "trust fund." Usually the instrument of gift specifies that the duration of the trust shall be forever, sometimes in quaint terms such as "even unto the end of time," or "as long as grass grows and water runs." Such wording creates a perpetual charitable trust—a unique type of social instrument provided for in equity jurisprudence.

It is possible, also, to create such a trust of a limited duration, or to authorize expenditure of the principal at the discretion of the trustee; but endowment gifts to colleges are commonly perpetual.

Funds placed in endowment without specification as to special purpose constitute the institution's general endowment fund. Those whose income is to be used only for one or more specified objects are called "restricted endowments," and each must be accounted for as a separate fund. Thus the total endowment of a well-established and wealthy institution can be visualized as resembling a cluster of grapes on the vine, albeit of markedly different sizes. Each is a separate trust. Once it was seriously debated whether these funds must be invested separately, or whether they could be "pooled" for investment purposes, with each to receive its proportionate share of the gains or losses produced; but this latter practice seems now to be generally regarded as permissible and legitimate.

Harvard's endowment approximates $1 billion in value, and there are perhaps 150 other colleges and universities in the United States having endowments of $10 million or more each, yet a big majority of all colleges in the country have little or no resources of this type.

Moreover, the relative importance of college endowments as sources of operating income has greatly declined over the past half century. When Trevor Arnett published his small book on *College Finance* in 1922, he expressed what was a commonly held ideal of that time—that a private college or university should have endowment funds sufficient to produce about half of its annual operating income. This ideal has never been realized on any appreciable scale. If any institutions in America have ever been in that fortunate position, probably no more than half a dozen have. It scarcely seems that such a goal will ever again be regarded as attainable.

The decline in the importance of endowments resulted, in considerable part, from the Great Depression of the 1930's and the accompanying revolution in Federal legislation and monetary policies. Prior to that time a well-managed perpetual trust fund might easily produce annual income at the rate of 6 to 8 per cent. The great and seemingly permanent drop in interest rates created conditions under which such a fund would do well to produce even 3 per cent during much of the Thirties and Forties. Not only was the productivity of invested funds cut in half, but the gradual and continued inflation which soon followed the Depression greatly reduced the purchasing power of the dollar and pushed up the cost of services and materials which colleges must buy, so that in the Forties and Fifties the drastically decreased endowment income would pay for less and less in an inflated market.

These conditions caused colleges to lose much of their former enthusiasm for building up endowments and to favor campaigns for capital improvements and for gifts expendable for current operation. In general the great philanthropic foundations veered away from the once-favored policy of making gifts for endowment of colleges and turned to "challenge grants" to stimulate college campaigns for gifts of currently expendable funds.

By the middle Sixties upward revisions of the discount rate by the Federal Reserve Board (intended to "tighten money" to curb too-rapid inflation) brought a substantial rise in interest rates, but already in 1967 the Board moved the discount rate downward again, and it does not seem probable that the interest rates of 1965 and 1966 will be permanently maintained.

It must be noticed, of course, that the level of interest rates is by no means the only determiner of the productivity of college endowments. A good deal depends, for one thing, upon the financial expertise of the investment officers and investment counsel that the institution employs. The large endowments are at a great advantage in this respect, for their size enables them to afford the services of well-organized and well-paid staffs of investment talent. The small endowment can not afford this expense, and often relies on the amateurish judgment of a committee of the college governing board with little or no paid professional counsel. Thus it was reported that a decade or two ago when most colleges were getting annual income of only 3 or 4 per cent on their small endowments, the large permanent funds of the University of Chicago were producing 6 per cent.

This disparity in the productivity of the endowments of different institutions intrigued McGeorge Bundy, who assumed the presidency of the Ford Foundation in 1966; and he announced in his first annual report, released early in 1967, that the Foundation would launch a major study of how colleges and universities might get larger returns from their invested funds.

Apparently well over half of all college endowment funds are now invested in common stocks. This is a comparatively recent development, brought about by the necessity of "hedging" against inflation. Two generations ago common stocks were almost universally regarded as "too speculative" as an investment of charitable trust funds; but the flow of economic history seems to have changed all that.[1]

The Boston Fund has also reported the 10 leading stocks in the portfolios of the 67 endowed universities and colleges reporting to

---

[1] *Citizens' National Bank* v. *Morgan et al.*, (N.H.), 51 A. 2d 841 (1947).

Table 2. How 67 leading universities and colleges were investing $6 billion in endowment funds in 1966, as reported by the Boston Fund.

Investments	Percentages
(1)	(2)
Common stocks	57.0
Bonds	28.9
Mortgages and real estate	6.3
Cash and liquid assets	2.2
Preferred stocks	1.1
Miscellaneous	4.5

it (Table 3). The list might be said to provide a glimmer of the prevailing emphases in the American culture: All are huge international corporations; three are oil companies; two are known chiefly as manufacturers of automobiles and trucks; two are manufacturers of business machines, and another is in somewhat similar light industry (cameras); one is in communications; and one is in soft drinks. Some of them are considerably diversified, in order to gain the advantages of "vertical organization of industry" or for other advantages.

The recording of actual dollar values of endowment funds is a somewhat erratic and unreliable business, because of the frequent wide disparity between "book value" and market value. Actual market value of securities changes daily, of course; and the market worth of real estate holdings and mortgages is not easy to appraise. Bearing these facts in mind, observe the Boston Fund's 1966 listing of seven of its respondents having endowments of more than $200 million each (Table 4). From other sources it would appear that Columbia University, Stanford University, and the University of Texas could be included in this classification, making a total of 10 institutions endowed with more than $200 million.

Without wrestling with the technicalities involved, but simply turning to page 754 of *The World Almanac, 1967*, the popular and useful annual reference work of long standing, we find a listing of about 120 institutions reported as having endowments of $10 million or more. Notice that 16 of these (about 13 per cent of the total) are public universities: 15 state universities and the University of Cincinnati, a municipal institution but recently "state-affiliated."

Table 3. The 10 most popular stocks held by 67 universities and colleges in 1966, in order of market value, as reported by the Boston Fund.

Stocks	Ranking
(1)	(2)
International Business Machines	1
General Motors	2
Standard Oil of New Jersey	3
Eastman Kodak	4
Texaco	5
Gulf Oil	6
Xerox	7
Coca-Cola	8
Ford Motor	9
American Telephone & Telegraph	10

Table 4. Market values of endowment funds of seven universities which exceed $200 million each in 1966, as reported by the Boston Fund (figures in millions of dollars).

Universities	Endowment Funds
(1)	(2)
Harvard University	$974.9
Yale University	469.5
Massachusetts Institute of Technology	374.3
Princeton University	311.4
University of Chicago	275.8
University of California	237.7
Northwestern University	204.9

The University of Texas is by all odds the most heavily endowed of all state universities, chiefly by virtue of the fact that the sovereign Republic of Texas entered the Union in 1845 upon an agreement that one million acres of public lands would be reserved for the endowment of the University.

Regarding the more than one hundred private universities and colleges having $10 million or more, a limited impression of the situation may be gained by observing the numbers in each of a few class intervals:

Table 5. Sixteen public universities reporting endowment funds of $10 million or more, 1966 (figures in thousands of dollars).*

Universities	Endowments	Universities	Endowments
(1)	(2)	(1)	(2)
U. of Texas	$451,528	Rutgers, S.U. of N.J.	$21,018
U. of California	219,952	U. of Oklahoma	20,072
U. of Virginia	85,000	U. of Kansas	17,481
U. of Minnesota	69,680	Purdue U.	15,931
U. of Washington	51,474	U. of Idaho	13,407
U. of Michigan	44,265	U. of Alabama	12,500
U. of Delaware	39,000	U. of North Carolina	12,000
U. of Cincinnati	27,779	U. of Vermont	10,212

Source: *The World Almanac*, 1967. New York: Newspaper Enterprise Association, Inc., 1967, p. 754, 912 pp.
*In most instances the figures represent book value, not market value.

Table 6. Private universities and colleges reporting endowment funds of $10 million or more, 1966, arranged in four class-intervals.

Class-Intervals	Number
(1)	(2)
Over $100 million	10
$50–$99 million	20
$25–$49 million	14
$10–$24 million	60

Source: Adapted from *The World Almanac*, 1967.

One source reports that 100 universities and colleges hold 92 per cent of the nation's $12 billion in university endowments, but it hastens to say that even the wealthiest ones do not find their endowment funds as great a pillar of strength as might be supposed. This source reports that Columbia University, for example, has quadrupled its endowment from less than $100 million 30 years ago to more than $390 million in 1966, but that in the latter year its endowment income covered only 22 per cent of its current operating expenses, compared with 42 per cent in 1937. Two-thirds of all the endowment funds, it says, are restricted to specific uses by their donors and can not be used for general operations.[2]

There are many technical matters involved in the investment and accounting of endowment funds that can not be gone into here. One intriguing question is: When in the course of investment, capital gains are made (as in the sale of real estate or appreciated securities), must these capital gains always be added to the principal and reinvested, or can they be used, in whole or in part, for current expenses? One simple and traditional view is that it is morally and legally wrong to do other than add all capital gains to the inviolate principal. It seems, however, that this is not always the practice; and it appears to be quite difficult to find any unequivocal statutes or court decisions compelling it. Seymour E. Harris has commented that "Erosion in the real value of income from endowment can often be reduced by investing for capital appreciation and then using some of the appreciation as income."[3] The reasoning apparently is that the investor has a choice of investing primarily for capital growth or primarily for high income; and having chosen the former, he finds the college in possession of capital gains it would not have had but for his acumen in making the choice. Further, he is obligated to make, in his best judgment, the best possible use of the fund for the benefit of the institution. Having foregone investment for high income in favor of capital growth, and having won the toss, he may perhaps feel he can enable the college in some sense to "have its cake and eat it too" by using part of the capital gain as expendable income, to take the place of the income it might have had if he had chosen investment for high income and foregone investment for capital gain.

Without taking too firm a position on either side of this matter, let us conclude with an argument quoted by Harris as a good one against the use of any capital gains for current expenditures. Capital gains are an unstable source of income, high in some years and low in others, so it would be a mistake to rely on income from this source

---

[2] *Time*, Vol. 89, No. 25, p. 79 (June 23, 1967).

[3] Seymour E. Harris, (Ed.), *Higher Education in the United States: The Economic Problems.* Cambridge: Harvard University Press, 1960. pp. 203-206. 252 pp. Also available as a supplement, August 1960, to the *Review of Economics and Statistics,* Vol. 42, No. 3, Part 2, 247 pp.

for recurring expenditures. Therefore a college should try "to avoid getting frozen into its budget a fixed expense which has to be met from a source such as capital gains." Says Harris: "If capital gains are to be used for current expenditures at all, they should be used only for extraordinary expenditures."

Further, some trustees say "We are the trustees for the benefit of students who are now here and for students who are to come, as yet unborn." The trustees hold a proxy for future students and must not yield excessively to the exigencies of the present. Harris remarks that this reinforces the argument for seeking capital gains, especially in an inflationary economy, but that these gains should be reinvested for future use rather than withdrawn and spent currently.

Further evidence that this is not a rigid policy of a large private university is afforded by a *Time* education writer who wrote in June 1967: "On the sound theory that the market value of Yale's $448 million endowment is growing each year at a roughly predictable rate, it (the Yale Corporation) has agreed that there is no great risk in applying part of the gain from about one-fourth of the endowment to current expenses instead of adding it to the principal. Result: $2 million more that Yale can apply this year to operating expenses."[4]

Thus the Yale Corporation apparently believes this is a matter for the exercise of its best discretion. Some others would say it should be regarded as morally and legally interdicted. Currently it must be regarded as one of the unsettled questions of college finance.

The University of Chicago had most of its endowment funds in a single investment pool, having a market value of $273 million on December 31, 1967. Effective January 1, 1968, it split this pool, placing $197 million (about 70 per cent of the pooled funds) in a pool styled the "endowment merger," including all funds that had been given to the university with the stipulation that none of the principal could be spent. "This fund would continue to be invested as previously with the aim of keeping the income as high as is prudent in relation to the need for maintenance of purchasing power over the long term."[5]

---

[4] *Time*, Vol. 85, No. 29, p. 84 (June 23, 1967).
[5] University of Chicago news release of March 5, 1968, quoting J. Parker Hall, Treasurer of the University.

At the same time, the university placed $76 million (about 30 per cent of the original single pool) in a new pool styled the "capital merger," comprised only of funds that were contributed with the provision that the university could spend all or a portion of the principal. The investment policy for the "capital merger" would be designed "to produce over the long term the highest available return, including realized and unrealized capital gains as well as ordinary income." This will result initially in a decline in current income, but the pool "would be expected to generate an increased amount of spendable funds over a period." Meantime, the trustees of the university have approved the spending of as much principal from the "capital merger" as is needed to produce the same amount of annual budget support as would have been earned if there had not been a split at this time in the pooled endowment funds. For example, if the newly established "capital merger" earns 2 per cent from traditional income and the "endowment merger" earns 4 per cent, then the plan is to withdraw 2 per cent of the principal from the "capital merger" for support of the university's annual budget, it being the expectation that capital appreciation will more than replace such withdrawals.

The general subject of endowment investments is of perennial interest. Early in 1968 the Ford Foundation announced the appointment of a nine-member Advisory Committee on Endowment Management, to study the management of college and university endowment funds, with a view toward discovering and recommending needed changes.

Chapter 11

HOW MUCH SHOULD THE
STUDENTS PAY?

PROVIDING the necessary financial support for higher education can be regarded as (1) the obligation of the students, or (2) the responsibility of the state or national governments or local governmental subdivisions, or (3) the task of private donors. These three sources may be combined in varying proportions; or any one of them may be left out, and the remaining two appear in different magnitudes.

The older predominant concept in the United States was that of the private nonprofit college depending chiefly upon student fees and private donors, and receiving nothing from the state other than the exemption of its property from taxation. To this picture there have always been some exceptions. Some of the Colonial colleges (all private) received some tax funds from the Colony and from local subdivisions, on a more or less intermittent basis; and this tended to be discontinued as anti-clericalism of the late eighteenth-century "enlightenment" led to the idea of the separation of church and state and the insertion of freedom of religion clauses in the national and state constitutions.

Even today Pennsylvania appropriates state tax funds as annual operating subsidies to three private universities and a dozen lesser institutions (among which are three private medical colleges), and is now the only one of the 50 states directly appropriating tax funds to private colleges or universities on any substantial scale. The beneficiary institutions are all nonsectarian. From 1880 to 1920 Pennsylvania similarly made direct appropriations to several denominational colleges, but in 1921 its supreme court declared that practice unconstitutional.[1]

Nearly all the states have constitutional provisions prohibiting state subsidies to nonpublic or religious institutions; and this has been the prevailing nationwide pattern for a century and a half. This scene has been modified slightly by the enactment of state scholarship laws in 20 or more states, providing to selected students who demonstrate both academic aptitude and financial need, limited tax funds to be used only for the payment of student fees. This carefully devised plan operates to enable the selected students, most of whom would make their way to college in any event, to attend, if they prefer, high-fee private colleges rather than low-fee public institutions, and encourages the private institutions to raise their fees at least to the level of the maximum subsidy. This in turn causes pressure on the public institutions to raise their comparatively modest fees, thus making it more difficult than before for nonscholarship students from low-income families to attend any college, and effecting a narrowing of higher education opportunity.

By far the largest state program of this kind is in New York, where the appropriations for various state scholarships aggregate some $75 million for the fiscal year 1967-68. A major fraction of this total is in fact an indirect subsidy to New York private colleges.

The Federal government, in contrast, has not felt any inhibitions of supporting private institutions with public moneys, at least under contracts and grants intended to purchase services which the government wants performed. Thus in the current vast program of subsidized research managed by several major Federal agencies, the 50 leading universities receiving most of the money are about equally

---

[1] *Collins* v. *Kephart*, 271 Pa. 428, 117 Atl. 440 (1921).

divided (25 public and 25 private), with the private universities getting a little more than half the funds that go to these 50.

The theory of this vast total of transactions is simply that the government is in the market to buy services from what it regards as the most competent sources, without any thought of subsidizing universities, either public or private. The effect, however, is a large-scale indirect subsidizing of graduate students and research professors and, in some 20 instances, of huge separate physical plants for research which are entrusted to designated universities for management and operation. In several instances this produces the odd current effect that a large private university is receiving more than half of its annual operating income from Federal tax moneys.

Contrast the two theories which are implicit in the preceding paragraphs: (1) it is simpler, more direct, and more efficient for a governmental unit (whether state or Federal) to establish and operate educational or research institutions of its own rather than to let contracts or make grants or otherwise subsidize other institutions to produce the services needed, and thus questions of constitutionality are avoided, and (2) it is better for the governmental unit, needing a "crash program" within specified areas of technological research, to purchase or otherwise pay for the needed research effort by agencies already equipped and experienced in such work (i.e., the selected universities), rather than to undertake to perform the work directly with plants and staffs of its own.

To the extent that the two theories are contradictory, they will probably furnish food for controversy for some time to come. That the second theory depends for its support in part on the phrase "crash program," especially since 1957, is obvious; that as operated up to the present it threatens the integrity of the universities, private and public, can hardly be doubted; and that an indefinitely continued "crash program" may not be the preferable organization of technological research, from the standpoint of efficiency and productivity, is beginning to be suspected.

Is it too much to hope for the gradual introduction of blanket Federal subsidies to the states, to be distributed among the universities and other institutions of higher education within those states at the discretion of the state legislatures?

The alternatives seem to be (1) to continue to drift into unitary national control of higher education or (2) to restore the responsibility and dignity of the states within a system of "creative federalism."[2]

To return to the history:—Every state has developed state universities and colleges which have collectively accommodated more than half of all students in the nation since 1950, now accommodate two-thirds, and at some time in the 1970's will accommodate three-fourths. When founded (mostly in the nineteenth century) most of these institutions were intended to be free of student fees. Thus was posed in stark form another basic issue: If a state determines to make available suitable higher educational opportunities to all its citizens, is it better to (1) establish public institutions as needed and support them sufficiently so they can operate tuition-free or at low fees or (2) keep all colleges, public and private, on a high-fee basis, and support and operate a vast system of scholarships, loans, and other student aids comprehensive enough so all or nearly all able students lacking financial resources will be enabled to attend the institutions of their choice?

The first alternative is strongly advocated by many public college and university presidents and trustees, and by the National Association of State Universities and Land-Grant Colleges, and the Association of State Colleges and Universities, among others.

The second alternative is urged by many private university and college presidents, at least on a moderate basis; and some of the less restrained among them have unqualifiedly argued that this alternative is the preferable use of state tax funds, and that all colleges and universities should charge student fees approaching or approximating the full cost of operation, with nearly all students receiving financial aid from tax funds. This, they say, would enable the private and public institutions to compete on an "equitable" basis. Some almost seem to hope secretly that the late-lamented "50-50 balance" between private and public institutions might be restored—a chimerical aspiration.

Shall all higher education be kept on high tuition fees, or shall *public* higher education move toward making tuition free? Proponents of these two divergent views are apparently influenced by drastically

---

[2] Private college interests generally oppose blanket grants to the states, because most of the state constitutions prohibit tax support of nonpublic or denominational institutions.

different assessments of the motives that lead men and women to seek higher education.

The one view: Education is a commodity on the open market—a consumer's goods which people buy for their own gratification. No one should expect to get it free, any more than he should expect to get food or clothing free. Its price may change with the state of supply and demand; it is properly "what the market will bear." People are moved to pay for schooling chiefly by selfish reasons—to get entry into a "prestige profession" or business where they may profit from the wants and misfortunes of others; to be able to outwit their less fortunate fellows in the social and economic competitions of life. As for women, they go to college primarily to find a husband well-placed financially and socially. Then there are others, men and women, to whom college is a "four-year loaf" in a country-club atmosphere—a pleasant way to waste time while gaining maturity. None of these motives is entirely reprehensible; but any and all of them represent a cramped, archaic, and erroneous concept of the role of higher education.

To a limited extent, education beyond the high school serves all the purposes just mentioned; but all these occupy only a small fraction of the total view. The individual may benefit from higher education for his own private reasons and purposes, but his private gains are far outweighed by the gains that concurrently accrue to the whole society. The view that follows is that the principal gainer is the whole public, through (in the ringing words of Daniel Coit Gilman) "less bigotry in the Temple, less suffering in the hospital, less fraud in business, less folly in politics." This is the basic argument for free tax-supported public higher education. Its benefits extend to every citizen, of whatever age, sex, or educational status; hence its cost should be equitably apportioned to all by means of a tax system adjusted to economic conditions. In short, higher education is essentially a public function and a public obligation—not a private privilege or a private caprice. It need not and should not be a public monopoly, but it is too important to the public to be left in any large measure to the vagaries of an unregulated private pricing-system. This is the broad, enlightened modern concept.

How the public weal may be damaged by the ascendancy of the older private-privilege view is often well illustrated by noting that many a student's ethics may be distorted and even his choice of career untowardly influenced by his knowledge that his education is being obtained at great private expense to himself or his family—perhaps that he will be saddled with a debt upon graduation. In many cases this will strengthen the all-too-common obsession that he must get quickly into a highly-remunerative occupation where he can "make a killing" and recover his private investment. Thus obsessed, he will certainly spurn the idea of preparing for a modestly-paid public-service profession such as teaching, research, or social work or public health work, though these occupations are chronically undermanned. Instead he will probably aim for the savagely competitive world of private business and finance or some profession closely associated with it, where spectacular financial success is possible; but more often than not he will wind up in middle life with ulcers or heart disease.

The question then becomes, it seems: Shall higher education be an agency for the perpetuation of the American way of life at its present levels, or shall it be at least in part a lever for the elevation of the quality of American civilization?

One must choose between the concept of higher education as primarily a private consumer's good, to be purchased and paid for individually, and the contrasting view of higher education as principally a benefit to the whole society and therefore an ideal object of productive public investment. More briefly, the choice is between tuition-fee support and tax support. The nationwide system need not be wholly the one or wholly the other. It is possible, and probably desirable, that a high-fee private college and university segment should coexist alongside a great and growing tax-supported free public sector.

This is now the case, and can continue, because private colleges can offer many choices and do many things that public colleges can not do because of constitutional limitations, Federal and state. Far beyond the foreseeable future there will be many people who prefer those choices and are willing to pay for them in the form of tuition fees. This guarantees against public monopoly of education, and is exactly what our constitution-makers intended in the bills of rights.

Some presidents of private colleges and some conservative economists who want the private colleges to have their cake and eat it too have generally not advocated direct tax support of these colleges, but have been fertile in devising schemes which would keep both private and public colleges on a high-fee basis. These are so numerous that they must receive some brief attention seriatim.

1. *Tax-supported scholarships, Federal and state.* State scholarships, have been discussed early in this chapter. The Federal scholarships for undergraduates under the Higher Education Act of 1965, known as "Opportunity Grants," are restricted to low-income students whose parents are able to contribute only $600 or less to their annual college expenses; these scholarships amount to $200 to $800 of Federal money annually, which must be matched by the institution from other sources of student aid. The program has a distinct "War on Poverty" slant and is commendable as far as it goes.

The program of National Defense Education Act (1958) fellowships for graduate students in science, mathematics, and foreign languages goes on without much bearing on the undergraduate level and without much impact on our main issue of free tuition versus high tuition fees.

2. *Government loans and guaranteed loans for undergraduates and graduates.* The Federal government and a considerable number of states have succumbed to the wave of sentiment for student loans, which received much impetus from the enactment of the loan features of the NDEA in 1958. Skipping the details of loans (NDEA) and guaranteed loans (Higher Education Act of 1965), which are in somewhat parlous and uncertain relationship currently because of a tight money market, note that loan systems result in the low-income student graduating with a debt of up to $5,000 to be repaid within 10 years with interest at 3 per cent. (Some state systems place no limit on the interest rate.) This initial handicap in life is heavily discriminative against young women, as well as discriminative against all students from low-income families, and is retrogressive in tendency.

The Higher Education Act of 1965 provided for a scheme under which private lending agencies would be encouraged to make "guaranteed" loans to students, at a rate not exceeding 6 per cent interest. While in school the student would pay no interest, and after graduation only 3 per cent, with the government paying the difference unless the student's family income exceeded $15,000 a year. Apparently it was hoped that this plan would supersede and supplant the system of government loans to students under the National Defense Education Act of 1958. Early in 1966 it appeared that banks were generally reluctant to enter into this business because the currently tight money market gave them other and more profitable uses for their money. This situation continued, and in mid-1967 proposals had taken form, backed by the Treasury Department, to make the plan more attractive to bankers by providing for higher interest rates or special fees in connection with each loan.

On August 31, 1967, Representative Wright Patman of Texas, Chairman of the House Committee on Banking and Currency, issued a statement, in part as follows: "The banks aren't satisfied with the six per cent rate, and have virtually stopped making these loans. In effect, they've gone on strike against students." At that time the American Bankers' Association, through its executive vice president, was urging that the banks be given a $35 extra fee on each student loan made. Representative Patman continued: "If the bankers' lobby plan is enacted, it will cost the taxpayers $400 million in fiscal year 1970. Every dime of that money will go to the banks. Unless the banks recognize their public responsibility, thousands of students will have to go without a college education. I know there are many banks that want to participate in this program and make the loans. I urge them to give every consideration to making college loans without seeking the additional payments."[3]

3. *Student-work opportunities.* The Higher Education Act of 1965 includes limited provisions for part-time employment of students under regulated hours, wages, and conditions, somewhat in the tradition of the student work program of the National Youth Administration (1933-41).

4. *Tax credits for tuition payments.* This device, which in the form of the Ribicoff measure would allow students or their

---

[3] Quoted in *Higher Education and National Affairs,* Vol. 16, No. 30, September 1, 1967.

parents to subtract up to a maximum of about $325 from their annual Federal income tax obligation (if any), would cost the government the loss of more than $1 billion annually in revenue, and is well disposed of by the comment that "there are better ways of spending a billion dollars for higher education." For example, $1 billion would be ample to make all public universities and colleges entirely tuition-free.

5. *Lifetime surcharge on earnings to repay student loans.* One group of private college presidents would have the Federal government lend all students applying, limited sums for their college expenses, taking in return a signed agreement that the student would pay a fixed percentage of his earnings for the rest of his life, along with his annual Federal income tax. Conceivably this could take the form of a fixed surcharge above the regular income tax obligation—but in any event it would involve vast numbers of unpredictable variations, from the case of the student who died on his graduation day to the one who made a million within 10 years and went on to become a multimillionaire, dying at the age of 101. Prudent and alert applications of actuarial science could doubtless enable the government to recover its investment and keep the enterprise solvent, but it could create a vast bureaucracy, larger, probably, than the huge social security system. Why all this vast complexity, when the simple solution would be to make public colleges and universities tuition-free? Apparently solely to keep all higher education on a high-fee basis, and thus permit private colleges to "live in the style to which they have become accustomed," while forcing public institutions into a similar mold of financing.

Simply, the proposal would tend strongly to discourage and diminish state tax support of public colleges and universities and to shift the support of all higher education from state taxes to private fees paid by the student—a shift backward toward earlier centuries. Incidentally, it would enthrone the Federal government as the father-figure lending agency, and inevitably a voluminous flow of rules and regulations emanating from a Federal source would come to determine in large part how much could be borrowed and under what conditions. It would be but a short step to offering selectively favorable conditions (such as partial forgiveness of loans) to students willing to study and practice certain sciences or professions, which in turn is only once removed from an authoritarian system in which every student is told what to study and what occupation to pursue, and is ordered from job to job within that occupation.

All these risks, together with the burdensome complexities involved, we are asked to undertake in order to keep all higher education on the antiquated high-fee basis, rather than go forward with the development of tax-supported tuition-free public institutions. Place the private institutions in their own sector, to subsist by their usual methods, and all else that this vast and complicated scheme purports to offer is already more than accomplished by the simple plan of tax-supported low-fee public universities and colleges; namely, the cost to the taxpayers of providing the education is eventually more than recouped in the form of additional taxes paid on the enhanced lifetime earnings resulting from the education.

And this does not mean the extinction of private colleges. Far from it. Currently they are growing in enrollments, income, and plant. Only their *relative* share in the total picture is declining—as it inevitably must. The issue could hardly be clearer. In order to enrich the private colleges, we are asked to brake the expansion of tax-supported low-fee public institutions, and put *all* higher education on a high-fee basis—to shift its support from the taxpayers (general public) toward the students, as though on the theory that they alone are its beneficiaries. This theory is false and deceptive.

From the foregoing it appears that a few simple tests can be applied to any tortuous scheme for financing higher education that is likely to be proposed.

1. Is it designed indirectly to channel tax moneys into private colleges (as in the case of tax-paid scholarships for tuition only, at any institution of the student's choice; or of tax credits for tuition payments)?

2. Is it designed to shift the cost of education from the general public to the student (as in the case of various student loan schemes; and the proposed Federal loans to be repaid by surtax on lifetime earnings)?

An affirmative answer to either of the foregoing questions means the scheme will tend toward a drastic raising of tuition fees, and a consequent *narrowing* of the total scope of higher educational opportunity in the United States. In such event, the whole society would be the loser.

It remains only to mention another consideration related to the present and future *quality* of higher education. Naturally to the lips of an orthodox economist comes the expression, "People will pay for what they value, and value what they pay for." The implication is that only high-fee schooling can be of high quality—that low-fee or tuition-free colleges will be swamped with hordes of unmotivated and incompetent students, and that hence their quality can not rise. Closely related to this is the plausible but fallacious notion that as the numbers of students balloon outward, reaching lower and lower into the family-income strata, academic quality must inevitably go down. Nothing is more trite than to say intellectual ability does not follow financial status; and in our day of universal high school education nothing could be wider of the mark than to suppose academic achievement parallels family income. Never provable by any rigorously scientific or pseudo-scientific method, it is nevertheless virtually certain that, on the average, the 6 million students beyond high school in 1967 (4 million of them in public low-fee or tuition-free universities and colleges and technical institutes) are at least equal and probably superior in thoughtfulness, alertness, comprehension, intellectual ability and academic achievement to their predecessors of a generation ago who numbered only one million.

Intellectual quality is extremely difficult to measure with precision and reliability. Pretensions of quality in an educational institution need to be regarded skeptically. Quality may easily be confused with prestige. In the face of these imponderables, the remark of Karl Jaspers that "every selection is an injustice" has peculiar force; truthful and appropriate is Sir Eric Ashby's laudatory comment, "In the United States, every high school graduate can get into some college or university, somewhere."

This nation will continue to have a dual system of higher education. Let the private sector manage its own affairs, academic and fiscal, with maximum autonomy. Let private colleges charge what student fees they will or must, or "what the market will bear" for the students

of middle-income and affluent families who prefer their particular offerings or atmosphere not obtainable elsewhere, or who are attached
to them by sentimental ties or religious predilections or other reasons.

Let them not seek to skew the whole nationwide system in their
own favor by trying to hamstring the vast and exploding public tax-
supported low-fee sector, or by trying to shift and keep the whole
system on a high-fee basis. Let them live and let live. The wave of the
future is an ever-larger low-fee and tuition-free public system, with a
minority private high-fee sector flourishing alongside. What should be
the student's share in the cost of his education? Except in a minority of
cases where he seeks a preferred atmosphere—nothing. Public higher
education is a public responsibility.

The public obligation to provide educational opportunity beyond
the high school at low cost to the student or entirely tuition-free is
recognized in every state. In recent years, when pressed by factions in
the legislatures to raise fees, some of the governing boards of the
nation's greatest state universities have responded with public declara-
tions of the obligation to move toward lower fees and free tuition.
Such a proclamation was made by the Board of Regents of the University of Wisconsin. In 1967 the Board of Regents of the University
of California, resisting the prodding of Governor Ronald Reagan,
voted 14 to 7 *not to adopt tuition fees*.[4]

In 1967 the Iowa State Board of Regents adopted a statement
which is reproduced here in full:

THE ROLE OF STUDENT FEES IN THE FINANCE
OF HIGHER EDUCATION

A Statement of the State Board of Regents of Iowa

May 12, 1967

1. The state university is an instrument of the open democratic society.
Its basic function is to open up opportunity to young men and women of all
socio-economic classes, and in so doing to provide an abundant supply of
educated people to serve our economy and our society.

---

[4] The University of California is tuition-free. Students pay, however, certain
other fees aggregating between $200 and $275 a year, placing the total of student
charges somewhat below the nationwide average of student fees at state universities.

One of the most significant American innovations and one of the most cherished American institutions has been free public education. The idea is well established that education at the elementary and secondary levels should be free to all regardless of socio-economic class. Since the founding of our public universities and especially since the land-grant movement starting in 1862, under Abraham Lincoln, it has been equally accepted that public higher education should be open to all at low cost. This tradition has been especially strong in the states west of the Alleghenies and is now spreading rapidly to the states of the Northeast.

The practice of charging tuition, even at the presently moderate rates, has emerged not from principle—educators have consistently opposed them—but simply because finance from tax sources has not been adequate to take care of university enrollments and to prevent deterioration of educational quality. Increased tuitions have been charged only as a last resort to protect the integrity of the education offered.

2. Even though tuitions at state universities are, on the whole, moderate, the present costs to students and their families are substantial. The costs include board and room, books and supplies, travel, clothing, and incidentals. These average $1,500 to $2,000 a year. Another cost is the loss of income because the student is not employed full time. This cost is as much as $4,000 to $6,000 a year. Any increase in tuition is on top of an already heavy cost, and would increase what is already a heavy burden to families and their student-children.

3. While a student loan system with liberal loans, long repayment periods, and low interest is surely an important part of any system for the finance of students, it is not socially desirable to load too much of the cost on students by means of loans—certainly not to substitute student loans for tax support of higher education. The students who need loans are those from families of modest income. It is neither equitable nor socially desirable to expect this group of young people to start out life with substantial indebtedness. The problem is compounded when two young people with indebtedness marry. The loan system is especially undesirable for women who are reluctant to go into debt knowing that the indebtedness may be a burden to a future husband.

The effort to shift costs from taxpayers to student borrowers is in reality only a shift from one kind of taxation to another. The new taxation in the form of repayment of loans places a special burden on those who have come from low-income backgrounds and need special help in starting out on their careers rather than the handicap of debt repayment.

Indebtedness at the end of a college career has the effect of undesirably restricting educational and vocational choices. A student with several thousand dollars of indebtedness tends to avoid low-paying vocations like teaching or the ministry, and he is often not in a position to enter the Peace Corps or the Job Corps or advanced study. To keep open the freedoms of occupational choice which is part of the American heritage, it would be best to use student loans with moderation and prudence.

4. It is often argued that those who benefit from education should pay a large part of the cost. In fact they do, because the burden of the cost of board and room, books, etc., as well as the loss of income while in college, falls largely on them. But society-at-large benefits from the nurses, engineers, scientists, teachers, physicians and the like who are the product of our universities. Society-at-large also benefits from the broad cultural advancement which derives from higher education, and it benefits from keeping the doors of opportunity wide open to its young people even if some do not or cannot take advantage of the opportunity. The broad social benefits are surely sufficient to justify public and philanthropic support of most of the cost of higher education. This has long been recognized not only by the traditionally low tuition in state universities but also by the practice of providing scholarships and other grants to help low-income students meet not only tuitions but other college costs as well.

5. Universities should clearly be responsive to the needs of the society they serve, and everyone recognizes the important role of legislatures in determining the amount of state funds to be invested in higher education. However, one of the fundamental principles of the governance of universities is that they should be free of direct political influence. That is why state universities are not part of state government but rather are governed by separate lay boards, and it is why universities are conducted as semi-autonomous organizations—sometimes as corporations. An important element in the freedom of the university is diverse sources of revenue of which one is state appropriation, and others are fees, federal grants, foundation gifts, and private donations.

Historically, the governing boards of state universities have controlled their own fees and their own fund-raising from non-state sources. These boards are close in touch with financial needs and are in a position to deal with a variety of donors. Any other arrangement has been found through experience to erode away the freedom of the University. Iowa has a superb record of maintaining the freedom of its Universities. This policy has resulted in three excellent institutions which have been consistently operated with concern for the interests of the people of the state. To encroach upon the freedom of the Universities at this time, by the Legislature's taking over in effect the function of fee assessment, would be a serious backward step.

6. It is sometimes argued that if private colleges can charge high tuitions, state universities should do the same. In reality there is no inconsistency between the two practices. It is only because open opportunity is provided in the state institutions that it is defensible for the private institutions to charge a large share of instructional costs to the students. Our dual system of education is highly desirable and the two parts are complementary. The job of the state university is to keep opportunity open to everyone who can benefit from higher education; the job of private education is to serve special constituencies, to assure diversity of control over higher education, to experiment, to set standards, and the like. Private education is

free to do these things precisely because public education exists to keep the doors of opportunity open to all. This does not mean that the public institution must be an inferior institution—only that it must be an "opportunity institution."

7. The proposal to raise fees drastically for students at Iowa Universities would discriminate against Iowa students as compared with those of other states. The fees for Iowa students are already high relative to those of most comparable Midwestern state institutions. In view of the relatively high fees at the three state universities in Iowa, further increases should be established only as a last resort. However, increased fees would be preferable to deterioration in the effectiveness of the three universities.

The most practical argument against the proposal is that it would cut the tax support of higher education below realistic levels. Higher education at this time needs solid increases in financial support from state appropriations, not only because the money is needed but because adequate state appropriations will help to attract needed supplemental funds from the Federal government and private foundations.

Chapter 12

TAX CREDITS FOR
TUITION PAYMENTS?

ONE OF THE MOST persistently advocated methods of meliorating the rising charges for tuition fees in private and public colleges has been a tax credit plan under which all citizens currently paying college fees and also Federal income taxes would be allowed to reduce their annual Federal income tax payments by specified small amounts, within a certain range of income brackets. That is, these persons would be permitted to cite their tuition payments, or a portion thereof, as a "set-off" against their individual income tax liability for the appropriate year.

"A tax credit is a direct reduction in the amount of federal income tax owed after all deductions from gross income have been figured and the amount of the tax due determined."[1]

It has been reported that more than one hundred bills have been introduced in Congress to provide various schemes of tax credits for college tuition payers; but the version that was most recently and urgently advocated by Senators Abraham Ribicoff of Connecticut and

---

[1] *Tax Credits for Educational Expenses.* A 10-page pamphlet, undated. Washington: National Association of State Universities and Land-Grant Colleges.

Peter H. Dominick of Colorado would give a tax credit of 75 per cent of the first $200 paid as tuition, 25 per cent of the next $300, and 10 per cent of the next $1,000. Thus the maximum credit for payments on behalf of any one student would have been $325 per year (and this would be reduced by 1 per cent of the amount by which the taxpayer's gross income exceeded $25,000).

Senator Ribicoff's measure failed of passage by narrow margins in at least three recent sessions of Congress and now seems unlikely to be enacted, though it will probably be pushed again in the next session. What are the merits?

1. Certainly the maximum of $325 would not be of overwhelming benefit to persons who are paying annual tuition fees to private colleges up to $2,000 a year.

2. Worst of all, it would be of no benefit at all to the large numbers of persons who have no Federal income tax liability at all, because their incomes are too small or their exemptions are numerous enough to wipe out their tax obligation. Many of these are the ones whose needs are more desperate than any others. This is why the National Association of State Universities and Land-Grant Colleges gave its pamphlet a subtitle: *How to Spend $1¼ Billion Annually in Tax Money to Help Those Who Need It Least.*

3. In fact, the purpose is by no means only to aid tuition-payers. It is largely to channel tax money into college coffers and to enable colleges to raise their fees substantially without adding new financial burdens on their students. This would start the restrictive spiral spinning again: private colleges boost fees; public colleges raise fees; parents and other tuition-payers are no better off than they were in the first place; with fees higher at all types of institutions the number of persons who can afford to pay them is smaller than before; opportunity for education beyond high school is narrowed and reduced; ground is lost in the path of progress toward universal higher education.

It is now estimated that the Ribicoff measure in its present form would cost the Treasury $1½ billion a year in revenue. It is opposed by the Treasury and opposed by the President, as well as by state universities and colleges generally.

It was advocated with considerable vigor by an informal group of about 20 private college presidents in the states centered about Chicago. However, President Kingman Brewster of Yale had come to a point where he said in his Camp Lectures at Stanford University in May, 1967: "The tax credit device is the most wastefully inequitable in the way it benefits many who do not need it and does not reach at all those who are below the taxable level of income."

The outspoken Senator Morse of Oregon is reported to have said simply: "There are better ways of spending more than a billion dollars a year for higher education." The National Association of State Universities and Land-Grant Colleges pointed out that it would cost less to give every student in every college and university in the nation $200 a year—though not necessarily advocating this.

In their Joint Statement of January 1967 the two national associations, having a membership of 300 state universities and colleges, said: "The Associations view the tax-credit proposal as inequitable from the standpoints of fiscal policy, educational policy, and national policy in general."[2]

Probably one of the best discourses on the recent history of the tax-credit proposals available in print in one volume is in Roger A. Freeman's *Crisis in College Finance? Time for New Solutions.* This 1965 book, though presenting a good deal of valid data on the financing of higher education, is unduly pessimistic about the amounts of funds that may come from the Federal and state governments, and its final 50 pages are devoted wholly to explanation and advocacy of the tax-credit scheme, so that it might perhaps seem that this was the principal purpose for which the book was published.

The author of the Foreword, President Landrum R. Bolling of Earlham College, introduces this small volume as representing the "hard-nosed approach of an avowedly conservative fiscal economist," and expresses the hope that it will precipitate widespread debate on the financing of higher education—a hope readily shared by many.

The chief shortcoming of the book is that it is "of little faith" regarding the ability and desire of the American public to support

---

[2] *Recommendations for National Action Affecting Higher Education: A Joint Statement.* Washington: National Association of State Universities and Land-Grant Colleges, and Association of State Colleges and Universities, 1967, pp. 23-24, 38 pp.

higher education largely by tax funds as well as by private gifts, and underestimates the knowledge and good will of the state and national legislatures in making their annual and biennial appropriations of tax funds for operating expenses of education beyond high school. This is a common error of conservatively oriented speakers and writers, during these years of rapid change. The appropriations of state tax funds alone for this purpose were more than tripled between 1959 and 1967, the average annual aggregate moving from $1.4 billion to more than $4.3 billion. This growth is far beyond Roger Freeman's most sanguine predictions, even for 1970. The same is true of the Federal contribution for 1967-68.

Some of the details of the inspiring story of state appropriations during the 8-year period 1959-67 appear in Chapter 24 herein.

My final comment on Freeman's little book is that he repeats the oft-heard overstatement that the private sector in higher education is about to disappear: "If current policies are not changed and present trends continue, we face within two decades the demise of much or most private higher education—aside from a few affluent prestige institutions" (p. viii). He somehow fails to notice that each year for the past 20 years the private colleges as a collectivity have had more students, more money, more facilities than ever before. Roughly speaking their growth has been at the rate of about 50 per cent every 10 years (while the public institutions grow at the rate of 100 per cent each decade).

The only "decline" suffered is a *relatively* slower growth than that of the public colleges, and hence a declining percentage of the total of all students, faculties, and facilities. This is inevitable. But it will not go on forever. Somewhere far short of zero the declining curve of percentages will level off and continue on a plateau. Why? Because within the foreseeable future there will always be millions of people who strongly prefer private colleges for many reasons which need not be repeated here, and who are able and willing to support them with tuition fees and philanthropic gifts.

Let me venture no guess as to whether the plateau will be at 25 per cent, or 20, or 15, or 10. For a long time to come there will be no actual absolute decrease in the students, faculties, facilities and financial support of the private colleges as a whole. Their decreasing *relative* percentage of the whole should occasion no undue alarm. There is no immutable dispensation from Heaven that the private and public sectors must forever be 50-50. Who says the private colleges can not fulfill their excellent and indispensable role in a pluralistic system without quantitatively occupying half the field?

One might raise a question as to whether, in the tactics of fund-raising, it is wiser to cry Wolf! and talk continually about the "crisis" in panic-stricken tones, or to take the positive stance and address prospective donors with confidence as from a position of strength. For example, the latter is what President Landrum R. Bolling did in his full-page appeal in *Time*,[3] for July 21, 1967.

"Something important is happening at Earlham College . . ." says he, and then proceeds concisely to describe six significant undertakings going on at his campus, their financial history, and the sums each could use to advantage.

"Just being a small college guarantees nothing," he says, "but a small college with imagination and a willingness to innovate and experiment, with teachers who care about teaching and about their students as human beings, and a community life of shared activities and concern for social and moral values, can provide an education both academically excellent and significant for human growth."

For such colleges there does not seem to be a drying up of philanthropy or a dwindling of patronage. Nor could any scheme be espoused which is devised indirectly to channel tax funds to them, such as the tax-credit proposals. However, the author would not ask an abolition of Federal and state scholarships, fellowships, loans, student work, and like student aids, if they were not unduly expanded in scope.

A few statistics of private giving appear in Chapter 15, *infra*.

---

[3] *Time*, p. 79 (July 21, 1967).

Chapter 13

DIFFERENTIATED TUITION FEES?

THE PHRASE FORMING THE TITLE of this chapter may have many meanings. College tuition fees in the United States are far higher than in any other country in the world. The only nation where this level is remotely approached is the Dominion of Canada.[1]

Generally speaking, charges for tuition in private colleges in the United States are roughly four times as high as those in public colleges. This is because most private institutions need substantial income from this source; while the public institutions are partly or largely supported from tax funds, and it was clearly the original intent in most of the states a century ago that they should be tuition-free, as the "capstones" of the free public school systems.

Within the private sector there are wide variations. A few such institutions charge no tuition fees (Berea College in Kentucky; Cooper Union in New York City), and until recently this was also true of Rice University in Houston. At the other end of the continuum the leading Ivy League universities are now charging abou $2,000 per academic year for tuition alone, and a few "way out" small colleges such as Sarah Lawrence in New York and Bennington in Vermont run to

---

[1] Exception: the University of the Province of Newfoundland is tuition-free.

$2,350 and $2,400 for tuition only. There are numerous variations between, with many in the $1,000 to $1,200 range. Parenthetically, room
and board for an academic year seem to range from $450 to at least
$1,350, reflecting at least three variables: (1) vast differences in quality,
(2) sectional differences in costs, and (3) the fact that some colleges use
the housing and feeding business as a source of profit.

In the public sector the range of tuition fees (for students able
to claim residence within the state) is less wide—from no tuition fees
in the California system of public higher education and for regular
full-time undergraduates in the City University of New York, and
$144 a year at the University of Texas, to $630 a year at the University
of New Hampshire, with the fees at the state colleges or regional state
universities usually on a somewhat lower scale in each state. Generally tuition fees are highest in the Northeastern states and become
somewhat lower progressively as one proceeds southward and westward, though there are exceptions to this generalization.

The most significant discrimination as to fees for regular undergraduates in state or municipal universities and public junior colleges
is that between "in-state" and "out-of-state" students—those who are
legally residents of the state, and those who are not.

Within the past decade there has occurred a wave of hysteria
demanding that fees for "out-of-state" students be raised again and
again, so that in almost all states they are now nearly or fully double
the fees for "in-state" students. (The out-of-state fee at the University
of Vermont in 1967 was $1,575. In several other state universities it was
in the $900-$1,200 range; for example, it was $1,200 at Michigan State
University at East Lansing.)

Generally there is really no justification for this differential, ignoring as it does that any excellent institution of higher education,
especially a university, must have students from other states and other
countries in order to avoid developing a condition of inbred provincial-
ism which would destroy its quality. The practice also disregards the
fact that migrating students are often somewhat more affluent than
the average, and the spending of $2,000 or more per year in the com-
munity and the state, even if part of it is locally earned, is itself a
boost to the economy. Probably a student living in the state for an
academic year is more of an economic asset than a summer or winter
tourist staying a few days or weeks. Yet we have the spectacle of states

advertising to attract tourists, while erecting high financial barriers against students from outside the state.

It has long been known that many nonresident students continue to live and practice their professions or carry on their businesses in the state where they attended college. A report made by the College Entrance Examination Board at the request of the Regents of the University of California in 1967 indicated that two-thirds of the out-of-state students at that university become permanent California residents.[2] From these data the report concluded: "Thus it is greatly to the advantage of both the state and the University that the University of California be able to recruit students, and particularly graduate students, on a national and even an international basis."

The imagined danger of being inundated by a flood of nonresident students may seem more real in particular situations such as where a university located on or near the border of its state draws a substantial portion of its students from the adjacent state. In such a case, President George Starcher of the University of North Dakota at Grand Forks (on the Minnesota boundary), which receives 1,000 students from Minnesota, has suggested, seriously and with unimpeachable logic, that Minnesota should appropriate each year to the University of North Dakota a sum equivalent to the cost of accommodating the Minnesota students there—so that in effect the institution would become a species of "bi-state" university, proportionally supported by the two states that supply most of its students.

A somewhat similar situation exists at the University of Idaho at Moscow, near the Washington state line. Recently it was reported that about 20 per cent of the undergraduates were nonresidents of Idaho, and that somewhat more than half of these were from the neighboring state of Washington. A disgruntled Idaho taxpayer sought to restrain and prohibit the Board of Regents of the University of Idaho from establishing any policy regarding the fees of out-of-state students other than one which would require them to pay fees substantially equal to the entire cost to the state of Idaho of providing their education.

Early in 1967 the suit was heard in the local trial court, and

---

[2] Reported in the *University Bulletin* of the University of California, Vol. 16, No. 6, August 21, 1967.

District Judge Merlin S. Young entered judgment against the plaintiff, and declared: "The nonresident tuition policy of the Regents is within their discretion and can not be said to be spending of public money for the private benefit of nonresidents of Idaho, as a matter of law."[3]

It appeared that the university's nonresident tuition fee was $500, and that the average cost to the state of accommodating one undergraduate one year was $1,200 to $1,400. Moreover, in the graduate programs the percentage of out-of-staters ran as high as 50 per cent in some instances, and instructional costs per student were of course markedly higher in the graduate programs than in the undergraduate schools.

The court observed that "No state university sets its nonresident tuition fees upon the basis of the actual cost of education of the student in that university," and concluded: "The Board of Regents does not attempt to set non-resident tuition upon a basis of costs per student or any other cost basis. It does use its best collective judgment to arrive at a figure for non-resident tuition which it believes will attract high-quality non-resident students to the University of Idaho. ... (It) believes that a substantial percentage of a college student body should come from outside of the state and that this is essential to prevent a university from becoming provincial in outlook and that non-resident students are necessary to attract a good faculty."

Noting that the benefits derived from the admission of Idaho students to other state universities on a somewhat informal non-resident reciprocal basis, and the benefits to Idaho universities received from the attendance of non-resident students, are real public benefits, the court remarked that "the public benefit derived from paying a substantial part of the cost of educating non-resident students is an intangible thing which can not be established in dollars and cents," and declared that such a problem of educational policy belongs to the board of regents, and no court should undertake to substitute its judgment for that of the board.

The vexatious business of determining which students are residents of the state for this purpose and which are not—of "separating the sheep from the goats"—has caused many controversies, and some of

[3] *Cobbs* v. *State Board of Education (acting as Regents of the University of Idaho* (Dist. Ct. of Third Judicial Dist.), Civil No. 36600 (January 16, 1967).

these have been litigated. It is significant that a case of this kind at the University of Iowa in 1966 was heard by a special three-judge Federal court as an alleged contravention of 42 United States Code, Section 1983. The thrust of the decision was that the presumption that a nonresident student intends to leave the state as soon as he completes his college course is rebuttable and susceptible of being overthrown by suitable evidence; and that in the case at hand the University of Iowa had interpreted the rule too rigidly, ignoring the student's declared intent to be a permanent resident of Iowa and various other averments pointing in that direction.[4]

Subsequently at least one practically-oriented university attorney has publicly advised state universities to avoid litigation of this matter; i.e., to be a bit flexible in individual cases if any indicia of merit are present. In the Iowa case the plaintiff's contention that charging differential fees to nonresidents is prime facie a violation of the "equal protection" and "privileges and immunities" clauses of the Fourteenth Amendment was not countenanced by the court; but these issues may arise again in other cases before other courts. There are also lawyers who believe the practice contravenes the constitutionally exclusive power of Congress to regulate interstate commerce. Undoubtedly there will be further litigation, and there is a distinct possibility that eventually the principle may be established that charging differential fees to nonresidents is indeed unconstitutional.

Certain it is that neither the framers of the Constitution nor the judges who have interpreted it for nearly two centuries, ever intended that barriers at state boundaries should be allowed to impede the free movement of persons for lawful purposes.

Within any university there is usually some differentiation of fees for some of the more expensive programs of instruction, especially courses in preparation for conspicuously highly-remunerated professions. For example, tuition fees in schools of medicine are almost always higher than in other schools in the same university (though not in proportion to their much higher costs). For laboratory sciences there is often either a small surcharge or at least a deposit required to cover possible excessive breakage of glass or other costly apparatus.

---

[4] *Clarke* v. *Redeker et al., Iowa State Board of Regents* (U.S.D.C., Ia.), So. Dist., Central Div., Civil No. 6-1773-C-1, January 9, 1967.

Differentiation on other bases has also been tried in various isolated instances. In the late 1920's Stevens Institute of Technology in Hoboken introduced differential charges based on the students' marks; i.e., the higher the grade, the lower the tuition fee, and vice versa. This proved hardly more popular or practical than the recently-jettisoned scheme of making male students' draft status depend on grades or examinations.

In mid-1967, after the Michigan legislature had been unusually parsimonious in its appropriations for operating expenses of higher education for the ensuing fiscal year, the Board of Trustees of Michigan State University at East Lansing (not to be confused with the Board of Regents of the University of Michigan at Ann Arbor) adopted an innovation that caused some titillation in the academic world: graduation of fees according to family income. No doubt it should be noted parenthetically that a somewhat similar result on a fragmentary scale and discriminatory basis has been achieved indirectly from time immemorial by selective awards of student aids; but not before, so far as is known, inclusively for all in-state undergraduates in a large public university.

Faced with an annual appropriation only one or two percentage points larger than for the preceding year, the trustees were confronted with a bitter choice: a stiff rise in tuition fees or a cutback of the university's planned operations. Many state university governing boards have faced this same choice in the recent years of rapid growth and have usually reluctantly ordered a boost in fees to prevent the university from deteriorating, while at the same time keenly regretting the fact that this would have the effect of excluding an unknown number of economically marginal students. This time the Board of Trustees of Michigan State, prodded by Don Stevens, a member of 10 years' standing who has long advocated free tuition, voted 5 to 3 to adopt the "sliding-scale" scheme.

Tuition fees had stood at about $350. The new plan requires all undergraduate "in-state" students to pay $501, unless they choose to produce a copy of the Federal income tax return showing that the family income is less than $16,667—in which event the charge will be reduced to 3 per cent of the family income, but not lower than $354 an academic year. Thus it seems that those having annual family incomes of less than $11,800 a year will not benefit directly; but the point is made that they will be relieved to some extent from "subsidizing the education of the well-to-do" who are now required to pay up to $150 a year more.

Needless to say, the plan may be susceptible of some adjustments for middle-income families having two or more children in college at the same time; and assuredly it will necessitate a vast amount of paperwork. However, it went into effect in September, 1967.

The Attorney General of Michigan, in opinions requested by a member of the legislature who is hostile to the plan, has said it does not contravene either the state or Federal constitutions; that the university can not compel a student or parent to exhibit his income tax return, but may offer him an inducement contingent on his doing so, as this plan does.

The scheme is of great current interest because it is a new and ingenious response to legislative appropriation-cutting—different, at least, from the docile acquiescence in flat fee-raising which has been the only response in the past.

The foregoing discourse is much compressed and oversimplified, but it indicates that differentiating fees can involve intricate and harassing difficulties. For public colleges and universities, the condition to be approached is free tuition, with ample support from tax sources and philanthropy.

Chapter 14

INDENTURED FOR LIFE?

SCHOLARSHIPS AND STUDENT LOANS are habitually lumped together as "student aids," though a scholarship is an outright gift, and actually a student loan is not a form of aid at all unless it is obtainable on more favorable terms than the going rates for commercial loans. There was an earlier day when commercial banks or other lending agencies were largely unwilling to consider student loans at all; but for many decades there have been charitable student loan funds available at many colleges and universities and from other private sources on varying terms.

In 1958, the National Defense Education Act put the Federal government into the student loan business on a substantial and expansive scale. It is of historical record that in the last days before the passage of that act, the provision for student *loans* was inserted in lieu of a plan of *scholarships*, at the initiative of the conservative Eisenhower Administration.

The fundamental difference between scholarships and loans is that the former place the entire cost upon taxpayers or donors, while the latter place the whole charge, plus interest, on students. The difference should be carefully pondered. It presents a basic issue. Any conceivable system of student loans has the inescapable tendency toward charging all or a substantial part of the cost of his education to the student. This carries with it the undeniable fact of discriminatory tendency against the economically underprivileged, which means, in varying degrees under varying circumstances, barriers against women students in general, and against the children of low-income families, of both sexes and all races, though proportionately to greater extent among nonwhites. It is precisely these barriers that are now recognized as the root cause of great economic and social waste through failure to develop the talents of the large numbers thus barred; to say nothing of the grave social and economic losses incurred by reason of destructive civil disturbances in urban ghettoes, and of public expenditures for welfare and correctional purposes made necessary by failure to provide adequately for the housing, health, education, and employment of the underprivileged.

For a decade there has been a tattoo of drum-beating for various schemes of student loans on a vast scale, led by certain conservative Ivy League economists who profess to perceive no difference between buying a family washing machine on the installment plan and borrowing to pay college expenses. Totally ignoring the public-service aspect of college attendance, and treating higher education as a consumers' luxury item, these gentlemen have written and spoken learnedly about "pricing systems" for determining tuition fees, and typically concluded, without adducing any particularly convincing evidence, that fees at private institutions should be "moved much closer to full cost" and at public institutions, "at least doubled."[1]

These gentlemen have performed a public service by insisting as early as 1958 that the total annual cost of higher education in the United States would mount to "$9 + billion, $11 + billion, or $13 + billion" by 1970, though those predictions have obviously already fallen short of the mark. Their predictions were far less accurate (not to say shockingly erroneous) and their service much less than wholly commendable when they plugged for "long-term loans" as a panacea in the financing of higher education, characterized other methods as "primi-

---

[1] This is the thrust of Seymour E. Harris' article, "College Salaries, Financing of Higher Education, and Management of Institutions of Higher Learning," *Bulletin of the American Association of University Professors* 44:589-595 (Summer, 1958).

tive,"[2] and predicted that by 1970 the aggregate of tuition fees would have to rise by an additional $3.2 billion a year, while the total to be expected from all governmental sources—state, local, and Federal—would not exceed one billion dollars more than what it was in 1957-58.

How great this last error was is partly revealed by the fact that the aggregate of *state* tax-fund appropriations *alone* for annual operating expenses of higher education in fiscal year 1967-68 in the 50 states was approximately $4.4 billion—more than three times what it had been eight years earlier in 1959-60, and well over $3 billion higher than it had been in 1957-58. Over the same eight-year period the *local* tax support of public junior colleges, municipal universities, and land-grant colleges increased by perhaps a quarter of a billion. The Federal contribution through numerous channels rose to an estimated $4 billion by 1967-68. The 1958 prediction of "not more than an additional billion a year" from all governmental sources by 1970 appears to have missed the mark by being about eightfold too small.

It is "hindsight" that provides the foregoing view; and no one enjoys calling attention to errors of his contemporaries; but the fact ought to be pondered that the same coterie of Northeastern academicians who made the incredible error just described, after having experienced a decade of actual demonstration of the ability and desire of the American public to support greatly expanded higher education mainly through taxation, are still exercising their utmost ingenuity to devise some scheme of student loans that will have the ultimate effect of throwing a great part of the cost of higher education upon the shoulders of the students.

Think of this, if you will at first, purely as a matter of social theory and public policy: *Should the financing of education at any level depend almost wholly on charity and on fees exacted from students and their families?* What would be the capacity and condition today of elementary and secondary schools, and indeed of higher education, if this theory had been applied over the past century? The author considers any such theory a relic dating from no later than the first half of the eighteenth century. It has little to commend it today except a glimmering hope that it could possibly check the

---

[2] Seymour E. Harris, in Dexter M. Keezer, (Ed.), *Financing Higher Education, 1960-1970.* New York: McGraw-Hill, 1959, p. 39, 304 pp.

decline of the relative size and scope of the private sector in higher education.

This would quite obviously, it seems, simultaneously restrict the breadth of opportunity and the scope of accessibility of higher education *as a whole*. There may be very respectable individuals who really desire to see such a narrowing of opportunity, but it is very likely that they are in a small—and a diminishing—minority.

Let the author not be misunderstood as being hostile to private colleges or universities; his position is that of an advocate and supporter of *all* higher education—of its expansion and augmented accessibility to all who can thereby benefit the nation and themselves. In comparison with that goal, real or imaginary conflicts of interest between the private and public sectors seem petty. The American Council on Education said, in a 1959 statement: "It is as shortsighted as it is false to promote one segment of higher education at the expense of another." The author's objection to any vast student loan system is twofold: (1) It is conceived to aggrandize the private sector, and to diminish the public sector; and (2) its tendency is to restrict rather than expand the opportunities available to all, because it shifts the major part of the costs of higher education to the student and his family, reversing the modern policy of having largely tax-supported higher education accessible to all at only nominal tuition fees or tuition-free.

The most recent proposal to turn to the rear and march toward the eighteenth century is that of the "Zacharias Panel," a small group scheduled to report in September, 1967, to the President's science adviser, Donald F. Hornig.[3]

Early fragmentary public notice of the proposed scheme (or of one closely resembling it) came in press stories following the delivery of the Harry Camp Memorial Lectures at Stanford University in May, 1967, by Kingman Brewster, Jr., president of Yale University. The three lectures composed a masterpiece of insightful discourse

---

[3] Chairman of the panel was Professor Jerrold Zacharias of Massachusetts Institute of Technology. Other members: Jacqueline Grennan, president of Webster College; Frederick H. Burkhardt of the American Council of Learned Societies; and Professors Andrew Gleason of Harvard, John Hawkes of Stanford, and George Stern of Syracuse University. Note that there is no representative of any *public* university or college.

on the nature and governance of higher education, with convincing emphasis against bureaucratization.

The final one thousand words of the third lecture briefly outlined a plan of lifetime loans, not precisely identical with the sketchy scheme later reported as the work of the Zacharias Panel in the press of early August, 1967, but the same in general principle. Avoiding any meticulous attribution either to Brewster or Zacharias or any individual whose name may have been associated with "anonymous quotations from a non-existent report," and recognizing that many details are at this writing unrevealed or undetermined, it is possible to discuss briefly the major essentials and some probable effects of the scheme if it were to be embodied in an act of Congress.

Aside from its generally reactionary tenor, some of the features of the scheme present difficult unsolved problems. Apparently no solution has been offered for the handicapping of women students. It seems clear that the millions of young married women who continue in remunerative employment after graduation would be obligated for the same proportion of their incomes as would male graduates, and that this would be highly regressive and discriminatory on account of the substantially smaller average salaries paid to women. As for the other millions who marry and do not continue in remunerative work, no answer has appeared. *If* they are to be excused from the obligation as long as they have no income, then working male and female graduates will be paying for the education of a large bloc of nonworking females; and any woman could get an entirely free college education simply by not having an income thereafter. Let us not speculate on what effects this might produce. If a way is devised to obligate women graduates who have no income, then this is open to all the objections to the "negative dowry" which makes existing loan programs so unsuitable for young women. (Our conservative economists and mathematicians seem strangely oblivious of the presence of women in the higher education picture.)

The scheme has some seeming advantages over previous loan plans: Collection would be wholly in the hands of the Internal Revenue Service (probably the most efficient agency of its kind in the world) and would be executed along with the Federal income tax, in a manner which would seem to promise maximum economy and would relieve the colleges and/or the private lending agencies of the troublesome task of collection. (One version would have the loans come from Federal funds; another as government-guaranteed loans from private banks or other agencies. The difference involves both ideological and pragmatic questions, but in either case the method of collection would be the same.)

One version estimates the necessary obligation as 1 per cent of income for 40 years for each $4,000 borrowed; another as 1 per cent of life income for each $3,000 borrowed. Since the total cost of a four-year schooling (board, room, books, clothing, incidentals, plus tuition fees and other fees) has already reached a minimum of about $14,000 at the high-fee institutions, and about $8,000 at the mythical average state university, and will go higher (and much higher if any scheme of this kind is adopted to encourage the raising of fees), it is manifest that the calculation of the necessary percentage of life income poses an actuarial problem of gigantic proportions. The vision of a Federal bureaucratic structure comparable to the magnitude of the vast social security setup begins to emerge, and it matters little whether it would be within the Internal Revenue Service or standing independently and maintaining the accounts of scores of millions of individual "clients."

One commentator has said that "with this modest burden proportioned to a person's actual earnings it should be possible to charge somewhere near the full cost of education," and "this would not grossly favor the high-fee institutions since the student would not welcome the contingent future liability for repayment unless he thought that for some reason the cost was worth it." This latter, of course, applies equally to any pre-existing student loan systems, and indeed to the whole present picture—the student undertakes whatever he thinks is worth the cost. This is why high-fee colleges are abe to operate and grow. The pernicious element is in the "charging of somewhere near the full cost of education" without distinction between private and public institutions. This may be all very well for the private sector, but it practically implies the quick destruction of the whole century-old tradition of tax-supported free public higher education, and the transfer of nearly the whole cost from the general public to the students alone.

Peculiarly enough, if the payment must be projected forward over a period of 40 years, in many respects the whole scheme parallels what actually takes place in public higher education currently, without any of the intricate mathematical exercises the proposed scheme would entail, and sans any of the vast apparatus of coercion it would necessitate, as well as clear of the dangers of diminished freedom that are inherent in it. Actually what happens is that the student attends a low-fee public institution and is graduated with perhaps some $4,000 to $8,000 of public money invested in his higher education. His earning-power, enhanced by that same education, by inflation, and by other factors, causes him to pay Federal and state income taxes in higher brackets than would otherwise have been the case, as well as taxes on sales, property, and other types at higher levels because of his added purchasing-power, so that with the passing of a few years, or a working lifetime at most, a majority of such persons will have repaid the full cost of their higher education, and more, in the form of added taxes. The whole society gains in actual dollars repaid, as well as in the great imponderable assets that can not be measured precisely in dollars and cents. What would be the advantage of abandoning this gloriously successful principle and plunging the whole enterprise into a morass of useless paperwork representing coercive obligations which in the normal course of events are discharged automatically and without any vast furor at all?

The only advantage is in the minds of a few persons who may believe that this sea-change would make life more comfortable and more secure for the private colleges and increase their competitive leverage.

One incisive writer[4] has said this trial balloon "will probably burst from its own expanding gases long before it is necessary to shoot it down. . . . We can see no benefit in changing the philosophy that society is the final beneficiary of education."

A colleague writing for the same journal[5] points out there is some interest in the life-indenture plan on the part of some officers of the U.S. Treasury and the Budget Bureau because it would eventually relieve the government of contributing to the support of higher education. This, he notes, would run counter to national policy for

---

[4] Dennis W. Binning, in *College and University Business* 43:31 (August, 1967).
[5] William Steif, *Ibid.*, p. 31.

more than a century; and it is the task of society to provide college education because society reaps large dividends from this investment.

"The student would carry a financial albatross around his neck all his life," and "not even those who are keenest on the proposal have yet figured out what to do with the female 30 to 40 per cent of the college population which marries and raises families." Finally, "While the plan would salvage hard-pressed private colleges, it also would end the distinctive and valuable competition between private and public institutions."

Public release of the text of the Zacharias Panel report occurred September 7, 1967. This version disclosed a preference that the lending agency be a public corporation created for the purpose and bearing the innocuously saccharine name of "Educational Opportunity Bank." The full text was printed in the September 13 issue of the *Chronicle of Higher Education* (Vol. 2, No. 1),[6] along with the text of a shorter statement severely critical of it, issued jointly by the two principal groupings of state institutions of higher education—the National Association of State Universities and Land-Grant Colleges and the Association of State Colleges and Universities. These associations circulated the full text of the Zacharias report to their members.[7]

Significant is a statement from the Washington headquarters of the American Council on Education, the 50-year-old national association of nearly 1,500 colleges and universities (private and public) and other associations and agencies related to higher education. The Council's President, Logan Wilson, commented:

"The Council has not taken a formal position on this or similar proposals which have been advanced by various individuals for well over a decade. We have not because it has seemed inconceivable that they could receive serious consideration either in educational or Governmental circles.

"We in this nation have believed, almost since our founding, that the cost of educating our young was the responsibility of society as a whole. We have moved steadily toward providing subsidized

---

[6] The biweekly national newspaper published by Editorial Projects for Education, Inc., 3301 North Charles St., Baltimore, Maryland 21218.

[7] Copies of the text may also be purchased at 15¢ from the Superintendent of Documents, Government Printing Office, Washington, D.C. 20202, under the title "Educational Opportunity Bank."

educational opportunity at ever higher levels for larger numbers of our citizens. The dividends returned to society on this investment seem obvious. It is the declared policy of the American Council on Education that a larger expenditure of public funds, both state and Federal, and a greater contribution by private philanthropy, in support of higher education is essential in order to minimize charges levied on individual students. The (Zacharias) panel's proposal would move the nation in precisely the opposite direction in an effort to relieve society of a commitment it has been increasingly willing to make.

"In 1963 Professor Edward Shapiro of the University of Detroit proposed a 'loan program' very similar to that now proposed by the panel. At the time critics with as diverse backgrounds as Professor Theodore W. Schultz of the University of Chicago, Representative Edith Green of Oregon, and John F. Morse, director of the ACE's Commission on Federal Relations, raised many practical, as well as philosophical, objections to the proposal. Most of these objections have been recognized in the recent panel report, but few have been overcome. They have been placed in the section entitled, 'Questions Requiring Further Study.' "[8]

---

[8] Quoted in *Higher Education and National Affairs*, the newsletter of the American Council on Education, Vol. 16, No. 31 (September 15, 1967).

PART FOUR

Chapter 15

SUPPORT FROM PRIVATE DONORS

In the long history of Anglo-American society, the legal concept of charity became viable some centuries before the idea of tax-supported education took root. Historians are now agreed that the concept of charity in a legal sense had its origins at least as far back as Biblical antiquity, and that it was recognized by English courts of chancery long before it was given its formal definition in the Statute of 43 Elizabeth (1601). The classic American definition (not greatly different from the words of the Elizabethan enactment) is by Justice Gray of the supreme judicial court of Massachusetts, in a decision of 1867: "A gift to be administered consistently with existing laws, for the benefit of an indefinite number of persons, either by . . . education or religion, or by relieving their bodies from disease, . . . or by assisting them to establish themselves in life; or by creating or maintaining public buildings or works; or by otherwise lessening the burdens of government."[1]

Hence the modern models of the charitable trust and the charitable corporation—the one springing from equity jurisprudence, the

---

[1] *Edmund Jackson v. Wendell Phillips and others*, 96 Mass. (14 Allen) 539 (1867).

other a creature of statute; both existing at the sufferance of the state, the one protected by the chancery courts, the other guided by the terms of its charter. Almost all private colleges are in fact charitable corporations, holding many separate charitable trusts. Colleges constitute a distinctive and prominent example of the species, but there are many other subtypes in the modern scene: philanthropic foundations, private charitable hospitals, libraries, church organizations, and associations of a hundred kinds for the promotion of health, recreation, education, and welfare, such as the American Red Cross, the Salvation Army, the Boy Scouts of America, the Girl Scouts, Inc., the YMCA's, the YWCA's, and a vast variety of others.

Nearly all state and municipal universities are public corporations capable of receiving and executing charitable trusts, practically all receive a stream of private gifts, and a few have substantial endowment funds derived largely from private sources. Many of them have also procured the incorporation of one or more "accessory" private charitable corporations, one of whose functions is to receive and execute charitable gifts on behalf of the university. This is partly because some donors are hesitant to make a gift to a public corporation, sometimes because a too-minute regulation of the university's fiscal affairs by the state creates real difficulties and uncertainties in the administration of charitable trusts by the university corporation directly, and partly for various other reasons.

The total of all private gifts to all colleges and universities in the United States during the one year 1965-66 was reported by the Council for Financial Aid to Education and the American Alumni Council as more than $1½ billion. (This is an estimate based on returns of data from 1,033 institutions from which a total of more than $1¼ billion was reported.)[2]

This aggregate of $1½ billion exceeds most predictions of five years earlier, when the total was about $1 billion, and the run-of-the-mill prophets were willing to project $1½ billion *by 1970*. It would now seem reasonable to suppose that the $2 billion mark will be passed, perhaps by a considerable distance, by 1970. There can be no question of the need. President Holgar J. Johnson of the CFAE is reported

---

[2] *The Chronicle of Higher Education*, Vol. 1, No. 16, pp. 1 and 12 (July 12, 1967).

as estimating that current operating budgets of colleges and universities are increasing at an average annual rate of 14 per cent. If that rate continues, it means practically a doubling of the total within five years; and just to keep abreast, the total of private gifts would have to double by 1970, plus whatever is given for permanent endowment and capital outlay. This is not impossible. The gain for 452 institutions that have reported to the CFAE consistently from 1954-55 through 1965-66 (a period of 11 years) was 221½ per cent—meaning that a multiplication of three and one-fourth times occurred, or that the total was more than tripled over 11 years.

The major sources of private gifts for 1965-66 and the contributions of each are exhibited here:

Table 7. Private gifts to 1,033 universities and colleges, by major sources, single year 1965-66 (figures in thousands of dollars).

Sources	Totals
(1)	(2)
General welfare foundations	$ 304,107
Non-alumni individuals	299,945
Alumni	265,558
Business corporations	195,705
Religious denominations	92,575
Non-alumni, non-church groups	59,086
Other sources	12,818
Total	$1,229,794
Extrapolated to all universities and colleges in United States	$1,535,000

Source: Council for Financial Aid to Education and American Alumni Council, as reported in *Chronicle of Higher Education* 1:1, 12 (July 12, 1967).

There appeared to be a very slight decline from the record total of $1,556 million for the preceding year, 1964-65. This seemed to be explainable at least in part by such factors as the distribution in 1964-65 by the James Foundation of its entire capital of some $33 million and by the circumstance that the same year marked the final payments by the Ford Foundation on its several large "challenge grants"—a program which it was beginning to de-emphasize in 1965-66.

Some knowledgeable observers are inclined to say that while the philanthropic foundations constituted the listed source of the largest total benefactions in 1965-66, this may not always continue to be the case in future years. As the source most promising for prospective rapid and ultimately very large expansion, they point to the business and industrial corporations; and it is undoubtedly true that this is a field destined for expansive development.

It seems that in 1965-66 183 state institutions received $234 million—about 19 per cent of the total, and a gain of nearly 25 per cent over the preceding year. Previous estimates had generally placed the proportion received by public institutions at about 15 per cent.

As in most economic and social statistics, a marked "concentration of wealth" appears in the record of private gifts to higher education. Twenty universities—16 private and 4 public, were the beneficiaries of more than $400 million in gifts—more than one-third of the total for a thousand institutions. Each of these 20 received from more than $10 million upward, Harvard being at the top with $44½ million. The state universities of California, Michigan, Wisconsin, and Delaware are in this favored list for the year 1965-66.

The analysts of the data from 1,033 institutions concluded that, as to the purposes of the gifts, about 31 per cent were unrestricted,

Table 8.   Twenty universities receiving the largest totals of private gifts, single year 1965-66, in thousands of dollars.

Institutions	Gifts	Institutions	Gifts
(1)	(2)	(1)	(2)
Harvard U.	$44,464	U. of So. California	$17,226
Mass. Inst. Tech.	40,740	U. of Michigan	16,781
U. of California	34,616	Brigham Young U.	15,181
Yale U.	27,717	U. of Wisconsin	13,731
U. of Chicago	26,413	Yeshiva U.	13,175
Cornell U.	25,125	Washington U. (St. L.)	12,781
New York U.	21,327	U. of Delaware	12,667
Stanford U.	21,226	Johns Hopkins U.	12,579
Columbia U.	18,815	Northwestern U.	11,748
U. of Pennsylvania	18,335	U. of Pittsburgh	10,724

Source: *Ibid*. (Original source is *Voluntary Support of Education 1965-66*. New York: Council for Financial Aid to Education, 1967.)

about 25 per cent for physical plant, 14½ per cent for basic research, 12 per cent for student aid, 6 per cent for faculty salaries, and 11 per cent for other purposes. Thus apparently only about a maximum of 65 per cent would be available for annual operating expenses (strictly "educational and general").

There is every reason to believe that philanthropic support of higher education will always continue, and in an increasing volume. It is heavily favored in the Federal Internal Revenue Code provisions for the deduction of charitable gifts from incomes and estates. This is firmly fixed national public policy. Courts at all echelons in all jurisdictions look with special solicitude on the inception and execution of charitable trusts. Many of the states have statutes designed to minimize fraud or ineptitude in fund-raising. The American Association of Fund-Raising Counsel, Inc., has a membership of 26 established firms, most of which have earned nationwide confidence and respect through careers of many years.

Perhaps most auspicious of all is the fact that increasing numbers of colleges and universities of every type are recognizing the function of expanding and improving contacts with prospective donors, and stimulating their interest in the future of the institution, as a top echelon administrative function (sometimes combined with the functions of public information and public relations, sometimes separately organized), which should be headed by an officer bearing the title and dignity of "Vice President for Development" or "Vice President for University Relations and Development," and who should be supported by a staff commensurate with the size of the institution. This officer should also have the confidence and respect of the faculty so as to attract its moral support and understanding of his task, and its voluntary assistance in appropriate ways. Progress toward those goals is taking place.

"The field of private philanthropy is still largely an untapped reservoir," says a *Time* education writer: "Only 23 per cent of college graduates give to their *alma mater;* only 600 of the nation's 5,000 large companies give significantly."[3] But President Nathan Pusey of Harvard is quoted, in a statement perhaps typical of private

---

[3] *Time,* Vol. 89, No. 25, p. 85 (June 23, 1967).

university and college presidents, as saying "The only place the money can come from is the Federal Government—that's inevitable."[4] In any event, all will agree that gifts from private donors will continue an important resource.

---

[4] *Ibid., loc. cit.*

Chapter 16

ALUMNI AS A SOURCE OF SUPPORT

A COLLEGE IS MUCH MORE than a temporary dwelling-place for a few months or a few years. It partakes of the characteristics of a clan or club or enlarged family within which a "sense of belonging" develops. Fraternities, sororities, athletic teams, journalistic and public speaking clubs, and a thousand other subunits afford closer associations in small groups, to say nothing of classes and of residence in dormitory units.

Individuals vary greatly in gregariousness and capacity for making friends; but even the most reserved or withdrawn find associations, formal or informal, which they enjoy and remember for the remainder of their lives. Sentiments of loyalty, gratitude, nostalgia, felt in diverse degrees by each former student, tend to grow with the passing years and to become fused into somewhat hazy but very pleasant impressions of college days.

Annual alumni reunions can become occasions of much hilarity as the idiosyncracies of classmates and professors are recalled, half-forgotten friendships renewed, and the "good old days" relived.

Every college of whatever type (except a new college which has no alumni) can benefit financially and in other ways from alumni support; and every college does so benefit. Generally speaking, as the college grows older the size of its alumni body steadily increases, and the number of individuals able and likely to make large gifts also grows.

Moreover, it has been demonstrated beyond question that annual giving, even in nominal or token amounts, becomes a habit that can be depended upon in successive years, and that may well produce progressively larger annual gifts, often culminating in a substantial testamentary bequest. Where large numbers are involved, as in the case of old or large institutions, the dependability of annual alumni campaigns becomes high, so that the alumni have often been aptly called "living endowment,"—meaning that they constitute a source of annual income as reliable as a prudently invested endowment fund. Ten thousand alumni who can be relied upon to give an average of $40 a year, for example, would be the equivalent of an endowment fund of $10 million. Even 1,000 alumni giving an average of only $20 a year would equal the annual income potential of an endowment of half a million.

Yale University is credited with being the first among American institutions to exploit systematically the potential of annual alumni giving, beginning before the turn of the twentieth century; and Yale has now been for some years regularly reaping $2 million or more annually from that source. The state universities can do equally well. Ohio State University, having conducted its annual alumni solicitation for half a century, now obtains more than $2 million each year.

The size of the annual harvest is, of course, limited by the size and age of the college, among other factors. The longer the annual campaign has been systematically and successfully made, the larger and more constant the product will be—assuming that reasonably good communication with alumni has also been maintained through a good alumni magazine, an active alumni association, local alumni clubs in cities, and other means.

While direct-mail solicitation will produce some results, a far more effective method is by telephone or face-to-face personal conversations by volunteers who are themselves alumni. This requires organization by tens and by hundreds and by thousands, somewhat after the Roman military model, to assure that every prospect will actually be engaged in conversation by a fellow-alumnus solicitor. If the local "centurion" is not personally acquainted with the prospect, he can usually find one of his own "soldiers" who knows the prospect well as a former classmate and who can persuade him as a stranger could not.

If there is a distasteful aura about the thought of "begging," even for the best of causes, it need hardly enter the transaction between the college and its own alumni, because rare indeed is the alumnus who does not feel some sense of actual indebtedness to his college. In the case of tax-supported institutions, he may indeed have long since discharged his dollar indebtedness in the form of additional taxes paid on higher earnings made possible by his college experience; but he will nevertheless forever feel an obligation to make gestures toward paying for nonpecuniary benefits unmeasurable in dollars. Apart from all this, if he has received regularly a good alumni magazine and other communications from his college, he can not avoid feeling an obligation at least to cover amply the cost of these services; and this may be the beginning of a habit that eventually leads to substantial gifts later in life.

Suffice it to say that any college or university, public or private, can ill afford to neglect frequent and continuous communication with its alumni; with persistence and good management this activity can be developed to produce priceless nonpecuniary advantages, to support itself financially, and eventually to become a dependable source of annual income for the institution.

If the institution is very small or very new, so that its alumni organization has no roots, then alumni solicitation during the first few years must be on a modest scale and may not be able at first even to pay the expenses of record-maintenance and mail communication; but if the institution is permanent and has a future, the few lean years should be used to lay prudently the foundations of alumni support, dollarwise and otherwise.

Chapter 17

THE PHILANTHROPIC FOUNDATIONS

MEN AND WOMEN of great wealth must sooner or later ponder the half-facetious adage, "You can't take it with you." Some may wish to guarantee that the family fortune will go on forever in the hands of their descendants. This is legally impossible in all Anglo-American jurisdictions because no donor or testator may lawfully extend any control over the disposition of the estate for longer than a specified limited time after his death. In some states this period is the duration of two "lives in being" at the time of the testator's demise.

The facts of biology also argue against perpetual retention of estates in the hands of direct descendants. It can be pointed out that each child has two parents, four grandparents, and so on, so that in theory the direct descendant in the tenth generation would have 1,024 ancestors in the first generation—that is, 1,023 contemporaries, male and female, of either parent in the first generation would have equal shares in the ancestry of the tenth-generation child. This severely dilutes the concept of the tenth-generation child as "the apple of the eye" of any one remote ancestor, and as belonging peculiarly to any one such progenitor alone.

This has sometimes been used as an argument for charitable

giving—an attempt to convince the prospective donor that he can best promote the welfare of his own remote descendants by contributing toward the general social progress of the successive generations. At any rate, a substantial number of possessors of vast private fortunes in the United States during the past century have devoted all or large portions of their wealth to the creation of charitable trusts or foundations.

Only a charitable trust can go on forever. All others are cut off by the Rule Against Perpetuities, which pervades the law of all Anglo-American jurisdictions. Yet not all charitable trusts are perpetual; they may terminate after a specified period by their own terms, or the instrument may authorize the trustees to determine whether to spend principal as well as income, and thus to determine how long the fund shall exist. But the classic form is that in which the principal or corpus must be forever held inviolate, and only the income expended. This is an awesome concept and creates a social agency of great dignity and usefulness, though the whole idea is not immune from criticism.

These "pools of wealth" dedicated to charitable purposes are known in the vernacular as "foundations," and some of them use the word in their official names; but unfortunately the word has also sometimes been adopted by trade associations, advertising enterprises, or even by profit-seeking businesses, and this tends to tarnish somewhat its pristine luster. However that may be, perhaps some 50 of the largest and leading charitable trusts in the United States enjoy substantial public favor, such that the names of at least several of them are "household words," nationwide.

Actually the total number of charitable trusts is enormous, and unknown with any precision. The largest available list is in the files of the U. S. Treasury Department, said to number 40,000 or more, of those which have applied for privileges of tax exemption under the Internal Revenue Code. No doubt thousands of others, usually comparatively small, are known only by instruments of varying ages, tucked into archaic files in 3,000 county courthouses from coast to coast. The Foundation Library in New York City has studied the foundations for many years, and issued several successive editions of a large directory, listing some 6,800 having assets of $200,000 or more, from which brief descriptive data were obtainable.

Various efforts are made to classify them as "general welfare foundations" and those whose charters or practices seem to confine their activities to narrower specific purposes; and the annual volume of gifts and grants from them is classified as for education (chiefly higher education), welfare, international activities, health, sciences, religion, and the humanities. The first of these objects (education) is the largest recipient. For the year 1966 it was reported that 6,300 foundations gave a total of $1.2 billion in grants to education (chiefly colleges and universities). Among larger grants of that year were $50 million by the Ford Foundation to 60 colleges and $6 million to the National Educational Television and Radio Center in New York; $1½ million by the Kellogg Foundation for continuing education to Columbia University; and $1½ million by the Carnegie Foundation for the Advancement of Teaching to the College Entrance Examination Board for research on a national system of college-level examinations.

During the six or seven decades in which the bulk of foundation activity has taken place, there have been many changes in the predominating emphases in the policies of educational foundations. Once the stress was on building up college endowment funds. This gave way to other aims. In 1955 the newly-active Ford Foundation devoted half a billion dollars to improve the salaries of college teachers. More recently it has committed large sums in the form of "challenge grants" to stimulate the raising of funds for annual operating expenses and capital outlays, usually to carefully selected "superior" private colleges.

This in turn was superseded in 1967 by other interests, one of which was announced to be an effort to study the management of college endowment funds and stimulate greater productivity through improved investment practices.

Another thrust now apparent among some of the major foundations is toward emphasis on the upgrading of "developing colleges," this phrase being a euphemism for substandard institutions hitherto weak academically and precarious financially; whereas until recently the emphasis tended to be largely on "building up the peaks of excellence" by reserving grants for colleges that were already traditionally among the "best."

A moment's thought will make it apparent that excellent arguments can be adduced in favor of either of these different policies; but perhaps now it is peculiarly appropriate that in a period of unprecedented expansion of higher education, attention should swerve toward the small and struggling colleges that have previously been least favored.

Philanthropic foundations have been much criticized on various grounds. It was once contended that trustees are required by statutes and sometimes by the terms of the trust instruments to handle foundation investments more conservatively than would an ordinarily prudent investor, and that this resulted in a large "pool of wealth" being held "stagnant"; that is, kept out of bold and somewhat speculative investments in new enterprises, and thus being something of a dead weight restraining economic progress. This contention has lost much of its force because the total of philanthropic foundation capital (perhaps $20 billion) is only a tiny fraction of the total of disposable wealth and also because restrictions on its investment are now generally much less strait than they were half a century ago.

A continuing source of adverse scanning of foundation activities, directed not so much toward the larger and well-established ones as toward the relatively newer "family foundations" and "company foundations," goes on in an effort to bring to light unethical or unlawful practices involved in their use for purposes of tax avoidance by their founders, and also their employment as vehicles to perpetuate and extend their founders' control of large business or industrial corporations through the purchase of voting stock and other security manipulations.

Prominent in this area have been several successive Congressional investigations and reports made under the aegis of a committee of the United States House of Representatives headed by Representative Wright Patman of Texas. It is also the duty of the Internal Revenue Service and of the Department of Justice to monitor these peccadilloes and to restrain them by appropriate administrative rulings, suits in Federal courts, and proposed amendments to the Internal Revenue Code and other relevant Federal laws.

Appraisal of the impact of educational foundations in a broad sense and over the decades is a complex and difficult undertaking. It would be easy to launch into a panegyric of praise, replete with laudatory examples. In this there would be a considerable element of truth. But it would not do to overlook the assertions from many quarters that the staffs and boards of trustees in general proceed timidly and without much disposition to make any significant breaks from conservative and traditional patterns of thought and practice in making grants for research or demonstration projects. It is possible to trace some important innovations in education to some landmark foundation grants, at least in part; but it is impossible to assess the exact weight of the foundation-supported activity in comparison with that of many other factors.

The theory underlying almost all foundation grants is that by selecting a project of "seminal" character and supporting it for a limited period (seldom more than a few years) it will be possible to demonstrate its permanent and widespread value so conclusively that it will become self-supporting—either from private fees or tax funds—and go on to spread its beneficent effects in ever-widening circles. In many instances in the past some such outcome seems to have been approximated in some degree; but in many more numerous instances a temporary foundation grant sustains some inept attempt at research or demonstration which limps along until the money is exhausted and then sinks without a trace, except perhaps an unreadable and unreliable report in a limited edition which gathers dust on a few library shelves.

It must be admitted that the work of foundation trustees and staff members (who facetiously call themselves "philanthropoids") is an unconscionably high-risk business; and a resoundingly successful coup in the form of a highly fruitful benefaction can be expected only occasionally. Trustees are almost always in and of the Establishment with a capital "E" and are thus not too predisposed to "rock the boat" by financing undertakings likely to produce any really revolutionary results in education or the social sciences. This is not to impugn their devotion to truth and the search for truth; only to note that truth does not reveal itself to all alike, and the *status quo* often takes on an exceedingly rosy hue when perceived from a plushy position.

The foregoing almost seems to point toward an obvious and hackneyed suggestion: That by some simple means which we need not pause to describe here, foundation boards take pains to see to it that there is more than token representation among their members of great segments of the population for whom they presume to play

God—that they insure that they will hear directly in their deliberations the voices of women, of persons under the age of 40, of Negroes, of persons in modest or stringent financial circumstances, of ordinary workers from factory, farm, or commercial outlet, of college students— in short, a few non-Establishment voices. Let the feudal concept of *noblesse oblige* be modified a trifle to make room for a little infusion of the modern concept of participation in decision-making by representatives of those for whom the decisions are ostensibly made.

Descending from Cloud Nine, what shall we say of the foundation world of today? All foundations might well emulate the practices of some of the leading ones in making full disclosure of their operations in informative annual reports, widely circulated; in selecting staffs of individuals highly qualified in the fields in which the foundation operates; and in placing, so far as practicable, their management on an impersonal basis, free of "cronyism" or class influence.

There is visible progress in all these respects. The great charitable trusts, old and new, can continue beyond the foreseeable future as uniquely useful servants of an open society, and as stimulators of inventiveness in the hugely expanding and enormously significant function of higher education in such a society. To college and university administrators, professors, advanced students: Study the foundations, offer them suggestions, ask them about ideas which you

Table 9. Fifteen philanthropic foundations, each having assets of $100 million or more, 1966 (figures in thousands of dollars).

Foundations	Assets	Foundations	Assets
Ford Foundation	$2,428,550*	Kresge Foundation	$172,829
Rockefeller Foundation	854,201	Commonwealth Fund	156,546
Duke Endowment	691,903	Danforth Foundation	145,576
W. K. Kellogg Foundation	491,523	Avalon Foundation	139,635
Carnegie Corp. of N. Y.	344,333	Mellon Foundation	121,969
Lilly Endowment	319,502	Carnegie Inst. of Wash.	115,318
A. P. Sloan Foundation	309,322	Old Dominion Foundation	105,062
Rockefeller Bros. Fund	210,342		

Source: Adapted from *The World Almanac*, 1967, p. 258. New York: Newspaper Enterprise Association, Inc., 1967, 912 pp.
*This figure represents market value; all others, book value.

think are creative. Learn the current special emphases of the large foundations and the smaller ones—especially the latter whose head-quarters are in or near your own community or state. Together they are an important element in the support of higher education from private sources.

Table 9 is only a thin slice off the top of the foundation pyramid. There are hundreds of others of substantial size, and many thousands of smaller ones, all encouraged and aided by Federal and state tax favors and overseen with solicitude by the courts of equity.

Chapter 18

CONTRIBUTIONS BY RELIGIOUS ORGANIZATIONS

MORE THAN ONE-THIRD of all the universities, colleges, and junior colleges in the United States have some connection with some religious denomination. The degree of a church's control over and support of a college varies widely. Some colleges are legally owned by the parent church conference and have no separate corporate identity. In such cases the college trustees are merely agents of the church. This has been the case with some colleges founded by some Protestant denominations, and is quite largely true of Catholic colleges, whether diocesan or operated by one of the several religious orders.

Mention of Catholic colleges in this context calls for immediate recognition of a number of facts peculiar to them:

1. Although there has been no regular custom of cash appropriations to them by the Church itself, and they have sought funds in the same manner as other private colleges—i.e., from student fees and from gifts from the several sources of philanthropy—yet they have generally had a very great continuing financial asset in the form of the unpaid services of priests, lay brothers, and nuns who often constitute large portions of their

faculties and administration. This is true both of the comparatively few colleges that are diocesan (owned and operated by a bishop for his diocese) and the larger numbers operated by one or another of the religious orders such as the Jesuits (Society of Jesus), the Congregation of the Holy Cross, the Vincentians, and many others, including orders of nuns operating colleges for girls. Priests or sisters under vows of poverty and celibacy receive only a modest subsistence, much less than the salaries of lay persons of equivalent education; and they transfer from place to place at the order of their ecclesiastical superiors and perform whatever duties are assigned to them. This circumstance has rather effectively frustrated the various accrediting associations and some students of the financing of private colleges who have sought to appraise institutions largely on the basis of faculty salaries or undertaken to place all colleges in some format of "uniform accounting."

2. It is true, however, that, especially among the larger urban Catholic institutions, increasing proportions of the faculties now consist of lay teachers employed in much the same manner as in non-Catholic colleges; and thus their financing makes a closer approach than formerly to what might be called "national norms."

3. It is also true that modifications are occurring in the structure of Catholic college and university governing boards. Formerly the model was frequently a small group (often three) of members of the priestly hierarchy, including the chief administrator of the institution, and operating subject to the orders of the bishop or of the head of the religious order, often resident in Rome. Now the tendency is to add substantial numbers of lay persons, either as a separate advisory board, or as a panel of the governing board itself. This move has obvious financial implications, as well as its ecclesiastical connotations of change in the Church-and-college relationship.

4. Lastly, two incidents of 1966-67 can hardly be omitted, though their bearings upon financing may be somewhat indirect: (a) a bitter revolt of faculty members, some priests and some lay, when 31 professors at St. John's University in New York City were summarily told their current one-year contracts would

not be renewed, and were given no specific reasons and no hearings; and (b) the occurrences at Webster College at St. Louis, where the extraordinarily intelligent and successful president, a sister in a religious order, requested, with the approval of her bishop, that she be released from the vows of the order and continued as head of the Catholic college, saying in effect that exclusively religious control and the spirit of an institution of higher education were incompatible[1]; and these dispensations were granted.

These relatively recent winds of change among Catholic colleges are indeed new as compared with the century of attenuation that has been undergone by the relations between Protestant denominational colleges and their parent church organizations.

As already noted, in a few cases the church is owner and governing body; but by and large, when litigated controversies have arisen, the courts have generally held that an incorporated college is an *educational* corporation rather than an *ecclesiastical* one, and that the college is not subject to control by the church except as unmistakably provided in the college charter. Among such cases is the decision of the Tennessee supreme court in 1914, denying the claims of the Methodist Episcopal Church, South, to certain controls over Vanderbilt University not provided for in the university charter. Thereafter the church severed all connection with Vanderbilt.[2]

Here we need not go into the charge, sometimes made, that in church-connected colleges piety tends to outrank intellectuality, and blind faith is prized above thought and reason. Rigid church control has been broken down in so many ways and in such varying degrees that the Court of Appeals of Maryland decided in 1966, wisely, that no blanket rule can be laid down as to whether a college is or is not an "establishment of religion" within the meaning of the First Amend-

---

[1] The words of President Jacqueline Grennan, in her statement of January 11, 1967: "It is my personal conviction that the very nature of higher education is opposed to juridical control by the Church. The academic freedom which must characterize a college or university would provide continuing embarrassment for the Church if her hierarchy were forced into endorsing or negating the action of the college or university."

[2] *State v. Board of Trustees of Vanderbilt University*, 129 Tenn. 279, 164 S.W. 1151 (1914).

ment to the Constitution of the United States, but that each case must be decided on examination of the particular facts.

Financial support from the church varies as widely as church control—from almost none to a substantial proportion. It has been reported that the largest Protestant denominations, such as the Methodist Church (11 million members), contribute relatively little *per capita* to the support of their many colleges—perhaps an aggregate of $1 or less per member per year; while certain small and close-knit denominations, such as the Seventh Day Adventists, the Reformed Church in America, and some others, tend to contribute much more annually *per capita* to the support of their few colleges—perhaps as much as $20 or more per member per year.

The teaching of sectarian religion and the maintenance and cultivation of a particular sectarian atmosphere are prominent among the services which a private college can lawfully perform, but a public college can not. Certainly there will continue to be many millions of parents who ardently prefer some infusion of sectarianism into the education of their children. Why, then, can not church support of denominational colleges have a new lease on life? It is true that state universities are not hostile to any religion, that they are hospitable to all sorts of denominational clubs among students and faculty, encouraging them to have houses near the campus and often permitting them limited use of state-owned facilities. But all this does not make a denominational college.

Even the current wave of ecumenicism need not militate against the sectarian college, but only stimulate it to a somewhat more tolerant and enlightened stance. The churches may well create opportunities for their cause in future generations if they recognize now that higher education is more important than ever before and redouble their efforts in behalf of their own type of college.

Addressing themselves to the financial responsibility of churches in higher education, Manning M. Pattillo and Donald M. Mackenzie wrote in 1965:

"The differences among churches in their support of colleges are enormous. Some churches provide almost no funds; others contribute more than 50 per cent of operating budgets and capital funds. One church underwrites its principal institution at the rate of $1,000 per student per year. The average is 12.8 per cent of operating budget."[3]

They concluded:

"Clearly, the differences among the churches in their support of higher education are not due to differences in economic status. In fact, the opposite is closer to the truth. The churches whose members have modest means often show the greatest financial responsibility in higher education.

"We think the time has come for most churches to reconsider their obligations to church-sponsored colleges and universities and to increase their appropriations substantially."

---

[3] Manning M. Pattillo, Jr., and Donald M. Mackenzie, *Eight Hundred Colleges Face the Future*. St. Louis: The Danforth Foundation, 1965, pp. 57-58, 74 pp.

Chapter 19

GIFTS FROM BUSINESS AND INDUSTRIAL CORPORATIONS

THE AGE OF VAST PERSONAL FORTUNES, when great business enterprises in private hands were comparatively unregulated and untaxed, has in large part given way to the era of corporate business. Huge industrial and commercial empires whose operations are nationwide and international in scope, with plants and offices in many states and foreign countries, are now the order of the day.

The great personal accumulations of the nineteenth century gave rise to several important private educational institutions—notably Cornell University, Tulane University, the University of Chicago, Stanford University, Carnegie University, Duke University, and Rockefeller University. The same class of benefactors also played large roles in the establishment of numerous other private colleges and added great sums to the endowments and properties of some of the older ones.

Personal benefactions of very impressive size continue to be made occasionally, but the wealth of the nation has come to be so largely in the hands of corporations, large and small, that corporation gifts must now become a principal channel of private giving if a modicum of the earnings of business and industry is to come regularly to the support of higher education, other than through Federal and state taxes paid by corporations.

Although members of the top managerial caste of large corporations are generally grossly overpaid in the form of fantastic salaries, bonuses, stock options, and other favors, and may acquire large personal accumulations, yet Federal and state personal income taxes tap their large incomes heavily and reduce the likelihood of the development of really enormous personal fortunes.

But charitable gifts by the corporations themselves are increasing, and for many reasons:

1. A concern having a chain store or a branch plant in a college town recognizes a certain obligation to be a "good corporate citizen" of that community, and to contribute to its worthy charitable undertakings.
2. A gift to an educational institution is in a sense a "purchase of good will" or a producer of favorable visibility in the same manner as an advertising outlay, for which large firms spend many millions annually.
3. Large corporations recognize that they must replenish their supply of "junior executives" from the ranks of recent graduates of colleges and universities; and hence in supporting these institutions, they are contributing to the development of their own future leadership.

Strangely enough, until about a decade and a half ago there was serious and persistent doubt that the board of directors of a business corporation could lawfully make a gift of any part of the corporation's funds, however small, except when specifically authorized by a vote of the stockholders.

It was also further questioned whether a charitable gift could be treated as a "business expense" and thus come out of the corporate income "before taxes" or whether it must come only from net income or profits. A third point thought to be dubious related to public utility corporations (such as railroads, telephone companies, gas and electric companies, and the like). It was agreed that since the rates charged by such companies to consumers are very closely regulated by the states and kept at levels barely high enough to provide a margin of profit, any substantial gift would eventually cause a rise in rates and would therefore actually be at the expense of the consumers;

and since the directors of the companies selected the beneficiaries of the gifts, in effect the consumers would be forced without their consent to finance gifts to beneficiaries not necessarily of their own choice.

All these qualms have largely disappeared. A New Jersey statute authorizing boards of directors to make charitable gifts not in excess of 1 per cent of capital and surplus in any one year was tested in the courts when the A. P. Smith Manufacturing Company made a gift to Princeton University. The result was an enlightened decision of the state supreme court sustaining the gift as not only properly authorized by the statute but also "under common law principles."[1] The United States Supreme Court declined to review the decision. There have been other decisions to the same effect. Some courts have ruled that comparatively small gifts by large utility companies constitute so negligible a fraction of the annual expenses as to have no appreciable effect upon rates and consequently to involve no inequity or injustice to the consumers. It may be said that the right of boards of directors to make charitable gifts as "business expenses" and "before taxes" is generally legally recognized.

As early as the late 1940's the coming increase in the importance of corporate gifts was foreseen by the late Frank H. Sparks, president of Wabash College at Crawfordsville, Indiana. The private colleges of Indiana formed the first state "college foundation" or voluntary association for the purpose of making united and orderly appeals to business corporations for gifts. There are now approximately 40 such associations—one in nearly every state except some of the sparsely populated states of the Mountain region where private colleges are so few that an association must necessarily cover more than one state.

These associations usually plan solicitation of corporation headquarters by selected teams of college presidents and formulate rules for the distribution of the proceeds among the participating colleges— often specifying that each college shall receive a certain minimum flat sum or percentage, and that additional receipts shall be allocated pro rata according to the numbers of students enrolled.[2]

---

[1] *A. P. Smith Manufacturing Company* v. *Barlow, et al.,* 13 N.J. 145, 98 A. 2d 581 (1953); appeal dismissed, 346 U.S. 861, 74 S.Ct. 107 (1953).

[2] For a concise history and survey of these organizations, see Benjamin L. Morton, *State and Regional Cooperative Fund-Raising Associations of Private Col-*

At first the well-known Council for Financial Aid to Education, with headquarters in New York City, functioned as a nationwide focus of liaison and information exchange. Subsequently this function seems to have been taken over by a new organization, also in New York, known as Independent College Funds of America. Although the statewide and nationwide organizations just mentioned have valuable achievements to their credit, and also a cheerful prospect, they do not encompass the whole field of corporation giving. Many business and industrial firms, large and small, make gifts for higher education through various channels. Many of them have extensive programs of scholarships, often limited to their own employees or their children. Some have the "gift matching" programs in which employees who make personal gifts to their alma mater or favorite college, not exceeding $1,000 in any one year, find the employer company ready to match the gift, thus doubling the amount received by the college.

Corporations having their headquarters offices or important branches in a college town often can be prevailed upon to make substantial special gifts to the local college.

Although corporation giving is trending upward, it is as yet far short of what it may well become. If all business corporations would give 1 per cent of their annual incomes before taxes, the accrual to the colleges would run into billions; whereas it has not yet reached one quarter of a billion. In his last years, Frank H. Sparks promoted this idea among industrialists in the Cleveland area, not entirely without some success. Conceivably it could eventually become a reality, nationwide.

In recent years many large corporations have turned to the device of creating a separate charitable corporation or charitable trust bearing the corporate name, as a vehicle for the parent corporation's charitable activities. This has the advantage of centralizing the development of gift policies somewhat aside from the mainstream of the corporate activities, and also offers various tax advantages regarding the assets and income of the charitable trust, and the transfer of assets into and out of it, as well as regarding the control of voting stock held

---

leges and Universities: A Study of the Organizational Development, Membership Characteristics, Financial Importance and Potential of the Associations. Ann Arbor: University of Michigan, doctoral dissertation, 1963, 211 pp.

by the charitable trust. These vehicles are commonly called "company foundations." Legally they constitute a type of philanthropic foundation; but in some instances it has been seriously questioned whether the charitable motive is really dominant, or whether it is entirely absent or largely overshadowed by motives of tax avoidance and manipulation of stock control.

In any event the charitable beneficiaries of these "company foundations" gain from the donations, whether or not the companies are motivated wholly by beneficent intents.

In view of the undoubted prospect that the bulk of the nation's industry and commerce bid fair to be under the corporate form of organization for a long time to come, the building of a custom of channeling a suitable fraction of corporation incomes and profits into the support of higher education is of the utmost importance. To the extent that this can be accomplished through voluntary giving, it tends to preserve the pluralism and freedom of choice essential in a free society, and to soften somewhat the compulsion of taxation. The history of the past 20 years is encouraging. There exists a mangificent opportunity for corporation officers and boards of directors to initiate further breakthroughs until it becomes universal corporate policy to support higher education regularly at a rate equivalent to 1 per cent of income before taxes.

Chapter 20

COMMUNITY SUPPORT FROM PRIVATE SOURCES

EVERY COMMUNITY, whether it be a large city, a country town or only a rural village, has civic leaders who are interested in its future. At their best, these people envision many avenues toward improvement of the general well-being of all the people. The vision is not always devoid of self-interest. Often the prophet sees a hoped-for increase in the value of his own property, an expansion of his own business, and other economic benefits to himself and his family.

These people know that a college is an asset to a community, not only as an opportunity for its young people and a lever of uplift for its whole culture, but also—from the purely economic viewpoint—as a magnet for added population and added dollars.

This is especially important during these years when new junior colleges are being established in the 50 states at the rate of from 30 to 50 annually, and the geographic spread of education facilities beyond high school is being enormously extended.

In our pluralistic society, there is more than one way of getting a new facility established or a needed project launched. One way is to get it through the ballot box; i.e., by governmental action and tax support. Another way is by voluntary action—by forming a private association or corporation and raising money from private sources. The marked American propensity for the latter method was noted with some astonishment and admiration by de Tocqueville, the keen French commentator, when he visited this country to study our political and social institutions about the year 1830.

All through the nineteenth century this proclivity was expressed in part through the founding of many private colleges in almost every state then in existence. And new private four-year colleges, as well as two-year colleges, have in a few instances been founded within the past quarter of a century. There are two views of this type of enterprise. In one view it is looked at askance and complaints are made that we have always had too many small weak colleges; that too many people are already going to college anyway; that new colleges are often poorly located with reference to the population and the needs and the sources of support; that the motives of the local promoters include much more of Philistinism than of a knowledgeable wish to advance education; and that heedless proliferation of small colleges tends to weaken the whole structure of American higher education and dilute its quality.

Coupled with these sentiments is an insistence that the creation of new colleges should be rigidly restricted by the state or by the ecclesiastical authorities, as the case may be, with the implication that in many cases the ambitions of local communities should be rigorously denied and no college initiated anywhere except after elaborate studies have elicited ample proofs that it will be an abundantly supported institution of good quality.

All will agree with this last thought insofar as it pertains to the discouraging of fraudulent "diploma mills." A free atmosphere for voluntary educational enterprises invites a "criminal fringe," as was discovered during the early years of the administration of the G.I. Bill of 1944, and has been noted before and since that time. Both the states and the numerous voluntary accrediting associations are reasonably watchful for these aberrations. The advocacy of tight restrictions on the founding of new colleges goes far beyond this level and embraces the less defensible idea that no college should come to birth unless it can be shown to have almost indisputable prospects of being able to achieve high standards of support, a minimum size, and at least average quality of instruction and other services.

These positions stem from a composite of sources: the lingering impression that education beyond high school must not be for the many, but only for the few; the centuries of the "economy of scarcity" and the panic engendered by the great Depression of the 1930's, when many small colleges were abolished—the belief that society can not afford universal higher education; and a certain stiff-necked adherence to certain standards of "quality" that were current a century and more ago, such as the "genteel" atmosphere, the notion that there is a positive relation between the quality of education and the practical uselessness of the subjects studied, and that "quality education" must always be painful drudgery, and never a joyous and independent experience of discovery.

Opposed to all these latter ideas is the view that we are now on the threshold of the era of universal higher education, whether we wish it or not; that virtually all young high school graduates are entitled to some education beyond high school, and that technological and cultural changes now occur so rapidly, and the average span of life has been so lengthened, that adults of various ages will increasingly find it necessary to add to and update their prior formal schooling; that in our affluent society these services can be financially supported with comparative ease; and that this is the way of progress.

It is evident that an increasing major segment of expanding higher education will be tax-supported; but this trend of our time must not lead to any denigrating of the value of local and private initiative and of voluntary enterprise in this field. Chambers of commerce, service clubs of business and professional men and women, labor organizations, church federations, and a host of other local associations and individuals are mighty reservoirs of good will, honest aspirations for community advancement, and financial support for worthy institutions. It is fortunate that we have not yet restricted the flow of this power or cut it off from the channel of the expansion of higher education.

The foregoing has been written with new private colleges or junior colleges in mind, but it applies as well to the support of older and well-established colleges, private or public, in their own communities.

Every local two-year college, even if tax-supported, needs the voluntary moral and financial support of private individuals and organizations. Few private four-year colleges, even if they serve a nation-wide and international clientele, would be wise to ignore the resources of good will and private giving in the town, county, or city in which they are located, including a radius of some 50 miles roundabout. Most such colleges will find that increasing proportions of their students reside within that radius, and that the college itself is increasingly regarded as an integral part of this community, much to its own advantage.

Accordingly members of the faculty, the administration, and the governing board may well devise ways of maintaining communication with local governmental functionaries, local educational authorities, and all types of local voluntary associations and civic-minded individuals. The college can benefit from making social and economic surveys of the area, projecting its probable development into the future, and freely circulating these data through local newspapers and broadcasting stations, as well as in face-to-face conversations and speeches at meetings and conferences. By identifying itself with its own community, the college constructs a form of assurance that a flow of private gifts from the people and the leaders of that community can be developed and augmented.

The same principles are applicable to public universities and colleges, from the locally-based junior college to the great state university. Although in part tax-supported, they need the marginal additions from private sources for the support of types of instruction and public service which state and local legislative bodies are often reluctant to underwrite.

No modern institution, save perhaps a handful of the greatest private universities that are truly national and international in their character and scope (and probably not even they), can properly take the stance of being "in the community but not of it." Nearly every type of college can well study its own immediate environment, and gain moral and financial support from the people of its own vicinage.

Chapter 21

SELF-FINANCING: TRUSTEES, FACULTY, STUDENTS, PARENTS, FRIENDS

THE HARD FACTS OF LIFE in the present economic order make it essential that the members of a college board of trustees be willing and able to assist materially in financing the institution. This explains in large part why boards of trustees are traditionally heavily overloaded with financiers and men of wealth, and men of other pursuits so placed as to be able to influence affluent benefactors. In general, trustees must be in and of "the power structure," and members of the "Establishment."

True, some boards include an impecunious labor leader or clergyman or housewife as a slight concession to the principle of representativeness, but this is relatively rare among private college boards except those still clinging to the obsolescent practice of filling the seats with ministers of the right denomination; and the housewife or labor leader is much more likely to be found on the board of a public institution, where there may be greater pressure for representativeness.

The wealthy members should be prepared to give periodically of their own means and should expect to solicit gifts from their affluent friends and associates. Those who are officers or directors of business or industrial corporations can influence their fellow-officers to make individual gifts, and the corporations to make corporate gifts.

Wealthy men are often members of several corporation boards of directors simultaneously. Thus they come into close communication with many of their own kind. Many of them are members of exclusive clubs where their opportunities for conversation among themselves are many. They often maintain two or more large homes and frequent the same social circles and tend to entertain each other at home and at sports such as yachting, skiing, polo, or motoring.

Not all men or women of wealth can be tracked to the same rarefied circles, but most of them have friends of their own kind with whom they can be influential if they choose. Thus one who is sincerely devoted to a college can attract to it not only his own contributions, but also munificent gifts from his relatives, friends, and associates. A small college which has a board of trustees composed largely of wealthy and influential persons really determined to advance its welfare "has it made" in a sense (provided it maintains reasonable academic freedom). This is the basis of such fund-raisers' maxims as "Ninety per cent of the money always comes from ten per cent of the donors."

Below the level of the board of trustees, an amazing variety of "bootstrap" financing devices have had some degree of success in various places. Accurate historians say the financing of higher education in the nineteenth century must be credited in substantial degree to the self-sacrificing faculties who worked for pittances. Even the meager stipends agreed upon were often partly unpaid, and "teaching was its own reward"—an occupation often heavily infused with evangelical fervor. Often there was an annual campaign in which all faculty members were invited to make gifts or pledges of small sums to the coffer of the college. In our day, in gift campaigns by large or small institutions, the contributions of faculty members are certainly not spurned; and rather frequently elderly professors who have comfortable accumulations provide for generous testamentary gifts to the college.

Another source of funds in some instances stems from the work of faculty members who, in the course of their use of the college's laboratories, shops, clinics, or libraries, make scientific or technological

discoveries or inventions which can be patented and exploited com-
mercially. Sometimes such a professor simply donates his rights to the
institution; in other instances his contract of employment provides for
a pre-determined sharing of the proceeds between himself and the
college or its agency set up for that purpose. As a matter of fact, many
large universities have nonprofit corporations created to manage such
matters, among others.[1]

An example from an earlier generation is the invention of the
Babcock tester for the butterfat content of milk, made by a professor
of dairy technology at the University of Wisconsin. For some time
that institution has had the University of Wisconsin Research Corporation, currently widely known for its profitable exploitation of the
chemical rodent-exterminator known as Warfarin. Another current
example is the interest which the Indiana University Foundation holds
in the popular Crest toothpaste, developed in Indiana University laboratories.

Faculties in all types of institutions can and do strengthen the
finances of the college and add to its physical assets in various ways:
by contributing to the housing and operation of a Faculty Club, by
organizing charitable efforts for the special benefit of needy students
and of foreign students, and by diverse other nonprofit enterprises in
different places. Voluntary efforts find many outlets.

Students and their parents are two of the college's "publics"
responsible for more of its financial support than is commonly recognized. Not much by way of material gifts can be expected from students during their short stay on the campus; yet the traditional "parting
gift" of each successive graduating class often adds something of
permanent utility and beauty to the physical assets. Even a student
organization as small as a departmental club of graduate students may
contribute a few hundred dollars toward a departmental library much
needed for their own accommodation but not otherwise obtainable,
and which will be of permanent advantage to the department and
to the institution.

There have been many cases in which students have themselves

---

[1] Archie M. Palmer. *University Research and Patent Policies, Practices and
Procedures.* Washington: National Academy of Sciences—National Research
Council, 1962, 291 pp.

organized cooperative ventures of diverse kinds, such as bookstores, student newspapers, residential housing and dining facilities, and others, initially financing them by purchasing small shares, and keeping them in successful operation by patronizing them, thus often obtaining some savings for themselves and adding to the educational facilities of the institution. In the long-run evolution of these types of facilities, the "student cooperative" probably represents an intermediate stage between the primitive state of affairs in which such services are available only from profit-seeking entrepreneurs, and the later stage in which they are obtainable from wholly college-owned enterprises as well as from private vendors. There are, however, many respectable economic theorists who believe the "limited-profit cooperative" is the best of all forms of organization for these services.

It is certainly trite, and also perhaps a kind of question-begging, to say that students become alumni, and generally continue as alumni much longer than the duration of their student days. For most of them "alma mater" has a real meaning, charged with much nostalgic and pleasant sentiment, throughout their lives.

This is because a college is, in varying degrees for different families and individuals, a tribe, a clan, an in-group bound by ties of diverse kinds and often of great tenacity. These ties may derive from like religious faith, enthusiasm for college sports, regard for distinguished or eccentric professors or administrators, college friendships that become lifelong attachments (including marriage), or a thousand other sources. If both parents were students at dear old Siwash, they are rather likely to want their children to attend dear old Siwash regardless of any obstacles, even if this means sending them half-way around the world. And if the parents or any bachelor uncles or maiden aunts in this family become affluent enough to consider philanthropic gifts for higher education, one scarcely needs a second guess as to what college will be the beneficiary.

For some families, attendance at some particular college is a status symbol of prime potency, coveted and treasured through several generations; and that college is automatically an object of family philanthropy. Such families often attend Commencement exercises, Baccalaureate sermons, and other ceremonial occasions at alma mater with total regularity, along with other families of like sentiments, and form a solid cadre of patrons whose loyalty is as unquestioned as that of Caesar's famed Tenth Legion. To the trustees and administration, these are the "salt of the earth"—an elite corps that is a basic element in assuring the college's continuance and development.

Every college, and especially if it is a private college with a history behind it, may expect occasionally and sometimes unexpectedly to receive a gift, sometimes small, sometimes large, "out of a clear sky" from some donor who may have lived as a recluse, or who may have been unknown to anyone connected with the college. The precise motives may never be known, but the general charitable intent will be clear. The newest college, during the enthusiasm of its founding, may receive gifts many and substantial from persons who have had no prior relation to it because it has not existed. All these can only be classified as "friends"—a limitless category not lending itself to narrow definition.

The traverse of "bootstrap financing" is incomplete without some mention of "gifts in kind." At a few colleges it has been expected that students and younger faculty members will contribute some manual labor to the institution. (Not to be confused with the plan at Berea College in Kentucky, where each student works for the college 10 hours a week and is paid by the college. This plan is adapted to the needs of the people of the mountain counties in several Appalachian states served by private tuition-free Berea College.)

Such work may sometimes take the form of construction labor under skilled foremen; and this is sometimes coupled with another form of "gift in kind." Costly construction materials have sometimes been obtained by direct appeal to the manufacturers or jobbers of these materials, who would not be susceptible to a request for a cash gift. A brick-maker may have his pride touched by a request for a gift of a specified quantity of his best bricks; a manufacturer of steel I-beams may be flattered by an appeal for a gift of a stated quantity of the appropriate product to form the frame or support the roof of a college building. So on with glassmakers, aluminum fabricators, lumbermen, paint manufacturers, concrete contractors, *et al.* Wilmington College in Ohio is said to have obtained more than one new building largely by this process.

Perhaps objection to the use of student labor may be anticipated from labor unions in the building trades; but there is some evidence that courts will hold that even a state university, to say nothing of a private college, is within its rights in using its own staff or student labor in construction work whenever this appears most practicable and economical.[2]

The variety of devices whereby ingenious friends of a college may bring financial gain to it, other than by means of outright gifts, seems inexhaustible. Witness, for example, the instance in which a small group of lawyer friends of New York University, led by John Gerdes, searched out a prosperous manufacturing concern whose owners were in a mood to sell at a price which would probably soon be recouped from the earnings of the business; they then formed a nonprofit charitable corporation of small capitalization, under a charter stating that no part of its income or property would inure to the benefit of anyone other than New York University, and that no stockholder would receive any dividends or any distributed assets. The new corporation then borrowed money and purchased the factory, and continued to operate it on a highly profitable basis, with the result that within a few years the business had been fully paid for, and the whole transaction had been spectacularly advantageous to the purchaser, and produced substantial gains for the university. This was done in at least two instances, once in the purchase of a macaroni factory, and once in the purchase of a shoe factory. The purchases were made in 1947 and 1948, and Federal courts decided that no Federal income taxes were due from the operation of these businesses by the charitable corporation which purchased them, from the time of the purchase until January 1, 1951, when an amendment to the Internal Revenue Code became effective, removing the exemption of such corporations.[3]

In these instances the university profited from the ingenuity of its friends who simply applied their business acumen and their legal expertise for its benefit.

Another type of transaction which has sometimes proved of substantial financial benefit to a college involves purchase of an industrial

---

[2]See *Inskip* v. *Board of Trustees of University of Illinois,* 26 Ill. 2d 501, 187 N.E. 2d 201 (1962); and *Montana Chapter, National Electrical Contractors' Association* v. *State Board of Education,* 137 Mont. 382, 352 P. 2d 258 (1960).

[3]The details of the transactions appear in *C. F. Mueller Company* v. *Commissioner of Internal Revenue* (U.S.C.C.A.), 190 F. 2d 120 (1951), and *Knapp Brothers Shoe Manufacturing Corporation* v. *United States,* 135 U.S. Ct. Cl. 797, 142 F. Supp. 899 (1956). They are also briefly discussed at pages 242-245 of M. M. Chambers, *The Colleges and the Courts Since 1950.* Danville, Illinois: The Interstate, 1964, 415 pp.

plant at a nominal price by a college, with an immediate "lease-back" for a long term to the former owner, who continues to operate it as before, paying periodic rentals to the college. Depending on the exact facts of the transaction, and the construction placed on them by the courts, the seller in such a case may gain spectacular tax savings by treating the difference between the nominal selling price and the market value of the property as a deductible loss in computing the Federal income tax. It must not be supposed, however, that court decisions in all such cases are favorable to this result.[4]

Yet another species of collaboration between a college or other charitable corporation and the owners of a prosperous private business was involved in the *Clay Brown* case, wherein the owners of a sawmill and lumber business near Ventura, California, transferred it to the California Institute for Cancer Research in a complex transaction which protected the Institute from any financial outlay or risk, while enabling the seller to escape payment of about $60,000 in Federal taxes. The case reached the United States Supreme Court in 1965, where by a vote of 6 to 3 the Justices decided that the transaction was lawful under current statutes, and if any change were deemed desirable, it should be made by the Congress and not by the Court.[5]

Justice Byron White wrote the majority opinion, and there was a specially concurring opinion by Justice John M. Harlan. Justice Arthur Goldberg wrote the dissenting opinion, in which he was joined by Chief Justice Earl Warren and Justice Hugo Black. Said Justice Goldberg: "The Court justifies the untoward result in this case as permitted tax avoidance; I believe it to be a plain and simple case of unwarranted tax evasion."

Bills were thereafter introduced in Congress to make similar transactions unlawful in the future, but the question seems to continue to be open as to whether devices of this kind can be used on a substantial scale for the financial benefit of charitable corporations.

---

[4]For details of one such case, see *Century Electric Company, Petitioner,* Docket No. 13115, decided in United States Tax Court October 31, 1950; and discussed at pages 121-123 in M. M. Chambers, *The Colleges and the Courts, 1946-50.* New York: Columbia University Press, 1952, 202 pp.

[5]*Commissioner of Internal Revenue* v. *Brown,* 380 U.S. 563, 85 S.Ct. 1162, 14 L.Ed. 2d 75 (1965). Discussed at pages 217-222 in M. M. Chambers, *The Colleges and the Courts, 1962-66.* Danville, Illinois: The Interstate, 1967, 326 pp.

PART FIVE

Chapter 22

SUPPORT FROM LOCAL TAXING SUBDIVISIONS

HISTORICALLY, the bulk of tax support for higher education has come from state tax funds appropriated annually or biennially by state legislatures. Now the Federal contribution through many channels has come to equal or nearly equal the aggregate of the state appropriations and may soon exceed them. Appropriations of tax funds by local subdivisions such as cities, counties, school districts, and junior college districts play a role relatively much smaller than either of the foregoing two major sources. There is a strong possibility, too, that the proportional contributions of local taxing subdivisions will decline, in comparison with income from other sources.

A handful of municipal universities (supported at least in part by city tax funds) has existed for more than a century. The history indicates that no expansion of their small number is probable, and that increasing major portions of their annual operating funds are coming from the state. As alert citizens can not fail to observe in these years, cities and other local subdivisions such as school districts face grave financial stringency, so that in all the populous states it has long been necessary for the state to make substantial and increasing annual grants-in-aid to assist these subdivisions in maintaining their necessary public functions.

This is due to the fact that the cities and counties necessarily depend for revenue almost wholly on property taxes, and it is scarcely practicable for them to levy and administer local income or sales taxes. Within the past decade, however, there has been something of a wave of state statutes authorizing local subdivisions to adopt these forms of taxation within closely specified limits, because the legislatures found themselves unwilling for political reasons to increase the rates of these taxes uniformly statewide. Some of the resulting confusion has been mitigated by providing in some states that any additional local sales tax, above the statewide rate, shall be collected by the state bureaucracy and the proceeds turned over to the local units levying the tax. The point is that these types of taxes are costly and difficult to administer by any unit smaller than the state.

There is much complaint about property taxes and demand for their downward revision, because property has become a relatively inaccurate and inequitable measure of taxpaying ability, far inferior to the income and spending of individuals and corporations. Property taxes can become confiscatory as against farm owners, whose property holdings are often of a value greatly out of proportion to their annual incomes. (A farmer owning land and equipment worth $100,000 may often have an annual income no larger than that of a skilled laborer or white-collar clerk who owns nothing.) The same is true of homeowners receiving only small fixed incomes, as from pensions or modest investments in bonds.

The age-old and continuing problem of avoiding these inequities, and of reforming the property tax in numerous other ways, from appraisal and classification to assessment and collection, is too cumbersome and formidable a task to be accomplished in 50 separate jurisdictions, except as a continuous process over a period of many years. Meantime the trend toward increasing state aid to the local units goes on, because fortunately the states are able to increase their annual revenues at a fairly rapid rate by levying, without undue hardship on the public, such revenue-producers as income taxes (personal and corporate) and general retail sales taxes, as well as taxes on alcoholic beverages, cigarettes and other tobacco products, and license fees on motor vehicles, severance taxes on the extraction of natural resources, and other miscellaneous revenue measures.

The multicampus City University of New York currently gets equal amounts of its annual operating income from the city and the state, and the state's proportionate share has grown greatly in recent years. Ohio's three municipal universities (Akron, Cincinnati, Toledo)[1] are asking for and getting increasing state aid. The University of Louisville presently obtains only 14 per cent of its total operating income from local taxation—the city of Louisville *and* the county of Jefferson—and has long operated virtually as a private institution, supported by student fees and private donations, with negligible state aid. Knowledgeable observers agree that it must eventually be largely state-supported.

Wayne State University (formerly Wayne University, in Detroit) was transformed into a state institution during a transition period 1956-59. The municipal University of Wichita has become a state institution in Kansas, and the municipal University of Omaha is now in the throes of becoming a campus of the University of Nebraska.

The establishment of any additional municipal universities seems improbable; but the City University of New York is adding additional campuses, and its traditions and repute are such that it will long continue as a municipal institution, with substantial state aid.

Nearly all the rural counties in the United States make some tax contribution to the operation of the nationwide Federal-state Cooperative Agricultural Extension Service, which at its inception under the Smith-Lever Act of 1914 was established on a basis of tripartite Federal, state, and local tax support. The staffs of this agency are employees of the Morrill Land-Grant universities in their respective states, serving as the implementing arm of the colleges of agriculture and the agricultural experiment stations, to carry their instruction and research findings to all the people of the states. Their record is one of magnificent accomplishment and affords one of the best concrete examples of higher education as a stimulator of industrial productivity and economic growth.

The local tax contribution to the Cooperative Agricultural Ex-

---

[1] In 1967 Akron and Toledo became state universities, and Cincinnati became "state affiliated."

tension Service never constituted more than a small fraction of the support of the land-grant universities, however, and its proportion has declined as the universities grew. Here again it seems that there is no expansive future for local tax support of higher education, but that the trend is downward at least proportionally.

It is in the support of the local public junior colleges (now often called community colleges) that local taxing subdivisions currently play their largest role. In a few states these two-year colleges are wholly supported and controlled by local public school districts and regarded as an extension of the public high school. This arrangement has been largely superseded in many states by the creation of new special junior college districts, with their boundaries drawn with regard to the maintenance of junior colleges as separate institutions, and hopefully in such a pattern as to make this type of institution easily accessible to all or nearly all high school graduates and adults in the state.

The junior college districts have their own boards of trustees and their own local taxing power, and are charged with the single function of maintaining public two-year colleges. Invariably the state statutes provide for at least some state aid for annual operating expenses, and some of the states also provide limited state support for capital outlays.

In New York, for example, the unit is usually a county, and for nearly 20 years a simple formula of financing has been followed: One-half of the capital funds come from the state, one-half from the county; one-third of the annual operating funds come from the state, one-third from the county, and one-third from the students as tuition fees. In California the pattern is different: Up to 1967 at least 75 per cent of annual operating expenses had been supplied by the local taxing subdivision on which the junior college was based; no more than 25 per cent by the state; and all junior colleges are tuition-free.

In 1967 about 25 states were making appropriations of state tax funds for annual operating expenses of local public junior colleges, the aggregate for the fiscal year 1966-67 being about $300 million. For the fiscal year 1960-61, six years earlier, the comparable total had been less than $60 million. The fivefold increase over six years is due to the amazingly rapid spread of this type of institution, and to the tendency of the states to increase their proportionate share in its support. For the fiscal year 1966-67, eight states appropriated $10 million or more each to this purpose: California ($66 million), Florida ($54 million), Washington ($29 million), New York ($25 million), Illinois ($23 million), Michigan ($17 million), Texas ($14 million), and North Carolina ($12 million).

Within the past five years at least three states which had developed respectable statewide networks of state-aided local public junior colleges have moved to relieve the local junior college districts of any responsibility for tax support of these institutions, and assumed full support out of state tax funds. Minnesota began this practice in 1963, and in 1967 somewhat similar statutes were enacted in Colorado and Washington.

Here again, then, there appears evidence that the future of local tax support of higher education probably does not promise much expansion, and that it may indeed eventually be entirely superseded by state support.

This may be viewed as simply another inevitable step resulting from broad economic and social changes which have caused the exercise of the taxing power to move upward in great part to the larger units of government.

With respect to the nationwide picture of the first two years beyond high school, it may be noticed that local public junior colleges as yet enroll only a minority of all students at that level—perhaps hardly more than one-fourth. There are several populous states—Wisconsin, Indiana, Ohio, Kentucky, Pennsylvania—where statewide networks of "regional campuses" or "university centers" or "commonwealth campuses" flourish as outposts of the state universities and perform much the same functions as local junior colleges, but are carried in the budgets of the parent universities and are hence state-supported. There are many of these "university regional campus" institutions in many states other than those mentioned, so that their aggregate number in a recent nationwide survey came to some 160.

Then too, there are some 10 states having one or several two-year colleges that are state institutions in their own right, not connected with any parent institution. Massachusetts has 12 "regional community colleges" that are really state institutions. Georgia has eight two-year state colleges. Oklahoma has seven and New York six (the Agricultural and Technical Institutes). Add to these some 30 two-year colleges recently transferred from local-and-state support to state support in Minnesota, Colorado, and Washington.

Some doctrinaire enthusiasts for the community college lament the possible passing of local support because they insist that the functions of the local two-year college can not and will not be properly performed in any other way than by the locally-supported and locally-controlled institution, unconnected with any "parent institution." Of course there is no conclusive evidence that all these functions can not be well performed under the aegis of another institution, either on its own main campus or on outlying regional campuses. On the contrary, there are hundreds of places where the service of the "community college" is thus performed; i.e., four-year or five-year institutions or large universities with full-fledged graduate schools are not automatically incapacitated for adding the functions of the two-year college, and there is ample scope for serious investigation and debate as to whether these functions are not better performed thus than by the unconnected local community college. It is not appropriate to enter that dispute here.

Chapter 23

STATE TAX SUPPORT

THE ONE LARGEST SOURCE of operating income for all education beyond the high school, public and private, is the annual or biennial appropriations of state tax funds by the legislatures of the 50 states.

The aggregate from this source for the fiscal year 1959-60 was about $1.4 billion; for 1961-62, $1.7 billion; for 1963-64, $2.2 billion; for 1965-66, $3 billion; for 1966-67, $3.5 billion. Thus it was more than doubled during the five-year period between 1961 and 1966. At the date of this writing (July, 1967) reports from 33 of the states have shown a consistent gain of more than 40 per cent for the fiscal year 1967-68 over the fiscal year 1965-66, two years earlier. This makes it appear reasonably certain that the total for 50 states for 1967-68 will be of the order of $4.3 billion — a tripling of the comparable figure for the fiscal year 1959-60, only eight years earlier.

The contribution of the states amounts to more than one-third of the total educational and general operating income of the aggregate of all institutions of all types, and slightly more than one-half of that of the *public* institutions.

The time may be coming, and perhaps soon, when the Federal contribution through various channels may exceed that of the states. This is not yet the case, partly because substantial parts of the Federal subsidies (even some of the research grants and contracts) include provisions for some capital outlays; and the exact total of these, as against grants for operation, is extremely difficult to ascertain with precision.

Another useful viewpoint from which to consider the total contribution from state tax funds is that of the proportion of each state's total revenues devoted to operating expenses of higher education. It has been reported that as of 1915, more than half a century ago, about 10 per cent of the national total of all state revenues was going to that purpose. After that year there came in successive decades manifold increases in state revenues and expenditures. The step-ups for highways, social welfare, public health, and some other functions greatly exceeded those for higher education, so that the 10 per cent figure declined until about the middle 1950's, when it reached a low point of 5 to 6 per cent.

Soon thereafter the great and continuing spurt in state tax support of higher education began, and the percentage turned upward. The total of state tax revenues for 1966 is reported as $29.4 billion. Recalling our figure of $3 billion as the contribution of the states to operating expenses of higher education in the fiscal year 1965-66, it would appear that the percentage was slightly above 10. Since that year the state tax support of higher education has patently increased faster than the growth of state tax revenues; therefore the percentage may now be of the order of 11 or 12. It can not be computed because the total revenue figures are not available for any year later than 1966.

Only now, after more than half a century, has higher education, by this measure, been restored to the position of relative importance among other state functions which it occupied in 1915.

This point of the competition among different public services for the state tax dollar is the crux of the state policy-making. Weighing and balancing the recurring needs annually or biennially as presented by the administrative officers responsible for preparing budget askings, comparing the needs of the several functions among themselves and with the revenue potentialities of the ensuing fiscal period, and making the necessary decisions constitute the core of the responsibilities of the governor and the legislature.

These elected representatives of the people must bear these major responsibilities, and can not evade or delegate them. The weight is onerous. The decisions call for superhuman knowledge and judgment.

It is hardly surprising that in the past the processes involved in making them have often been far short of ideal. For example, proceeding in accord with the "slicing of the pie" theory, very often espoused by governors, legislators, administrative department heads, and others, has done untold damage.

Slicing the pie: First obtain from a reliable source a dependable estimate of the total revenues for the ensuing fiscal period. Next, place the figure on the chalkboard and draw a circle around it. This is the pie. All that remains is to parcel it out to the different departments and institutions. This intensifies the competition, because everyone assumes that the total available is definitely limited to the figure stated. If any slice is enlarged, this means that some other slice must become smaller. Major attention is therefore devoted to defending the allocations of the preceding fiscal period—the *status quo*. In this atmosphere it is difficult to get a hearing for the funding of any entirely new needs or for expansion of any existing services. Bitterness and recriminations are likely to develop, and one department head may say to another (perhaps with some justification), "You expanded your service at the expense of mine."

The process as sketched may superficially seem logical, but it is in fact an inverted, upside-down image of what the budget-making process should be. Note that the needs of the state do not receive priority. Before studying the askings of the departments and institutions, the governor dodges that responsibility by placing an arbitrary limit on them. I have personally observed more than one state where the presidents of the state universities and colleges did not seriously compile their askings until the governor had given each one a "ceiling." This is a particularly reprehensible situation if the governor has campaigned on a platform of "No new taxes," as has often been the case, but now happens less frequently as the electorate becomes more knowledgeable.

Priority should be given to the needs of the state for the next fiscal period—not to the *status quo* nor to a ceiling imposed by estimated revenue under an antiquated pattern of state taxes. After the governor and his budget staff have studied the *needs of the state* and approved what the governor honestly regards as a true estimate of necessary expenditures, *then* is the time to compare it with estimated revenues. If it can be fitted within estimated revenues, there is no problem; if not, it is then the duty of the governor to propose means of raising sufficient additional revenue. Many governors have done this with courage and success. Ideally, the state's tax system should be under continuous study by tax study commissions set up by the governor or the legislature (or both jointly) so up-to-date recommendations of needed changes will continuously be at hand to inform the public and guide the legislature. It is a maxim that any state revenue system is always susceptible of improvement to make it more equitable or more productive, or both. Economic change makes this inevitable.

The state budget-making process is improving. Year by year there is a closer correspondence between askings and actual appropriations. The ancient practice of "padding" the departmental or institutional requests—inflating them far beyond any reasonable expectation of fulfillment in the hope of thus obtaining the sum needed after a drastic reduction of the request, has already largely disappeared. The statesmanship of governors, the competency of their budget staffs, and the quality of legislators are all vastly better than they were a generation or a century ago. If they were not, the splendid gains in state support of higher education over the last decade would hardly have occurred on such a scale, though in any event popular demand would have forced very substantial gains.

Many other absurdities have been largely eliminated from the budget-making process. One is the well-intended but wholly misguided requirement that all state departmental and institutional budgets be set out on antiquated identical forms, ostensibly to facilitate interdepartmental comparisons, but actually useless for that purpose because of the diversity of the functions. For colleges and universities this meant two budgets and double clerical and fiscal technical work, because all colleges and universities use for their operating budgets the classifications developed and refined over many years by committees of leading college business officers, subsidized by philanthropic foundations, and published in volumes issued by the American Council on Education, as mentioned in Chapter 7.

The current tendency is for the governor's budget staff to tolerate this deviation from statewide uniformity, recognizing that it is the product of decades of cooperative study and practice, and not of any contumacious whim. Today the persons who serve on governors' budget staffs are much less likely to be inexperienced youngsters or tired hack politicians than they were a generation ago. Many of them are on a high level of intelligence and integrity. Through a voluntary national association of their own they strive to build up their professional stature and improve their performance. They have already moved away from some of the clownish crudities which often marred their practices in earlier years.

Such is the apparent degree of suspicion regarding state departmental and institutional budgets that some of the states, including the most populous one—California—, not content with a full-fledged executive budget office, have also set up an entirely separate legislative budget office, fully staffed, to constitute an added hurdle. This office in California annually publishes a printed volume of 400 to 600 pages as its analysis and review of the developing state budget for the next fiscal year. Well-written and intelligently organized with many specific recommendations, this volume is usually decidedly negative in tenor.

In the work of budget analysts, whether executive or legislative, there is the difficulty of insufficient time in which to hold urbane and deliberate hearings for the heads of all departments and institutions, and to carry on the communications which might easily cause mutual misunderstandings to vanish. In times of rapid economic and social change, it seems hardly wise to expect an institution to submit its annual budget request a full year in advance of the probable time of appropriation; but the compression of the intervening time often means that intercommunication must be deficient, and that scheduled hearings must be somewhat perfunctory, in which event they often tend to degenerate into a sort of ill-tempered and ill-mannered "trial by combat." Anyone who has attended many such hearings in different states must gain an impression that hasty and testy arguments between opposing parties do not constitute the best possible way to arrive at the truth. A way should be found to encourage budget directors and analysts on the one hand, and state university and college presidents on the other, to join their intellectual capacities in studying what is best for all the people, rather than to look askance at each other as adversaries, sworn either to beat down the requests under any circumstance, or to hold them up, come what may.

A development which may or may not foretell some improvement in the process is the recent and current stress on the so-called performance budget or program budget, the thrust of which is to achieve a relationship between operating costs and annual output. In the field of education, the "output" of an enterprise over a period of a fiscal year or a biennium can mean nothing more nor less than "educational value added." This concept can not be precisely measured in dollars, even in its most mundane part; and at best a large part of it can be appraised only in terms of values unrelated to monetary considerations.

It would seem, then, that the effort to match costs with output in higher education will probably always labor under very severe limitations. It can be done in a crude way, with results that may easily be meaningless or misleading unless the figures are confined to the narrowest possible connotation. For example, a statement that two colleges with 3,000 students in each show an average operating cost of $1,500 per student per year for each, can mean just that and nothing more. It says nothing about the quality and real value of the educational experience at any level in either college. It does not say whether the "mix" of students according to different types and levels of instruction in the two colleges is similar or markedly different. In short, it takes no account of institutional differences and provides no allowances or deductions for institutional idiosyncrasies.

If the "output" of colleges or universities can be measured only in that manner, or similarly by counting the degrees granted or the semester credit hours earned, as though every unit were of identical value and therefore ought to be produced at a standardized cost, then the worth of the accounting effort must be restricted to extremely small dimensions. This is too obvious to be labored further.[1]

If in one large state a regional state university in one corner offers costly instruction in ferrous metals technology and industrial engineering because there are large steel mills in its vicinity, and another stresses expensive instruction in agriculture because it is in a productive agricultural region, while a third in an urban location provides advanced work and research in the multiple problems of city life, and a fourth is developing a scholarly and respected Institute of Tax Research, does it make sense to apply a rigid "formula" in allocating tax funds to these four institutions as though they were all identical? Seymour E. Harris has answered this in one way. Despairing

---

[1] A technical discussion is presented in R. N. McKean and M. Ansehn, *Problems, Limitations and Risks of the Program Budget*. Santa Monica: RAND Corporation, 1965, RM-4377-RC.

of accurate "quantifying" of educational productivity, he groaned: "Well, if we could only find out what the product is and define it, and if we could only know what the input is, then the problem would be relatively easy."[2]

Henry M. Wriston put it unerringly when he said, "Every time a formula is substituted for responsible judgment there is official defeasement. Rules make decision easy but rob it of wisdom."[3]

It should be clear that the push toward the development and the use of "formulas" for the allocation of state tax funds to higher education is an abdication of reason—a balking at the task of studiously hearing and weighing the claims of different institutions, and the claims of higher education as against those of other public functions at the given time—, with the askings of higher education to be explained and justified by those who understand best the nature and workings of higher educational agencies—the presidents of the state universities and colleges. These are usually men of high competency, chosen with great care and relatively well paid for a large and difficult set of responsibilities. Is it wise to brush them aside and rely on a "formula" which tends to reduce the whole state system to treadmill uniformity?[4]

The current bandwagon answer in the American states is to set up a central "super agency," either in the form of a single statewide governing board which governs *all* the institutions of all types (the institutional governing boards having been abolished), or in the form of a central statewide board which stands above the institutional governing boards and "coordinates" them in some manner, either by allocating appropriated funds among them or by advising the governor and the legislature in that regard. Fortunately many of these central

2 Seymour E. Harris, *Education and Public Policy*. Berkeley: McCutchan Publishing Corporation, 1965, p. 165, 347 pp.

3 Henry M. Wriston, *Academic Procession: Reflections of a College President*. New York: Columbia University Press, 1959, p. 112, 222 pp.

4 A skeptical and rather dim view of "formulas" is provided by L. Bradford Gregg in his December, 1966, summary report on *State Budgeting for Higher Education in the Midwest*. Bloomington, Indiana: Indiana University, December 27, 1966, pp. 9-11. Chicago: Council of State Governments, 1966, 12 pp. lithoprinted.

The classic defense of the use of formulas is James L. Miller's *Budgeting for Higher Education: The Use of Formulas and Cost Analysis*. Ann Arbor: University of Michigan, Institute of Public Administration (Michigan Government Studies, No. 45), 1965, 228 pp.

agencies of the "coordinating" type as yet have little or no authority beyond the duty of making recommendations; but most of them slyly reach out for more power by importuning each successive legislature, and most of them are slowly increasing the size of their staffs and the amount of tax funds at their immediate disposal, after the well-known manner of "Parkinson's Law."

A new echelon of bureaucracy is coming into state government, tending to place a new barrier of distance between the state universities and the governors and legislatures—the direct representatives of the people to be served.

It is debatable, and doubtful, that this new and added echelon is actually any more successful in giving knowledgeable attention to the development of higher education than are the state budget analysts in the state department of finance. Especially is this doubtful in several states where the "coordinating board" is composed exclusively of laymen, with no representation of public university or college presidents or trustees; and where the principal staff officer for the "coordinating board" has no great educational stature and is dominated by the board and little respected by the presidents.

An alternative, and more promising, method of receiving and deliberating sensibly on the claims of higher education as formulated by those who know most about higher education, would be the establishment of a permanent staff for a joint interim subcommittee of the appropriations committees of the two houses of the legislature. The joint interim subcommittee, consisting of a few key members of each House, would meet perhaps monthly or oftener to keep aware of developments in higher education and, enlightened by the full-time labors of its professional staff in stimulating liaison, fact-finding, and public information about higher education, would always be ready, shortly before and during legislative sessions, to deliberate intensively and hold hearings culminating in recommendations to the legislature regarding budget askings for higher education at appropriate times.

After all, passing upon requests for state tax funds is a legislative function which need not be delegated. The method suggested would avoid the accretion of a new bureaucratic echelon in the executive branch, and would tend to keep the necessary central statewide functions related to the support of higher education in immediate propinquity to the legislature. The "lay board" would be a joint subcommittee of legislative leaders, thus shortening the chain of communication between the institutions and the legislature, which is desirable.

Would this destroy the unity of the "executive budget system" and undercut the governor's influence in his own administration? Not necessarily. The budgets of the judicial branch and of the legislative branch are not integrated with the "executive budget"; and there is a convincing theory that public higher education should properly be regarded as a "fourth coordinate arm" as it is in the law of Michigan, Minnesota, and California—meriting a degree of independence comparable to that of the judiciary.

University presidents and many members of university governing boards and faculties deserve and receive as much public respect as judges of the state judicial system, because of their personal eminence and the importance of their functions. It is incongruous that in the matter of their budget askings they should be relegated to a place several echelons removed from the legislature and the governor by a system which superimposes: (1) the staff of a statewide "coordinating board"; (2) that board itself, which in some states is not permitted to include any representatives of the institutions of higher education; (3) the budget analysts of the staff of the executive budget director, often both undermanned and underqualified; (4) the executive budget director himself; (5) the governor; and (6) in several populous states, a legislative budget analyst, serving a joint legislative budget committee. This chain can be too cumbersome.

Indiana, by the way, has a somewhat simplified picture in which the joint legislative budget committee customarily holds its meetings in the office of the executive budget director and the two authorities work closely together. With 4 major state institutions of higher education and some 15 "regional campuses" at strategic concentrations of population in the state, Indiana has no statewide board of general jurisdiction over public higher education. Representatives of the four universities have direct access to the state budget authorities, and to the governor and the legislature. There is a Commission on Higher Educational Facilities, such as is required by Federal law of every state prerequisite to participation in facilities grants and loans; and a State Scholarship Commission of recent creation. Both of these receive the good will and cooperation of the 30-odd private colleges, as no heavy-handed "coordinating board" could.

This chapter must conclude with some notice of the question of direct appropriations of state tax funds to private colleges. Elsewhere we have observed that this practice has recently occurred in no more than a handful of states, Pennsylvania being the only state where it is followed on a regular and substantial scale. In 1967 and early 1968 a few private college executives, including Chancellor Allan M. Cartter of New York University and Chancellor Peter Sammartino of Fairleigh Dickinson University, were advocating the extension of this policy. Cartter suggested that perhaps the state tax contribution to the private colleges should bear a ratio of 1 to 4 to the state tax support of public institutions[5] (meaning, no doubt, *per unit of product* as measured by some such scale as degrees granted at different levels, or costs of instruction per student at different stages).

Parenthetically, it is interesting to observe that Cartter also raised his voice above the rumble of the bandwagon, to "caution against the trend toward centralized state systems of higher education with inflexible formula budgeting." His conviction that neither private nor public institutions should be confined in the harness of fiscal straitjackets seems sound.

In March, 1967, Governor Nelson A. Rockefeller of New York appointed a Select Committee on the Future of Private and Independent Higher Education in New York State.[6] A preview of the 16 recommendations of its report appeared in the *New York Times* January 31, 1968. The practical gist was that the New York State Board of Regents

---

[5] Allan M. Cartter, address to joint district meeting of the American Alumni Council and the American College Public Relations Association, as reported in *The Chronicle of Higher Education*, Vol. 2, No. 10, p. 1 (January 29, 1968).

[6] The committee's five members were: McGeorge Bundy (President of the Ford Foundation), Chairman; James B. Conant (President Emeritus of Harvard University); John A. Hannah (President of Michigan State University); the Rev. Theodore M. Hesburgh (President of the University of Notre Dame); and Abram L. Sachar (President of Brandeis University).

It is noteworthy that only one of the five members—John A. Hannah—was representative of a *public* university; and that New York is central in a compact group of seven contiguous states in the Northeast, each of which has from 50% to 80% of all its students enrolled in private institutions. This is not typical of the nation as a whole, but is the "stronghold" of private higher education in the United States.

should obtain annual appropriations of state tax funds and disburse them to the state's 143 private institutions of higher learning, the appropriate total for the year 1970 being estimated as $33 million. The allotment to each eligible institution "should be calculated on the basis of earned degrees conferred annually, with differentials for the appropriate levels and types—approximately proportional to the average differences in costs."

The suggested $33 million (of which $1 million would be allocated to the Board of Regents for "planning, standard-setting, and surveillance") would amount to only a small fraction of the total annual operating expenses of New York's private colleges. Even if only 100 institutions were qualified, the average institutional allotment would be only $320,000; though it might rise to several millions for a few of the largest private universities in New York, which confer large numbers of graduate degrees.

Another feature was a recommendation that "When the Board of Regents determines, after an inquiry which it has initiated, that new or expanded graduate programs are required to meet specific manpower needs, it should consider contracting with private institutions for such purposes, as an equally attractive alternative to expansion of public institutions. Its recommendations in each case should be made on the basis of the institutional resources available, the comparative costs and other relevant factors."

Noting current advocacy by the Board of Regents of a large expansion of the "scholar incentive program" of aid to individual students (and not wishing to set up competition between that program and its own recommendation of direct aid to the institutions), the committee declared: "Both programs are clearly essential."

Regarding the pushing of the panic button concerning "the plight of the private colleges," the committee maintained a cool position. In a letter to the governor and to the chairman of the Board of Regents, it was quoted as saying it began its inquiry "in the face of a widespread belief that private higher education, in New York as elsewhere, faced an imminent financial crisis of disastrous proportions." But, it continued, "We have not been able to substantiate this notion, and indeed one of our more important findings is that no one really knows precisely the exact financial condition" of the state's private colleges and universities.

The committee estimated, however, that by 1970-71 the yearly gap between income and expenditures for all of New York's private colleges and universities would be $30 to $35 million, and on this estimate its principal recommendation was based. In the early months of 1968 no one could predict how the legislature of 1968 would respond to this report; but certainly its publication was a major event of the year in the area of financing higher education.

The recommendations received the immediate and unqualified indorsement of Governor Rockefeller. But even if they were to be promptly enacted by the 1968 legislature, which seemed somewhat doubtful, they could be implemented only as to the 60 nonsectarian private colleges in New York, and not as to the 83 colleges having religious denominational affiliations until 1970 at the earliest; for a clause of long standing in the New York Constitution forbids payment of state tax funds to denominational institutions, and the procedure for amending the constitution requires that a proposed amendment must be approved by two successive legislatures and then submitted to popular vote at a statewide election. Thus if the amendment should be drafted and approved by both the 1968 and 1969 legislatures, it would not be voted upon by the people until November, 1969.

In this present chapter we limit ourselves to the subject of *state* tax support of higher education by direct appropriations. In Chapter 29, on "The Federal Involvement," happenings of 1967 and 1968 relevant to the probable expansion and the changing nature of the role of the national government are to be observed.

Chapter 24

EIGHT YEARS OF PROGRESS

THE RESPONSE of the 50 state legislatures in tripling state tax-fund appropriations for annual operating expenses of higher education in the short period of eight years between 1959 and 1967 was, as already noted, unforeseen and unpredicted. Even after the fact, it has been remarkably little publicized.

The 50 states did not all make the same rate of gain over the eight years, nor would this be expected. The weighted average rate of gain was about 213 per cent—indicating that for the nation as a whole the amounts were substantially more than tripled (200 per cent gain equals tripling). The range, however, was from 73½ per cent to 449 per cent—from less than doubling to more than quintupling.

Some interesting observations can be made by arranging the highest quartile of the states in descending order of their rates of gain (see Table 10). At the top is New York—the nation's most populous during most of the period, but now second in population.

1. A glance will show that seven of the states (New York, New Jersey, Pennsylvania, and four New England states) are in the Northeast. This is the result of the fact that each of those states was in a low position as to tax support of higher education in 1959, and each has made and is making great strides in a con-

191

scious effort to provide quality public higher education for its
people. This is evidenced by the swift development of the
conglomerate State University of New York and the City University of New York; new life for most of the state universities
in New England; new state junior colleges in Massachusetts,
Connecticut, and Rhode Island; and other features of the
"Northeastern revolution" in higher education.

2. A second glance shows Alaska and Hawaii, both small in population and of recent admission to statehood, with the exhilara-
tion of that event and the gusto of pioneer development. Hawaii
has the additional spur toward international educational service
that comes from being at the "crossroads of the Pacific" and
the presence of the wholly Federally-supported East-West
Center.

3. The remaining four states are Southern or Border states. They

Table 10.   The top quartile of states, measured by rate of increase, 1959-67,
in state tax-fund appropriations for annual operating expenses of
higher education (figures in thousands of dollars).

States	Year 1959-60	Year 1967-68	Eight-Year Gain	Per Cent Gain
(1)	(2)	(3)	(4)	(5)
N. Y.	78,546	431,212	352,666	449
Me.	3,356	18,167	14,811	441¼
Hawaii	4,958	26,320	21,362	431
Ky.	14,954	74,371	59,417	397¼
Mass.	12,167	57,667	45,500	374
Conn.	12,273	53,655	41,382	337
Pa.	43,471	179,212	135,741	312
R. I.	4,477	18,401	13,924	311
Alaska	2,111	8,619	6,508	308
N. J.	21,982	83,758	61,776	281
Tenn.	17,022	64,472	47,450	279
Mo.	24,744	92,855	68,111	275
N. C.	28,419	106,550	78,131	275

Source: *Appropriations of State Tax Funds for Operating Expenses of Higher
Education, 1967-68.* Washington: Office of Institutional Research, National Association of State Universities and Land-Grant Colleges, 1967, 30 pp. mimeo.

too were in low positions in 1959, and are determined to come up fast. Some of the same enthusiasm prevails in the whole region. Kentucky has made commendable progress since enacting a 3 per cent general sales tax in 1960, but even yet the relation of total tax collections to personal incomes in Kentucky is one of the lowest in the nation.

Missouri, with the state university at a small city, long left higher education in the two big cities (St. Louis and Kansas City) to private universities and the local public school districts; but it is now positively developing state university regional campuses in both—having taken over the private former University of Kansas City and established a state university campus in St. Louis as well. The city and county of St. Louis compose a junior college district developing a three-campus junior college in the metropolitan area.

If we turn now to the lowest quartile of the states, various observations also leap out (see Table 11). Michigan is the only state above average population, except perhaps Louisiana; all the others in this group are definitely not heavily populated, and some of them are among the smallest in population.

1. Geography plays a part here, too. A contiguous bloc runs from Oklahoma to the Canadian border, thence westward through Montana, Wyoming, and Idaho to Oregon. This embraces nine states and a vast area of high plains and mountains, mostly in the northwest quadrant of the continental United States. Generally speaking, these states have had a relatively slow growth of population (some of them have had temporary losses); and some of them seem to be more or less chronically economically depressed. The "westward tilt" has largely passed them by and poured people into the southwest quadrant instead. There is considerable valid connection between this situation and their comparatively slow gains in support of higher education. It should be noted that some of these states, especially Kansas, North Dakota, and Oregon, have traditions of generosity and of faith in the value of their state universities and colleges. North Dakota has at times devoted a higher percentage of state tax collections to the support of higher education than has any other state.

2. Michigan also has a great tradition and takes pride in what

Table 11.   The lowest quartile of states, measured by rate of increase, 1959-
             67, in state tax-fund appropriations for annual operating ex-
             penses of higher education (figures in thousands of dollars).

States	Year 1959-60	Year 1967-68	Eight-Year Gain	Per Cent Gain
(1)	(2)	(3)	(4)	(5)
Mich.	$95,599	$231,567	$135,698	142¼
Kans.	25,036	59,003	33,967	135½
Ore.	28,719	67,305	38,586	134½
La.	40,062	93,123	53,061	132½
N. H.	3,973	9,201	5,228	131½
Ida.	8,799	20,101	11,302	128½
Wyo.	4,955	11,123	6,188	125½
Nebr.	15,217	33,248	18,031	118½
N. D.	9,368	19,888	10,520	112¼
S. D.	8,128	16,992	8,864	109
Mont.	11,230	21,375	10,145	90¼
Okla.	27,014	46,858	19,844	73½

Source: *Appropriations of State Tax Funds for Operating Expenses of Higher Education, 1967-68*. Washington: Office of Institutional Research, National Association of State Universities and Land-Grant Colleges, 1967, 30 pp. mimeo.

was until recently the second largest state system of higher education in the nation (second only to California, though California now has more than twice the population of Michigan), including the renowned University of Michigan at Ann Arbor and the largest separate land-grant university (Michigan State University at East Lansing), as well as 10 other excellent institutions. Michigan now shakes down into fourth place, however, being outstripped by the more populous states of New York and Illinois. Starting from a high point in 1959, Michigan has suffered two slow-downs within eight years, partly because of bitter partisanship in the legislature. A four-year stretch of slow gains occurred from 1958 through 1962, with partisan infighting and deadlock between Democratic governors and Republican legislatures. Then came a time of fair progress from 1963 through 1966; but 1967 was again a year of parsimony, with only minuscule gains over the preceding year.

3. New Hampshire alone among the New England states is in the lowest quartile, quite clearly because it is conspicuously without a modern state revenue system—no general sales tax and no income tax except on dividends, which produces negligible returns. (For a time in the Sixties New Hampshire and Nebraska, alone among the 50 states, shared the dubious distinction of having neither an income tax nor a sales tax—the two types that are the largest revenue-producers for most of the states today. A recent expedient in New Hampshire was the installation of a state lottery, which proved somewhat disappointing as a revenue-producer.

4. Louisiana, in the Deep South, has a highly productive severance tax but probably does not utilize some of the other types to the extent practicable. The state income tax is rated low, but the total of tax collections per capita is higher than in any adjacent state. Support of higher education was at a comparatively high level in 1959.

The foregoing brief comments afford only inklings of the useful information that might be adduced by extensive and intensive studies of the tax support of higher education in each state in relation to a variety of relevant economic and social conditions in that state and region.

Adverting again to the progress of the 50 states during the eight years, 1959-67, let it be added that none of the states having the highest rates of increase of population during the period 1950-1965 appears in the top quartile of gainers in support of higher education—illustrating that it is difficult to keep abreast of rapid population growth with revenue systems and appropriations. Four of the outstanding states in population growth were Nevada, Arizona, Florida, and California. Each made only second or third quartile rates of gain in support of higher education: Nevada, 220 per cent; Arizona, 229½ per cent; Florida, 217 per cent; and California, 183 per cent.

California's rate of gain is well below the nationwide weighted average of 213 per cent, despite an increase of population in the state of something approaching 50 per cent every 10 years. The statewide system of public universities, colleges, and junior colleges was already in an advanced stage in 1959 and benefiting from a high level of support, at least at its top segment; and even until beyond 1967 the

70-odd public junior colleges were largely supported by local taxing subdivisions—a factor of considerable weight.

We turn now to more general considerations, involving the relations between rising enrollments and mounting costs of annual operation.

The impressive fact that appropriations of state tax funds for annual operating expenses of higher education in the 50 states have been tripled within eight years (1959-67) calls for comment. The rise was from $1.4 billion in 1959 to more than $4.3 billion in 1967—a gain of almost $3 billion.

1. It discomfits and dumbfounds the many who were saying in 1957-58 that the unprecedented appropriations of that year were the "last straw"—the absolute all-time maximum that the states could afford—and the timid economists who were then predicting that it might be barely possible that by 1970 another billion a year could be obtained from all governmental sources—Federal, state, and local.

2. It gives rise to a question: Why do annual operating costs rise faster than enrollments? For during the eight years when annual operating costs were tripled, annual enrollments in higher education were only approximately doubled. Confront this question head-on. There are several factors that add up to a compelling answer:

   a. Continuing inflation, gradually lowering the purchasing-power of the dollar, means higher costs for salaries, wages, equipment, and supplies each year.

   b. Although faculty salaries have doubled in the past dozen years, the market is now more keenly competitive than ever before, and the largest faculty shortage in history exists and impends; and faculty salaries are not yet "caught up" to comparability with compensation in the other learned professions. Hence salaries (half of the total of annual operating expenses) have risen and will continue to go up about 6 per cent to 7 per cent per year—about twice as fast as the rate of general inflation.

   c. The explosion of new knowledge forces universities and colleges to modify and modernize their courses and to add new courses, departments of instruction, interdisciplinary

units, and specialized institutes at much more frequent intervals than formerly. As every man of business knows, a
new enterprise is an "island of high cost" during the first few
years of its existence, until it becomes properly staffed and
equipped and well-known.

d. Another result of the explosion of knowledge is the flood
of new and astronomically costly apparatus and equipment,
much of which is already indispensable: computer services,
electron microscopes, new copying, duplicating, and projecting devices, and television receivers, to name only a few,
and not to mention the separate streams of novel devices for
physical, medical and dental instruction and research.

e. An important aspect of the great and continued rise of enrollments is the fact that students are now continuing longer
in college and larger proportions of them are going into
and completing the upper division, graduate, and graduate-
professional studies. This raises the "center of maturity" of
the whole institution, and also forces upward its annual
operating cost, because unit costs in the upper division are
necessarily about twice as high as in the lower division, and
at the doctoral level in the arts and sciences or engineering or
medicine they are from 6 to 10 or more times as high.

The foregoing are a few of the reasons that combine to
cause annual operating costs to rise faster than enrollments.

Vague and uninformed intimations that they can be quickly countervailed by "the economy of scale," as would occur in
a factory producing standard bolts; or by huge increases in
the student-teacher ratio, aided by motion pictures and television; or by forcing students to do more independent study
without benefit of instruction—all must be discounted at least
for the immediate future.

The audio-visual "educational hardware" can greatly enrich instruction, and spread its range of diffusion; but no one
soundly supposes it can soon displace a single professor or
assistant. Independent study, with some regular association with
a tutor, is one of the best possible methods of learning, but
also the most demanding of tutorial time and therefore the
most expensive of all.

3. A second question: Why is the annual operating cost of higher education taking a growing share of state tax receipts, and a larger percentage of the Gross National Product than ever before? The answers are self-evident:

a. In the half-century since 1920 the percentage of the population of appropriate age getting some education beyond high school has increased fivefold. Since 1950 it has more than doubled; and at the same time the percentage of youth of college age in the total population has also greatly increased. Higher education is simply a much greater enterprise in comparison with the population and resources of the nation and the states. Instead of an average of 5 to 10 per cent of the annual revenues of the states, it will cost more. Instead of 1 per cent or less of the Gross National Product, 2 or 2½ per cent will be invested in the annual operating expenses of higher education. This will be an increasingly productive investment.

b. Education beyond high school, of all grades from preparation for technician-level occupations to the highest graduate and professional instruction and research, is now indispensable for the maintenance of an upgraded manpower supply. It is the mainspring of an upward spiral of economic growth. It is the source of advancement in public health, an enlightened public awareness of social and political issues, and a generally more sensitive and humane civilization.

With these considerations in mind, the great increases in the public investment in higher education are not cause for alarm, but a matter of congratulation. They will continue through the 1970's, without hardship, because some of the gains come automatically from economic growth without changes in taxation. The state revenue systems are susceptible of almost constant improvement to make them more productive and more equitable and can become thrice as productive as they now are. Only the deepest pessimism would deny that within a few years a larger proportion of the huge Federal revenues can be allotted to domestic concerns, including higher education. There are overwhelming evidences that increasing support of education beyond the high school is rooted as a paramount public policy of the states and the nation.

Chapter 25

STATE REVENUE SYSTEMS

IN TERMS OF THE THREE LEVELS of government, the state level now offers the brightest prospects for the improvement of tax patterns and the expansion of public revenues.

At the Federal echelon there is already in operation a taxing system of huge productivity. The current problem is that of reaching a situation in which most of the vast annual income will not have to go for policing the world and subsidizing other nations, but can be used for domestic public purposes, among which higher education has a prime place.

The local taxing subdivisions within the states have had their revenue-raising potentialities severely limited by technological and social changes, and it has become quite evident that most of them will have to receive increasing financial aid from the state and Federal levels to enable them to operate and maintain their necessary public services. There is room for much improvement in the administration of property taxes, on which the local units chiefly depend; but such improvements are difficult and slow, and do not in any event promise ever to make most of the local units financially self-sufficient.

State revenue systems offer the best promise because in general the state is the smallest governmental unit that can hope to levy and administer efficiently the types of taxes that are the best revenue-producers in the present society: sales taxes, general and selective; income taxes, personal and corporate; licensing of motor vehicles and of drivers; severance taxes; succession taxes and others.

The nationwide total of state tax revenues rose from $13.4 billion in 1956 to $29.4 billion in 1966—considerably more than double. To keep this fact in perspective, note also that the rise over the same 10 years in *per capita* state taxes was from $80.34 to $150.60—less than double (the lesser rate of gain was obviously accounted for by the increase in population). Over the same period the rise in the amount *per $1,000 of personal income* was only from $40.74 to $55.51 —a much less impressive gain (explained both by increase in population and inflation of personal incomes). It is clear that over a single decade the states more than doubled their revenues by increasing the actual incidence upon personal incomes by only about 36 per cent. This resulted from the fact that each year there were more people and larger per capita incomes. In a time of population increase and economic growth, some of the augmentation of revenues comes without any new levies or increases in rates.

In 1966, 40 states were using general sales or gross receipts taxes, and these accounted for more than one-fourth of all state revenues (26.8%). Fifty states had selective sales on motor fuels (15.7%); 48 states taxed tobacco products (5.2%); 50 taxed alcoholic beverages (3.4%); and 50 had other selective sales taxes (6.9%). Thus the foregoing group of general and selective sales taxes brought in 58 per cent of all state revenues.

Sales taxes can produce large amounts of receipts promptly. They are regressive; i.e., they bear proportionately most heavily upon low-income families or individuals, because these people generally have to spend all their incomes to purchase necessities. For that reason some general sales tax statutes exempt such common necessities as foods not consumed on the premises, prescription drugs and medicines, and children's clothing below specified prices. For the benefit of farmers, a few states provide for the exemption of their purchases of agricultural machinery, fertilizers, insecticides and herbicides, livestock feeds, and other necessary farm supplies.

On the other hand, there is some tendency to broaden the coverage by embracing rentals of hotel and motel rooms, hotel or restaurant meals, telephone and telegraph services, and fees for professional or technical services. Sometimes the total receipts from professional work or business services are covered—and then the general sales tax is called a "gross receipts" or "gross income" tax; but this type is not found in many states.

The selective sales tax on motor fuels is used in 50 states, with the receipts usually, though not always wholly, pre-allocated to highway construction and maintenance. Taxes on alcoholic liquors and tobacco are supposed to exert some slight controlling effect on undesirable personal habits inimical to public health. Other selective sales taxes are usually aimed at luxury items such as cosmetics, expensive clothing, high-priced tickets of admission to amusements, and the like.

The generally regressive character of sales taxes persists, even when some basic necessities are exempted; but note that in 1966 all general and selective sales taxes produced 58 per cent of all state revenues. Note also that the general sales tax rates in different states varied from 2 per cent in eight states to 5 per cent in Pennsylvania. In 1967 Rhode Island joined the "5 per cent club," and likewise California. As a matter of fact, New York has a 2 per cent statewide rate and additional 3 per cent general sales taxes locally in New York City and Rochester, so that more than half the people of the state are subject to the composite rate of 5 per cent.

By 1967 general sales taxes had been adopted by four additional states—making a total of 44. The recent additions were New Jersey and Virginia in 1966 and Minnesota and Nebraska in 1967. The six states now having no such tax are all of comparatively small population, the largest being Oregon. The other five are Alaska, Delaware, Montana, New Hampshire, and Vermont.

A reliable maxim is that a state revenue system should be diversified, consisting of several types of taxes, so the inequities and insufficiencies of any one may in some instances be countervailed by the merits of others. Such a varied composite might also normally be expected to withstand the shocks of economic dislocations better than a system depending exclusively or too heavily upon one type of tax.

The regressiveness of sales taxes can and should be counterbalanced by *graduated* income taxes. In 1966, however, only 36 states had personal income taxes and 38 had corporation income taxes. Unfortunately, too, some of these tax statutes provide for *flat rate* income taxes, not *graduated*. This robs the tax of most of its progressive effect, i.e. the tendency to bear proportionately heavily upon the well-to-do.

Massachusetts can not enact a graduated income tax until a constitutional amendment is adopted. In 1967 the legislature approved this proposal for the second time in different sessions (as required by the constitutional procedure for amendment) and it can now be placed on the ballot at a popular election. Michigan also has a constitutional provision prohibiting a graduated income tax, so the new income tax statute enacted in 1967 after long insistence by successive governors for two decades necessarily provides only for a *flat rate* income tax for individuals and corporations.

The story of Nebraska in the middle 1960's is intriguing. Up to 1965 Nebraska was getting one-third of its revenue for *state* purposes from the property tax. (Most states had long since ceased to use property taxes for *state* functions.) It had neither a sales tax nor an income tax of any kind. It enacted an income tax in 1965, to become effective in 1967. In 1966 this was subjected to a popular referendum and overwhelmingly defeated. At the same time the electorate adopted a constitutional amendment prohibiting the use of the property tax for state purposes, thus leaving the state without any major source of revenue for state-level services.

The legislature of 1967 enacted a sales tax *and* an income tax, not fixing the rate of the income tax, but providing in effect that it shall be determined for each year at such level as may be necessary to make up the difference between all other revenue receipts and the amount deemed necessary to be expended for that year. This is a new way of guaranteeing a balanced budget. Hitherto it has been accomplished by ruthless cutting of budget requests to fit estimated revenues. To be sure, the sensible device of fixing the tax rate after determining the necessary expenditures is used at the local level for property tax rates; but such a provision for a "sliding-scale" income tax rate at the state level is rare indeed. It seems to mean that Nebraska, which has been as reactionary as any state in matters of taxation and budgeting, has at last decided to reverse the upside-down way of estimating revenues and then "cutting the pie," and instead to embark upon the sensible practice of first determining necessary expenditures and then tailoring the revenue to fit the needs.

A similar idea cropped up in Pennsylvania in 1967. The state had no individual income tax. Governor Shafer urged the enactment of a "standby" income tax of 1 per cent on personal incomes, to become effective only if and when the state's expenditures exceeded the rate of $1.9 billion per year.

In the states having income taxes, there are very wide variations in rates, amounts of income exempted, and numerous other features. There is a recent tendency, however, to simplify the matter by following the provisions of the Federal income tax statute and making the state tax due simply a modest percentage of the Federal tax paid. This automatically carries the *graduation* and obviously is unlawful in states whose constitutions forbid a graduated income tax.

Another important improvement in the administration of state income taxes has already swept many states, probably a majority of them. This is the adoption of the principle of requiring employers to *withhold* a large portion of the estimated tax due from each of their employees and to pay these withholdings to the state promptly at short intervals, after the manner of the well-known Federal income tax withholding system. The adoption of this scheme results in a "windfall" during the first year after its initiation, by telescoping the due dates for the past year and the current year. A more durable benefit to the state, however, comes from the fact that thousands of small taxpayers who have never before bothered to make a return, and perhaps have not even been aware of their liability, become regular taxpayers because the paperwork is done by their employers' accounting and clerical staffs.

Individual income taxes produced 14.6 per cent of all state revenues in 1966, and corporation income taxes turned in another 6.9 per cent of total revenue receipts, making a total of 21.5 per cent for state income taxes. Add this to the 58 per cent brought in by sales taxes, and it becomes evident that approximately four-fifths of state revenues are presently coming from these two types. Yet sales taxes are the largest single source of revenue in only 31 states, while income taxes hold that place in only 13 states. Strangely enough, five states were using the gasoline tax as their largest single source—Nebraska, New Hampshire, New Jersey, Oklahoma, and Texas. The names of these five are readily recognized as those recently most reluctant to adopt either sales or income taxes, other than on a basis so narrowly selective as to be almost negligible; but at least three of them have made changes in 1966 and 1967 which will probably now remove their dependence on gasoline sales as their largest single source.

Louisiana, alone, uses the severance tax on the extraction of minerals, gas and oil, and other natural resources as its largest single source of revenue. It has a sales tax at the lowest rate (2%), and individual and corporation income taxes at modest rates. It is probably doing a better job than any other state in taxing the exploitation of its irreplaceable natural resources. Oklahoma and Texas are also getting substantial revenue from this source. Many other states fail to use it at all.

The foregoing oversimplified sketch affords a pale idea of the complexity and diversity of 50 state revenue systems. The paramount point is that they are all susceptible of improvement. This would be true even if they were all perfect today, for swift economic and social changes would soon make them out-of-date, inequitable, and relatively unproductive. State taxes must be constantly studied and adjusted to fit the economy of today, not of last year or of the nineteenth century. The potentiality is there. As state expenditures rise, state revenue systems can be revised to become more productive and also more equitable, without unduly burdening individuals or families, or strangling economic growth. A grasp of this problem in some detail should belong to every citizen from high school age upward.

One type of study which would seem to be of tremendous interest and value was once published by the Southern Regional Education Board for the 16 states of the Southeast, entitled *Revenue Potentials in Southern States* (Kenneth E. Quindry, 1962, 54 pp.). The technique is to find what portion of its revenue each state derives from each type of tax and compare this with the proportion other states in the region or in the nation obtain from that type of tax. There are many legitimate reasons why these proportions will vary considerably among different states, and there is no thought of reducing all state tax systems to uniformity; but such a study is sure to reveal certain probable lacunae in the various systems and point to their possible improvement. The relation between total tax collections and per capita incomes in each of the 50 states provides a brake to prevent excessive overestimation of tax potentials in any one state.

It would be decidedly in the public interest if studies of this kind could go on constantly in every state and every region throughout the nation, with a constant flow of findings universally available for examination and discussion by all citizens. With respect to the ability of our states to provide improved public services, including the expansion and upgrading of public higher education, we do not yet "know our own strength." We are on the threshold of a new decade as excitingly expansive as the one now approaching its end.

Chapter 26

STATEWIDE "COORDINATION" IN
PUBLIC HIGHER EDUCATION

As EARLY AS THE LAST DECADES of the nineteenth century the
notion appeared that several state institutions of higher education in
the same state should have their control centralized in a single lay
board. In the middle 1880's South Dakota set up a sort of supervisory
board to oversee its several institutions, each of which had its own
governing board. In 1896 the institutional governing boards were
abolished, and full governing powers vested in the statewide central
board—misnamed Board of Regents of Education, though it was concerned with higher education and had nothing to do with the state
system of elementary and secondary schools.

A state of vast distances, sparse population, no cities, and slim
resources, South Dakota in the Eighties and Nineties had a difficult
problem of providing state colleges at places reasonably accessible to
all its people. In those days duplication of undergraduate offerings
was regarded as reprehensible or intolerable, and apparently the answer
was to settle for a clutch of specialized or fragmentary institutions:
a land-grant college, an embryonic university, a school of mines, and
several normal schools—all under a single board to insure that none
got out of its special groove. The probable connections between the

legislation of 1896 and the financial panic of 1893 would be an interesting topic of research.

Florida made a somewhat similar move in 1906, as did also Iowa
in 1909. Probable effects of the panic of 1907 on Iowa's legislation
would also bear investigation. During the second decade of this century
similar state-level structures for public higher education were set
up in Mississippi (1912), Montana and Idaho (1913), and Kansas and
North Dakota (1915). Both of the two last-named made the mistake of
creating a salaried state board to govern not only state institutions of
higher education, but also a variety of others—penitentiaries, state
hospitals, and schools for the handicapped—a mistake which was eventually corrected by both states.

The eight states just named are all in the West or South, and all
were at the times mentioned comparatively large in area and small in
population. The next burst is associated with the Great Depression
beginning in 1929: Oregon, 1929; Mississippi, 1932 (in the meantime
the consolidation of 1912 had fallen into desuetude); and Georgia,
1931. Parenthetically it may be added that in acts of 1931 and 1933
North Carolina created the Consolidated University of North Carolina (three campuses, later four), but left a number of other state
colleges untouched, and hence is not in the group making the sweeping
consolidation of *all* institutions under one statewide board. In 1939,
little Rhode Island, then having only two state institutions a few miles
apart, consolidated the government of both in one statewide board of
trustees.

The next such move was by Arizona in 1945—having only three
state institutions, as is also the case with Iowa. Arizona was the twelfth
state in the series (North Carolina being excluded as inappropriate).

In 1948 when the Board of Trustees of the State University of
New York was created to govern a conglomeration which now consists
of some 31 state colleges, including four "university centers," and was
given some supervisory powers over some 28 or more two-year local
public "community colleges," the consolidation of control in a state
agency appeared in the nation's most populous state at that time. Each
of the state institutions, however, has its own governing board with
closely limited powers; and the whole setup is in a sense not new to
New York, because prior to 1948 essentially the same powers now
belonging to the Board of Trustees had long been exercised by the

"Board of Regents of the University of the State of New York and State Board of Education," which dates as far back as 1784 and which continues to be nominally superior to the Board of Trustees. These factors, and others, place New York in a class by itself. The only other state having a claim to inclusion in the category of 12 previously discussed is New Hampshire—among the smallest in area as well as in population, and having only one small state university and two tiny state colleges—which in 1965 simply abolished the two college boards of trustees and declared the two colleges henceforth to be branches of the university.

Thus the maximum number of states having a single statewide governing board for all public higher education is 14; and the adoption of this scheme in those states was spread over a stretch of 70 years, from 1896 to 1965, with some clustering at periods of financial panic. Most of these states are relatively small in population, and at least two of them are small in area. It can scarcely be said that their scheme has made any rapid nationwide sweep, or that it demonstrates any overwhelming popularity. In fact, it has gained but a single small state during the past 20 years.

As everyone knows, it has been largely superseded by a scheme which involves no abolition of institutional governing boards, and no creation of a statewide governing board, but instead merely the establishment of a statewide board which will govern no institution or group, but will exercise certain coordinative functions. Since 1934 this has occurred in more than 20 states; but they should hardly be categorized in an undifferentiated group because of great variations in the nature of their functions and the manner of their exercise.

In order to comprehend this variety it is desirable to contemplate it briefly "in the round" before inspecting the states specifically. The basic dichotomy is between persons who believe the coordinative functions must be performed as an exercise of force—of coercive power—and those who believe the public interest will be better served if these functions are performed by the use of noncoercive persuasion and permissive methods such as the facilitation of liaison and of public information, accompanied by fact-gathering and the preparation of advisory reports.

Under the first view, state university and college presidents, faculties, and governing boards are hopelessly engrossed in rampant empire-building "institutionalism" and can not be trusted to consider the public higher educational needs of the people of the state as a whole. Someone is needed to "knock heads together" and issue orders which the universities and colleges must implicitly obey. Institutional autonomy must go by the board in these times of "interdependence." Some writers and speakers appear to become quite ambivalent by paying lengthy lip service to autonomy, and in the next paragraph declaring that every institution must now submit the task of determining its own services to a statehouse bureaucracy—not, mind you, to the judgment of the representatives of the people elected to the legislature and the governorship. Underlying this is the notion that only thus can the most value be had for the dollars spent to maintain and operate facilities of public higher education.

Under the other view, an authoritarian hierarchy, after the manner of a military or profit-seeking organization, is not only out of place but also harmful in higher education, destructive of morale at all levels and inimical to the spirit of the free search for truth, without which a university is a travesty. High morale is indispensable to the best service of an educational institution, and the best index of the productivty of educational dollars invested there. Morale can not be forced; it can only be fostered. Therefore meat-axe "coordination" by "chopping off fingers and toes," if intended to promote economy and efficiency in a college or university, is self-defeating.

Proponents of this view do not deny the need for certain statewide coordinating functions, nor do they question that ultimate authority rests with the legislature and the governor. They would not have this authority abdicated or delegated. They would have a central statewide agency with a small full-time staff to facilitate liaison among the state institutions, to prepare and circulate a flow of publications concerning the condition of the statewide system, for the information of the public and the institutions and the current state government. This agency might be the permanent staff of a joint legislative committee on higher education or the staff of a joint council of the university and college presidents and representatives of their governing boards. The first of these alternatives would obviate the addition of a new echelon of bureaucracy in the administrative branch. The main principle is that the agency, wherever based, would have *no statutory coercive powers;* it would be wholly an *advisory* agency—an agency of research, liaison, public information, and recommendations regarding the future development of public higher education in the state.

With the foregoing contrasting concepts as a backdrop, one can next consider a few of the principal "coordinating" functions most commonly assigned to the central statewide board and observe the manner of their execution. These are relating to (1) budget askings (*revising* askings, or *recommending* specific revisions); (2) the initiation of new and additional schools, divisions, or departments of instruction, or new degree programs; (3) student fees, admissions requirements, and yearly calendars.

Look at each of these three areas briefly, with some appropriate examples:

1. Almost all the 20-odd states authorize the central board to "recommend the general level of support," and impliedly to propose specific changes in the institutional budget askings, leaving the actual appropriation of state tax funds and their allocation among different institutions to the discretion of the legislature and the governor. There is one outstanding exception: an Oklahoma constitutional amendment of 1941 which forbids the legislature to appropriate any sums for higher education to any agency other than the Board of Regents for Higher Education, which then must distribute the funds among 18 state colleges and universities. This bald power of the purse, one would say, makes this "coordinating board" the most power-laden one of its kind in the nation.

   In Ohio, where a superimposed Board of Regents was created by statute in 1963, the legislature has thus far retained its habit of determining separate appropriations to each of the major and older institutions, but has on occasion left apparently unlimited discretion to the Board of Regents in allotting appropriated funds among newer and smaller institutions, sometimes making the appropriations before the institutions were in existence.

2. Many of the states have made some attempt to empower the "coordinating board" to wield authority in the approval or disapproval of new departments or degree programs as proposed by the various institutions. Almost everywhere this has been largely a failure (as it should be), for numerous reasons.

a. No state board wants to meddle with every new "course," of which most colleges have hundreds, and large universities, thousands. This is too far down the scale of detail. But it is easy to create a department of instruction *de facto* by introducing the appropriate courses; and then the emergence of the *de jure* department awaits only a shifting of labels, which sometimes need not necessarily occur at all. At the Oregon State College (now Oregon State University) of 40 years ago, it was wisely decided to teach a course in United States constitutional law as an element in a good liberal education for many upper-division students. It was offered under the label of "Advanced American Government," because the prevailing "division of labor" among the state institutions forbade the land-grant college to teach any more than a minimum of courses having any elements of law. The same factor prevented the college from emphasizing the liberal arts, so it grouped some of its excellent liberal arts departments in an organization called the "Basic College." Not only "Advanced American Government," but the whole political science department, was placed in the School of Commerce. Elsewhere whole major schools or colleges have naturally developed by similar processes. Courses and departments of technology can evolve into a needed school of engineering, as at Southern Illinois University. Departments of biological and related sciences can evolve into a needed school of medicine, as at Michigan State University.

b. At large universities there is an almost constant "coming and going" of specialized institutes, interdisciplinary programs, and other centers of new studies, many of which attract substantial subsidies from philanthropic foundations, industrial corporations, or agencies of the Federal government. This kind of activity is of the essence of a university, regardless of whether it brings in subsidies or not; but a state "coordinating board" is in a particularly embarrassing position if its delays or negative recommendations not merely frustrate the efforts of the most alert professors, but also cause the loss of substantial grants from outside sources.

c. No real university can or will submit to the strait jacket implied by the power of an absentee "coordinating board" to dictate its program. It will circumvent it overtly or have it thrown off formally, as was done in North Carolina in 1959, when the State Board of Higher Education, created in 1955, was finally restrained by the legislature after four years of bitter conflict with the Board of Trustees of the University of North Carolina. The act of 1959 specified that only the legislature itself has power to make orders regarding the addition or deletion of programs of the university.

3. With regard to such matters as student fees, admissions requirements, and yearly calendars, there is a marked tendency among the "coordinating boards" to reach out for power—a species of "creeping centralization." The Illinois Board of Higher Education, created in 1961, asks for authority to impose *uniform* minimum entrance standards for freshmen at all campuses of the six state universities. This would obviously have the effect of restricting the choices of many Illinois students—they would have to attend a junior college, or a private college, or go outside the state. A more recent request for authority to "freeze" the freshman enrollments of all the state universities at the figures prevailing in 1970 is of precisely the same tendency. While attending a junior college in his home town is markedly more economical for the student and his family, there is simply no credible evidence that it is any more economical for the taxpayers who support the junior colleges and the state universities; and certain it is that in many junior colleges the facilities and opportunities can not for several years become of a quality and diversity approaching those available to lower-division students in the state universities. The junior colleges will unquestionably develop rapidly in size and quality; but meantime the surge to divert students forcibly to them and away from the universities spells restricted opportunities for many students. This is costly to the state in the long run.

The foregoing paragraphs are for the purpose of illustrating that up to the present many of the activities of "coordinating boards" have been exercises in futility and self-defeat. Examples could be multiplied many times. A traverse of the 20-odd states would fill an encyclopedic volume. Fortunately many of the boards are exclusively *advisory*, as is the California Coordinating Council for Higher Education created in 1960; or have little more than advisory functions. Sometimes the situation is quite ambiguous, as in Michigan, where the constitution of 1963 makes each of the state universities and colleges constitutionally independent in the management of all its funds, and designates the State Board of Education as a "coordinating agency" for all public education from kindergarten through graduate school. Manifestly the board can exercise this function only in an *advisory* capacity with regard to higher education.

The anomalous and almost self-contradictory wording is the result of a compromise between bitterly contesting factions in the constitutional convention—one of which insisted on the continuation and expansion of the principle of institutional autonomy which has served Michigan so well for more than a century, while the other espoused the *embourgeoisement* of public higher education. Similar compromises often occur in state legislatures, producing statutes that are ambiguous and difficult to interpret without an understanding of the conflicts that underlie them. One must believe, however, that the urbane and humane principle of progress by voluntary consensus will eventually prevail in statewide coordination of higher education, even in the states whose statutes provide for a rigid authoritarian structure. Structure is far from all-important—much less important than the spirit pervading the individuals who man it and the spirit of the times in which it functions. These factors point toward less crude coercion and useless overcentralization, and more mutual confidence and cooperation. This trend is profoundly intertwined with the problem of getting maximum educational productivity per dollar invested.

That autonomy and flexibility are essential to the performance of a university's real functions is well understood by the members of the governing boards, the administrators, and the faculties and students of all great universities, private and public. It has seldom been better expressed than in the words of Kingman Brewster, Jr., president of Yale University:

"A distinctive feature of a university as a gathering place of intellectual talent is that it defies programmatic purpose. Like the government of a free society, so the government of a university finds its purpose in the development of capacity and opportunity of its citizens, not their direction into some centrally planned grooves."

Chapter 27

THE CAMPUS UNDER
STATEHOUSE CONTROL

EXCEPT IN TEN STATES whose state universities have constitutional autonomy (Michigan, Minnesota, California, Idaho, Nevada, Arizona, Oklahoma, Colorado, Utah, and Georgia), a maze of fiscal controls from the state capitol is directed at the state institutions of higher education, a result of the half-century-old wave toward centralization in state governments which had an impetus about 1910 to 1912 and has spread intermittently ever since, though some indications of abatement began to appear about 1960.

In general the tightest apron strings are found in New England, New York, and New Jersey. Among the other states the condition varies widely from almost complete freedom for the universities in Indiana and Missouri all along the intermediate scale.

The scene may be examined in capsules: (1) legislative controls, (2) state emergency boards, (3) budgeting, (4) internal auditing, (5) purchasing, (6) uniform accounting, (7) state architects and departments of public works, and (8) state civil service statutes and regulations.

In some states there are constitutional restrictions on the adding of "riders" to appropriation bills, but in others there is a considerable history of harassment by the device. It is also possible for legislatures to make "conditional" appropriations, and thus deprive a university of control of appropriated funds. Thus when the Mississippi legislature of 1928 appropriated $1,600,000 for capital improvements at the University of Mississippi, and in the same act created a special state building commission to administer the fund, the act was sustained in court,[1] though there was ostensibly little reason for it other than to keep the expenditure of the money in the hands of the politicians currently in control of the statehouse.

Another type of legislative control is through minutely itemized appropriation acts. An example of stringent control strictly interpreted was afforded by Illinois in 1943, when the supreme court declined to order payment of the salary of the eminent jurist, Sveinbjorn Johnson, who had long served in a dual capacity as professor of law and university counsel at the University of Illinois, because there was no specific item for "counsel" in the current appropriation act.[2] The same decision, however, held that the university is a public corporation constituting a legal entity distinct from that of the state, and entitled to employ its own legal counsel; and directed the attorney-general to withdraw from a pending case in a lower court where he was attempting to intrude himself as university counsel.

How a change for the better regarding itemization of appropriations can take place within a few years is strikingly demonstrated in a 1957 decision by the same court, when commercial television interests sought to defeat the operation of a university broadcasting station on the ground that it was not expressly provided for in a line-item appropriation. The court evinced understanding that a university must have some latitude and flexibility in adjusting its service to new times. Said Justice House, for the full court: "There is nothing unusual in the University's power, in the objectives to be obtained, or the cost thereof in the construction and operation of a television station. We take judicial notice of the fact that our great universities, through experimentation and research in many scientific fields totally beyond the

---

[1] *Trotter* v. *Frank P. Gates and Company, et al.*, 162 Miss. 569, 139 So. 843 (1932).

[2] *People ex rel. Board of Trustees of University of Illinois* v. *Barrett*, 382 Ill. 321, 46 N.E. 2d 951 (1943).

comprehension of normal man, are the prime sources of discoveries for the betterment of mankind. How then can we say that the University of Illinois should be restricted to specific authorizations such as this?" He continued: "The General Assembly can not be expected to allocate funds to each of the myriad activities of the University and thereby practically substitute itself for the Board of Trustees in the management thereof."[3]

In furious pursuit of the "fetish of the balanced budget," many states have set up some species of "emergency board" (usually composed of the governor and a few other principal state officers, *ex officiis*) empowered by statute to reduce the quarterly or monthly allotments of appropriated funds to the universities and other institutions and departments if and when current revenue receipts fall below the estimates on which the appropriations were based. This perpetual uncertainty effectively deprives university presidents of a portion of their freedom to plan the year's operations and is thus actually wasteful of public funds, though it may tend to guarantee that there shall *never* be a deficit at the end of a fiscal year.

Some states also provide that at midnight on the last day of a fiscal year any funds unspent or unobligated, in the hands of a university or other state agency, are automatically and instantly recaptured for the state treasury. This almost inevitably produces a more or less hectic effort to spend or obligate the last dollar during the final weeks or days of the fiscal period—an annoyance which a good administrator should be spared—and is often in a real sense self-defeating of its own purpose, which is presumably to promote economical management.

Of much the same tendency is a more recently-begun practice, in a few states, of appropriating a "conditional reserve" fund to an emergency board or perhaps to a central governing board or coordinating board for higher education, to be doled out to the institutions if and when their enrollments exceed the estimates on which their budget askings were based. This has the disadvantage of diminishing the presidents' latitude for planning, and the added detriment of treating

---

[3] *Turkovich* v. *Board of Trustees of University of Illinois*, 11 Ill. 2d 460, 43 N.E. 2d 229 (1957).

educational planning as a mechanical process in which no account is taken of varying levels and qualities of instruction and research.

As to the mainstream of annual or biennial state budgeting, no one questions that the institutions of higher education, even where constitutionally independent, are and should be properly expected to participate in the process in much the same manner as other institutions and agencies of the state—without, however, allowing anyone to lose sight of the fact that higher education is a public function quite different from any other (a "fourth coordinate arm of the state") says the supreme court of Michigan).[4] As already noted in Chapter 7 herein, the science of college accounting has been painstakingly developed over half a century and more, and there can be no point in compelling universities to exhibit their budget requests on antiquated forms that are uniform for all agencies and departments of the state. Such a requirement simply necessitates the maintenance of two accounting systems at about double the expense of maintaining one.

A number of states (not those having constitutionally independent universities, nor several others) maintain centralized internal *pre-auditing* of all expenditures. This usually means that all requisitions for disbursement of university funds are scrutinized in a statehouse office, and all checks are signed by a fiscal officer having no connection with the university. This practice is not only unnecessary, but is inseparable from a certain time-lag under the best of circumstances, and often is responsible for needless long delays that are irritating and often productive of actual financial losses, to say nothing of the losses of program quality and of morale that they occasion. All the pre-auditing that is necessary can be done best and most economically by the institution's own pre-auditor or comptroller; it is done that way at most of the nation's greatest state universities, and this has a certain relationship to their greatness.

Pre-auditing is to be distinguished from *post-auditing*. No one doubts for a moment that an annual post-audit (after the fact) should be made by some competent agency totally unconnected with the institution—either a state office charged with that function, or a private

---

[4] *Sterling* v. *Regents of the University of Michigan,* 110 Mich. 369, 68 N.W. 253, 34 L.R.A. 150 (1896).

firm of accountants and auditors, preferably specializing in college accounting.

Centralized state purchasing, if compulsory for universities (which in most states it is not), is especially subject to the accusation of involving delays and disputes causing large losses of dollars and morale in state institutions of higher education. Educational purchasing is a science in itself and has been developed almost as a distinct profession, with its own national associations, in somewhat the same manner as in the case of college accounting. There are often circumstances in which certain university supplies may be bought advantageously through a central state purchasing office (especially large purchases of more or less standard products which the state also buys in large quantities for its other agencies and departments—perhaps fuel oil or coal, perhaps motor vehicles, perhaps furniture); but it is unquestionably absurd to think of state central purchasing of library books and periodicals, or of unique laboratory equipment or comparatively uncommon items of scientific apparatus, to say nothing of purebred livestock for the university farms. The practicable solution is the practice now followed in many states: The universities are not required to use the central purchasing office, but are authorized to do so in all instances where they deem it in their own interest and in the best interests of the public.

It is in the area of building construction that much streamlining and simplifying of relationships between campus and state is badly needed almost everywhere. A college has plans and specifications carefully drawn by its own salaried architect or by a contracted firm of architects, but is informed that these plans must be thoroughly inspected and overhauled by a State Architect or a similar functionary in a State Department of Public Works or State Building Commission. If his inspection is any more than a perfunctory one to assure compliance with the state building code safety and health provisions, it is quite likely to involve delays, disputes, and duplications of work that make it expensive in time and money. College architecture is a profession in itself, distinguished chiefly by its cognizance of the peculiar needs of educational institutions and its responsiveness to the legitimate wants of professors and students. This does not necessarily mean a flair for Neo-Gothic and walls of heavy masonry. Even boxlike steel-and-glass shell-type structures need to be planned by university architects in consultation with presidents and professors.

There are some encouraging signs here, too. When Governor Nelson A. Rockefeller discovered that the lag between authorization and opening of doors for new college buildings was in some instances as long as six years, he succeeded in removing the matter entirely from the red tape of the Department of Public Works and brought in General Traub, a retired Army fiscal officer, to expedite the large long-term building program of the State University of New York, thus compressing the delay toward the normal dimensions of two years, even in a large centralized statewide organization.

In probably a majority of the states, but by no means in all, the nonacademic employees of the universities and colleges are under the jurisdiction of some species of civil service commission or state personnel board, which, operating under a civil service statute, makes rules for examining, recruiting classifying, promoting, and retiring state employees, including establishing salary schedules for the different grades, providing grievance procedures, hearing cases of dismissal, and related functions. All this is usually less than satisfactory from the university viewpoint and frequently results in pathetic blunders and delays, due in large part to the circumstance that the commission is usually an "absentee lord" with its main office many miles from most of the universities and colleges, and with its own officers and employees as many miles (figuratively) from an intimate knowledge of the nonacademic personnel needs and practices of universities.

The constitutionally autonomous state universities do not suffer this annoyance. For example, the Arizona Board of Regents of State Universities was created by a legislative act pursuant to Article II, Section 2 of the Arizona Constitution. It derives a degree of autonomy from the constitution. Thus when a statute of 1948, enacted by popular initiative, created a state civil service system in which nonteaching employees of three institutions would have been embraced, the act was declared to be to that extent unconstitutional and void because the power of the Board of Regents to appoint and supervise the employees of the institutions could not be encroached upon by the legislature.[5]

A peculiarly obnoxious form of state administrative control is

---

[5] *Hernandez* v. *Frohmiller*, 68 Ariz. 242, 204 P. 2d 854 (1949).

that which forbids a university either to operate presses or to contract for printing and requires all such work to be requisitioned through a so-called state printer who lets contracts. In 1944 the Wisconsin supreme court made an unnecessarily narrow and literal interpretation of a statute currently in force which required that all state printing be procured by the state printer on order of the state director of purchases. A private printing company, miffed at the fact that the University of Wisconsin College of Agriculture and the University Extension Division were operating presses, sued to enjoin the approval of university vouchers for the wages of printers and for purchases of printing supplies.

Strangely blind to the fact that printing and publication have been traditional functions of universities for 500 years, intimately connected with their freedom to seek and disseminate truth, the court refused to consider whether the constitutional requirement that contracts be let to the lowest bidder actually prohibits any printing by the university, and based its decision solely on the absence of any statute affirmatively authorizing printing by the university. It waved aside the argument that the presses in question were used for work supported in part by Federal funds, and that printing was essential to the efficient conduct of that work. As to that: "If the statutes do not permit administration in the most convenient and economic or effective way, the administrative agencies must secure statutory authorization before administering it in any other way."[6]

Contrast that viewpoint with its opposite, which is characteristic of the Missouri supreme court. Speaking of the Board of Regents of a state college, in a case involving a different issue but of roughly comparable import, the Missouri court said: "While in a sense the board is an agent of the state with defined powers, the importance of its duties with their attendant responsibilities is such as to necessarily clothe the board with a reasonable discretion in the exercise of same. This is inevitably true, *first*, because of the difficulty in framing a statute with such a regard for particulars as to cover every exigency that may arise in the future; and, *second*, because a restriction of the board's powers to the letter of the law would destroy its efficiency, and

---

[6] *Democrat Printing Company* v. *Zimmerman*, 345 Wis. 406, 14 N.W. 2d 428 (1944).

to that extent cripple the purpose for which the institution was created. Legislatures, therefore, moved by that wisdom which is born
of experience, whether conscious or not of that aphorism that

'New occasions teach new duties;
Time makes ancient good uncouth'

have contented themselves with defining in general terms the powers of
such boards as are here under review, leaving the discharge of duties
not defined, and which may, under changed conditions, arise in the
future, to the discretion of the board."[7]

The point of all the foregoing is that in too many states and in
too many ways state universities and colleges are needlessly shackled
by fiscal controls from the statehouse that, if intended to promote
efficiency and economy, are actually self-defeating and the cause of
dollar losses as well as of serious imponderable losses. Milton Eisenhower's Committee on Government and Higher Education expressed
the idea in the title of its cogent brief report—*The Efficiency of
Freedom*, and Malcolm Moos and Francis E. Rourke of its staff
supported it with the classic study of the field—*The Campus and the
State*.[8]

There is no reason why state universities should not have the
degree of autonomy that private universities have; indeed some of them
(Michigan, California, Minnesota, and others) have it; so that the
Governor's Committee on Higher Education in New York in 1960
pleaded that the State University of New York be disentangled from
the snarled red tape of state bureaucracy and enabled to act "with the
spirit and style of our great public universities."

---

[7] *State ex rel. Thompson* v. *Regents of Northeast Missouri State Teachers'
College*, 305 Mo. 57, 264 S.W. 698 (1924).

[8] Malcolm Moos and Francis E. Rourke, *The Campus and the State*. Baltimore:
The Johns Hopkins Press, 1959, 400 pp. Committee on Government and Higher
Education Report, *The Efficiency of Freedom*. Baltimore: The Johns Hopkins
Press, 1959, 44 pp.

Chapter 28

INTERINSTITUTIONAL AND INTERSTATE COOPERATION

IN THE COMPLEX MODERN WORLD it may be said that no institution of higher education, however large and complex or however small and specialized, can operate optimally by depending solely on its own resources and ignoring channels of interchange with other institutions.

Geographic propinquity affords one stimulus to mutually profitable cooperation. Several colleges in and near Richmond, Virginia, have carried on organized interchanges for at least a quarter of a century. More recently the Kansas City Regional Council for Higher Education has achieved many advantages for the private and public colleges in the nearby parts of the two states of Kansas and Missouri.[1] There are other similar examples in other parts of the country.[2]

---

[1] In 1967 *The Acquainter*, a monthly mimeographed "international newsletter for regional councils for higher education" intended to "establish a systematic communications link for academic consortia across the nation" was initiated by the Kansas City Regional Council for Higher Education, 4901 Main Street, Suite 320, Kansas City, Missouri.

[2] Hundreds of such arrangements are listed in Raymond S. Moore, *A Guide to Higher Education Consortiums: 1965-66*. Washington: Government Printing Office (OE 50051), 1967, 175 pp.

One such is the College Consortium of the Finger Lakes in upstate New York, which includes the public Corning Community College and the public Mansfield State College (Pennsylvania), as well as Elmira College and some other nearby private institutions in New York.

Another is the joint efforts of the University of Massachusetts and three private colleges—Amherst, Mount Holyoke, and Smith—in bringing to birth the emerging new private Hampshire College, and in accomplishing advantageous interchanges among the members of the group.

The point to be exploited is that neighboring colleges are never alike, but each has something which could be shared with its neighbors with economic advantage to all; and often each, or at least some, will feel a critical need for some innovation which would be uneconomical for any one of the institutions alone and at its own expense, but which can be easily financed and advantageously put into operation at the joint expense of several. Joint use of lectures, bilateral or multilateral exchanges of specialized professors and students, cooperative availability of specialized library resources, and synchronizing of calendars and class schedules to facilitate interchanges are only a few of the devices used to avoid imprudent expenditures and make possible new services without overstraining the budget of any one institution, and thus presumably to give the participating colleges the maximum educational services for each dollar of expenditure.

Physical proximity is not in all cases necessary for interinstitutional cooperation. In the Midwest there is the Midwest College Association with its office at Chicago and embracing 10 private colleges in the four states of Wisconsin, Minnesota, Iowa, and Illinois;[3] and the Great Lakes College Association, with its office at Detroit and including 12 private colleges in Ohio, Michigan, and Indiana.[4]

More recently organized (1966) is the Central States College Association, composed of 12 church-related colleges dotted across

---

[3] Beloit, Lawrence, Ripon; Carleton, St. Olaf; Coe, Cornell, Grinnell; Knox, Monmouth.

[4] Eldon L. Johnson, former president of the Great Lakes College Association, now vice president of the University of Illinois, has discussed the potentialities, limitations, and prospects of "Consortia in Higher Education." *Educational Record* 48: 355-62 (Fall 1967).

eight North Central states from Indiana on the east to South Dakota on the west, including 2 Roman Catholic institutions and 10 of various Protestant denominations. Possible avenues of cooperation are almost limitless, ranging from joint recruiting activities to joint fund-raising to joint provision of a semester or a year in Europe or Latin America for students who apply for it and qualify for it. This latter is an enterprise already actually carried on by the older consortiums of this type.

On another level is the Council on Institutional Cooperation which involves the "Big Ten" universities of the Midwest (nine state universities in the seven older North Central states, plus Northwestern University, a private institution at Evanston, a suburb of Chicago). The University of Chicago is also added, so that the group is sometimes informally called the "Council of Eleven." These are all large universities having important full-fledged graduate schools generally conferring 100 or more doctoral degrees annually, and the chief impetus for the founding of the consortium about a decade ago (with the aid of a small Carnegie Corporation grant) was to stimulate cooperation among graduate schools toward the aim of developing optimally and economically the advanced graduate programs for the maximum benefit of the whole region and the nation.

The essential idea is that highly specialized doctoral and post-doctoral instruction and research are costly, and therefore a large number of such programs should not be developed indiscriminately by a dozen big universities in the same region; but that the group should constantly take account of the resources already available and in use at each institution, consider the wishes and potentialities of each for further development in the numerous specialized fields, and by informal agreement encourage each institution to go ahead with the particular programs for which it is best equipped and the programs it is most likely to develop successfully, while refraining from initiating programs which may already be well-developed in one or more of the other institutions.

This would ultimately bring about a more or less permanent but yet not inflexible "division of labor" among the 11 universities, so that a large number of different advanced specialties would be developed, each in an appropriate place or places (considering the volume of need or demand, the initial capacity and support, and other relevant factors), with a minimum of unnecessary or inadvertent duplication within the region. Theoretically this would enable more effective development of all or many of the advanced specialties at less cost to the region than would occur if there were no agency of intercommunication among the universities, and if each proceeded with insufficient knowledge of the present and planned achievements of the others. Its supposed bearing upon the efficient and economical use of educational dollars is therefore quite clear. The accompanying features include various measures to facilitate interchanges of specialized faculty members in accord with the developing regionwide plan, and measures permitting advanced students to transfer, when necessary for the best pursuit of their specialties, without financial barriers such as out-of-state fee differentials. This can be done on a reciprocal basis, apparently without objection from the legislatures in the states concerned.

Note at this point that although the Council on Institutional Cooperation (C.I.C.), runs across the boundaries of seven populous states, it is *not* an *interstate* compact, but an *interinstitutional* arrangement.

Apparently somewhat similar to it is the more recent Mid-America State Universities Association, embracing some eight state universities, in Missouri and the next tier of states to the westward, as well as Colorado.

These regional associations of state universities are distinct from, and clearly different from, the regional *interstate* compacts, of which there are three: (1) the Southern Regional Education Board (Atlanta), including 15 Southeastern states; (2) the New England Board of Higher Education (Durham, New Hampshire), six New England states; and (3) the Western Interstate Commission for Higher Education (Boulder, Colorado), the 13 westernmost states, including Alaska and Hawaii.

These organizations are officially recognized in the statutes of the states involved, and each member-state makes modest annual appropriations toward the support of the headquarters office and activities. Some of the states also appropriate additional sums in payment of balances due from them for various educational services performed for their citizen-students under the aegis of the regional interstate agreement—such as payments by a state having no medical school, for the education of its medical students in other states.

In addition to the programs of student interchange, each of the regional interstate boards maintains a staff for the promotion of interinstitutional studies and liaison, and of public information regarding the status, needs, and plans of public higher education in each of its states and in its region as a whole.

During their short periods of existence (the oldest, in the Southeast, dates only from 1949) they have had considerable success in issuing informative publications, conducting regional meetings of state legislators, and otherwise informing and stimulating the public about the uses and necessities of higher education.

Thirty-four states are members of one or another of the three regional *interstate* compacts. Seven others are represented by their principal state universities in the Council on Institutional Cooperation, and five others in the Mid-America State Universities Association, both of which are *interinstitutional* consortiums. Apparently only four states—a bloc in the "middle Atlantic" region—are currently not represented in any agreement of either of these regional types: New York, New Jersey, Pennsylvania, and Delaware.[5]

Three of these states are so populous and have such large numbers of private and public institutions of higher education, that the thought of a new mid-Atlantic interinstitutional council or interstate compact embracing the four would seem appropriate.

Beyond all this is the relatively new Compact for Education which aspires to include all the states and already has a majority of them as members. This is an *interstate* compact, but differs from the three familiar regional compacts because it takes for its purview not merely higher education, but education at all levels—from nursery school upward. It was initiated in 1965 with considerable flourish of trumpets and roll of drums stemming from the great devotion and energy of Terry Sanford, former governor of North Carolina, who had demonstrated forward-looking and bold leadership on behalf of public education during his administration as governor, and who is now based at Duke University as head of a Carnegie-financed research project on the improvement of state governments.

---

[5] Delaware was originally a member of the Southern Regional Education Compact, but withdrew within recent years, thus reducing the number of states in that organization from 16 to 15.

Carnegie Corporation of New York, which also subsidizes the researches of James Bryant Conant and his staff based at Princeton, New Jersey, was first to proffer a grant toward the support of the new compact until it could become self-supporting from fees paid by its member states. The idea of such a compact was first publicly broached by Dr. Conant in his small book, *Shaping Educational Policy*, published by the McGraw-Hill Book Company in 1965. Apparently much of this small volume was based on the work of one or more overzealous political scientists on Dr. Conant's staff, who recited overdrawn and convoluted tales of alleged political chicanery in education at the state level in selected states, particularly stressed what Dr. Conant called "disarray" in public higher education, and stimulated him to laud inordinately California's "master plan" and New York's educational bureaucracy as models for other states to follow.

The book was harshly critical of the regional and national voluntary accrediting associations and advocated that their functions should be taken over by state governments. It gave short shrift to the many decades of work by the great national voluntary associations in higher education, such as the American Council on Education, the Educational Policies Commission, the National Association of State Universities and Land-Grant Colleges, and others, and decried the alleged lack of a "national policy in education." This led up to the proposal of a nationwide interstate compact for education, which was the main thrust of the volume, though not elaborated in detail. The proposal would have been more palatable if it had not been prefaced by so heavily overdrawn a picture of woe.

The compact was met with widespread skepticism by leaders in public higher education, who had not been consulted on the inception of the plan. Some misgivings were felt in many quarters on the ground that the structure of the commission (governing body of the compact) did not provide with certainty for representation of public higher education. (Each state's delegation is to be composed of the governor, two members of the legislature, and four citizens appointed by the governor.) Only the passage of years will demonstrate whether a body so constituted will or will not be sufficiently representative of the different levels and types of education.

Equally crucial, and perhaps more so, is the problem of recruiting and maintaining an able staff, selecting avenues of research, and producing reports and pronouncements that will command respect. Whether this paramount purpose will be frustrated by conflicts among the widely varied political, partisan, personal, and educational interests represented remains to be seen. There is probably merit in the effort to get governors and legislators personally involved in nationwide consideration of educational problems.

Each of the four *interstate* compacts has as a prime object the encouraging of *interinstitutional* cooperation; but equally or perhaps more important is their aim of involving politicians and the public in such manner as to increase popular knowledgeability regarding higher education.

Innumerable examples of interinstitutional interactions could be cited at the level of *intra*state relations. Consider the recently-developing foundation-subsidized program for the establishment and strengthening of cooperative contacts between selected predominantly Negro colleges and neighboring predominantly white institutions. Observe also the Texas Association of Developing Colleges, formed in 1966 by six private four-year predominantly Negro colleges as a cooperative self-help agency to maximize limited resources and achieve economies through joint endeavors.

Indiana, long noted for successful joint efforts by private and public colleges, and by the public colleges among themselves, supplies two emerging illustrations. The Indiana legislature, at the suggestion of the public universities, appropriated $600,000 for the biennium 1967-69 for the development of a telecommunications system linking the four state universities among themselves and with their regional campuses and with other colleges in Indiana as the system grows. High fidelity television will be employed; and "slow-scan" television will make it possible for educational messages to be copied before they leave the screen. Students far removed from a teacher may use electronic blackboards that will contain voice circuit for explanation by the instructor. Both teletype and facsimile machines will be elements in the system. Colleges and universities will be able to multiply and expand the productiveness of the investments they already have in especially distinguished professors, unique specialized equipment, and costly books and periodicals, as well as courses of instruction not otherwise obtainable.

The advantages of this system will apply in many fields of knowl-

edge and in many types of curricula, but at first perhaps none will
be more important than medicine. Indiana University's College of
Medicine at Indianapolis, though the nation's largest, has in recent
years been unable to muster within the state enough opportunities
for internships and residencies sufficiently attractive to hold more than
half of its annual crop of graduates. The fact that half of the new
M.D.'s leave the state for internships and residencies in other states,
and many of them never return to practice in Indiana, has become a
matter of concern. To meet this situation the Indiana Plan of Medical
Education has been devised. It is expected that several leading hospitals
in various centers of the state will be linked in the telecommunications
system and will in other material ways be helped and encouraged to
become on a limited scale teaching hospitals affording attractive internships to graduates of Indiana's College of Medicine.

Medical education in Indiana will then become a somewhat decentralized enterprise on a statewide basis, rather than exclusively centralized in one place. The cooperating hospitals will also be subcenters of
postgraduate instruction for practicing physicians. Another feature
of the plan contemplates that some of the preclinical instruction of
medical students will be decentralized to other public and private
colleges in the state that have excellent instructors and equipment
for teaching the biological sciences. This could eventually enable the
College of Medicine in Indianapolis to approach a doubling of its
previous annual output of graduates, without a proportionate expansion of its facilities. For first steps in the development of this composite
plan of medical education, with first emphasis on the medical internships program, the legislature of 1967 appropriated $2½ million for
the biennium 1967-69.

The sums appropriated for the telecommunications system and for
the internship plan (aggregating more than $3 million for the biennium)
may seem substantial, but the total is a drop in the bucket compared
with the cost of establishing and operating a new medical college,
generally estimated at $50 million ($25 million for the plant and $25
million for operating expenses for the first five years). Perhaps there is
no better example of the relationship between financing higher education and ingenuity in devising voluntary cooperative relationships.

PART SIX

Chapter 29

THE FEDERAL INVOLVEMENT

NATIONAL SUPPORT for higher education began before the adoption of the Constitution in 1789. The Congress of the Confederation, in the Northwest Ordinance of 1787, provided for the reservation of blocks of public lands for the endowment of "seminaries of learning" in the territory that eventually became the five East North Central states of Ohio, Michigan, Indiana, Illinois, and Wisconsin.

The Constitution itself, limiting the powers of the Federal government and maximizing those of the states (Tenth Amendment), makes no mention of education. From this it can be reasoned that it was intended to be exclusively a state responsibility; but the evolution of the society has long since brought the view that public education is of so great importance to the nation that there can and indeed must be Federal participation in its financial support, and that this can be soundly warranted under the Preamble clause which states one of the major purposes of the Federal Union as being "to provide for the general welfare."

As late as 1857 President James Buchanan vetoed the first version of the Morrill Land-Grant Act of Congress because he thought it was unconstitutional; but five years later this view was wholly discarded when the Congress again passed the act and it was signed by President Abraham Lincoln in 1862.

This act, and the long train of statutes which followed it during the ensuing century, brought into practice the policy of *categorical* grants for education. To be sure, the act of 1862 stipulated no narrow category of education exclusively, but it did unquestionably contemplate a certain new emphasis on agriculture and the mechanic arts, and military science.

Some of the subsequent acts were much narrower. The Hatch Act of 1887 provided only for agricultural experiment stations. The Smith-Lever Act of 1914 was concerned only with support for agricultural extension services. The Smith-Hughes Act of 1917 was concentrated on aid for the education of teachers of agriculture and home economics. More recent vocational education acts have expanded this purview to embrace other categories, such as "distributive education," but always the emphasis has been *categorical*, not *general*.

This emphasis led to the complaint that Federal support of specific categories of education inevitably produced some distortion of a state's total program of education by giving a financial advantage to the Federally-supported types. Especially was this true under some of the acts which made state *matching* of the Federal grants a prerequisite to obtaining the Federal money. This compelled a state to channel some of its own tax funds into the support of the favored category in order to receive the Federal aid, and in fact amounted to a coercive external control of the state's total educational program, skewing it in favor of the Federally-aided types of education. The aroma of this kind of transaction is repulsive to many thoughtful persons. Comparatively few wish to see Federal *control* of public higher education, whether it be direct or by such transparent circumventions as just described.

Can there be Federal support without Federal control? There *can*, and there *must be*. The thoroughly putrid adage, "He who pays the piper calls the tune," must go into the garbage can where it belongs. Irreversible technological, economic, and social changes have brought about the situation in which the national government collects more tax proceeds than all the state and local governments combined. There is no efficient or satisfactory way of drastically modifying this situation. The exercise of the taxing power simply must be largely by the national governmental unit because of the large-scale organization of industry, the mobility of the population, and other factors in a shrinking world. This means that large portions of the Federal revenues, not needed for the external functions of the national government, must come back to the states to help support their essential domestic functions, including higher education. But this does not mean that increasing national control of higher education must be centralized in the national capital, tending toward unitary government and the destruction of creative federalism.

If this analysis is correct, it points toward a less exclusive emphasis on *categorical* support of higher education and a beginning of *general* support. This could be accomplished in several ways:

1. Professor Walter W. Heller of the University of Minnesota (who served for a time as Chairman of the President's Council of Economic Advisers) has suggested a rebate to the states of a fixed small percentage of Federal income tax collections, as an unrestricted "bloc grant" to each state, to be expended for any public purposes at the discretion of the state, without Federal interference.

2. Another possibility would be a tax credit against an individual's (or corporation's) Federal income tax of any sums (or a large percentage thereof) paid by him to his state under a state income tax law. This would be similar to the Federal tax credit of 80 per cent of state succession taxes paid against the amount due under the Federal estate tax law. Adopted some 40 years ago, this measure speedily encouraged all the states except Nevada to enact succession taxes, putting to an end the silly competition then rampant among them to attract wealthy residents by having negligible succession taxes, or none.

3. Frank Fernbach, representing the viewpoint of organized labor, fears that unconditional bloc grants to the states might be misused, perhaps even spent for advertising and related efforts to lure industrial plants from other states. (This could be obviated by making the bloc grants for higher education, but otherwise unrestricted.) He also fears that unconditional bloc grant funds, going into the general fund of the state and being commingled, could no longer be followed for the enforcement of Federal standards which now apply only to Federally-

supported expenditures—such as antidiscrimination and minimum labor standards. He also insists that the grants should be
distributed to the states not in proportion to their totals of
Federal income tax payments, but in accord with some formula
that would assure that the wealthier states would get less than
this share, and the poorer states would get substantially more.
He points out that many of the present categorical grants are
on such a basis. Also he notes that the present categorical
grants, especially if they require matching with state funds,
encourage the states to increase their own efforts, whereas he
fears that unconditional bloc grants might cause some states
to lessen their own support of public functions. He would
not rule out increased Federal revenue-sharing with the states,
but he would place it second to the maintenance and expansion
of the current complex system of categorical grants.

To what conclusion can we come? Perhaps the feasible reform
at this stage would be to retain and expand the present categorical
grants and make a gradual beginning of raising the categories to an
intermediate level of generality—broader than the present categories,
but not to the logical extreme of being unconditional, unrestricted,
and usable by the state for any public purpose. The middle ground
might be a new series of grants for the broad category of *higher
education*, with all allocations within that field (education beyond the
high school) at the discretion of the state, and with the proviso that
the state's own tax support of the broad field be at least 10 per cent
larger than the average of the two immediately preceding fiscal years.

The foregoing would, at least for the time being, not supplant
or diminish any categorical grants or institutional grants to public
or private institutions of higher education within the state. It would
not disrupt the existing pattern of grants, but would supplement it.
I believe it would obviate most of Frank Fernbach's objections to
unconditional bloc grants, while at the same time getting a step away
from the very undesirable too-detailed categorization, which inevitably
means external control. It might seem appropriate that such a step be
taken first for higher education, on account of the conspicuous repug-
nancy between education at this level and detailed external control.

Since the Depression of the 1930's there have been more or less
continuous (but sometimes intermittent, because of early exhaustion

of the short-term funding) available loans for capital outlay by colleges and universities, from a succession of Federal agencies. In the early Thirties the Reconstruction Finance Corporation made some loans of this kind; and later they were made on a considerable scale by the Public Works Administration (PWA). During World War II for a time construction was practically halted by scarcity of materials and labor. After the war, construction loans were soon to be had from the Federal housing finance agencies. A great impetus came with the enactment of the Higher Education Facilities Act of 1963, providing for grants to three types of institutions, and loans—in each case covering only a part of the cost of the facilities and obtainable only for the construction of buildings for specified purposes.

To four-year colleges, public or private (and private junior colleges and technical institutes), grants were available for buildings for the teaching of mathematics, engineering, science, modern foreign languages, and for libraries. Public two-year colleges, and graduate schools, public or private, were each placed in a separate classification regarding grants. Loans were available to all reputable institutions, for any kinds of instructional facilities except those for the teaching of religion or theology. A separate act of somewhat smaller scope made special provision for facilities for medical and paramedical education.

To qualify for these grants and loans the institutions are required to apply to a state commission which has the duty of determining priorities and recommending to the U.S. Office of Education which applications should be granted and in what order. In many states a new body, often styled "Higher Education Facilities Commission of the State of _____," was created for this purpose. In some others having a statewide board or council of higher education this body was designated for the purpose of meeting, or possibly remodeled to meet, the Federal requirement that the state commission be broadly representative of all types of higher education in the state. Each such commission develops an ongoing "plan," including a more or less objective "formula" which takes into account the past, present, and probable future growth of the enrollment in each institution, its present facilities and their suitability and the degree to which they are currently utilized, and other factors bearing on a proper determination of priorities.

The restriction to buildings for specified purposes is rather un-realistic and a trifle absurd—a fruit of the excitement of "Sputnik" and the international arms race. Few college buildings are used for precisely the same purposes throughout their useful lives, as the in-stitution grows and the older buildings become obsolescent as new ones are added. This would appear to be another example of a too-detailed categorization (except, of course, the prohibition of financing buildings for theology or religion, which would be in flat violation of the "establishment clause" of the First Amendment to the United States Constitution). Federal loans for student-housing facilities con-tinue to be available from the Housing and Home Finance Agency.

In the realm of academic facilities, the attempt to skew the nation-wide picture in favor of facilities for mathematics, engineering, science, and modern foreign languages is an unnecessary encroachment upon the control of the institutions and a disturber of their morale as their faculties see new facilities financed for those areas while the arts, the humanities, and the social sciences "make do" as second-class citizens.

The same sort of skewing occurred in the early years of the program of graduate fellowships under the National Defense Education Act of 1958 and is also a prominent feature of the vast program of contracts and grants for research available from half a dozen or more huge Federal agencies: the Atomic Energy Commission, the Depart-ment of Defense, the National Aeronautics and Space Administration, the National Institutes of Health, the National Science Foundation, and the U. S. Office of Education. A small particular example of this attempted distortion of the educational and vocational choices of individuals is afforded by the current provision regarding National Defense Education Act student loans, which now provides that bor-rowers who become teachers in public or private schools or colleges at any level will have 10 per cent of the loan forgiven for each year of actual service as a teacher, up to 50 per cent of the loan. This in effect bribes a student to choose teaching as his prospective profession by giving him half of his college expenses as a gift in order to get him to take the other half as a loan, unless he changes his mind about teaching. This can readily be regarded as a mass interference with individual freedom of choice which ought not to be countenanced in an open society and does not comport with the approved methods of selection and preparation for a learned profession of greatest importance to the public welfare. The preferred way to get competent people into the teaching profession is to make the profession reasonably attractive as to compensation, working conditions, and social status— and no system—however ingenious—of bribing young people to prepare for it, can force them to remain in it. Millions of persons educated for teaching never actually teach, or teach only for a short time. The connection of education with vocation is happily not too close in this country, except perhaps for a few professions such as medicine and dentistry.

Among the acrid criticisms of the whole vast complicated complex of Federal support to higher education which has grown up in a decade or two are:

1. It is badly skewed in favor of comparatively few large universities (private and public, about 50-50), and against the institutions of medium and smaller size and repute—especially against the small liberal arts colleges.

2. The research contracts and grants, and indeed every other channel of Federal support to higher education, involve mountains of unnecessary red tape and a superfluity of auditing the expenditure of trivial sums, so ubiquitous as not only to annoy the scholars and administrators involved, but actually to hamper the scholarly and scientific work.

3. The system of charging "overhead" or "indirect" costs, under different voluminous rules issued by each Federal agency, overlain by certain blanket prohibitions enacted by Congress, and complicated by immensely detailed regulations of the Bureau of the Budget and the General Accounting Office, usually does not fully reimburse the university or college for the use of its own resources in the subsidized project.

4. By all odds the most serious caveat is that by accepting a continuing series of short-term grants and contracts from various sources—on such a scale as in some instances to amount to half its annual operating expenses—the university is fragmenting its integrity as an academic and scientific organism and in large part surrendering its ultimate control to the external agencies upon which it is becoming dependent for funds.

This last apprehension is shared equally by thoughtful administrators and scholars in private and public universities and colleges. It is undoubtedly one of the most influential factors underlying the weird scheme originating recently in the Ivy League, under which Federal loans would be available to all students, who would repay with fixed percentages of their incomes throughout their lives; all institutions, public and private, would go on a high-fee basis ("near to full cost"); and virtually the whole cost of higher education would ultimately fall on the sudents.[1] This might be one avenue of escape from Federal financial support and the accompanying dangers of external control; but it seems safe to say it is a step that will not be taken. It is attractive only to private institutions, and totally repugnant to all who are attached to the principle of free public higher education in the American states, supported by the whole society through taxation rather than by the students alone through fees.

Each of the four complaints just enumerated is valid to a degree, but none is so incurable as to justify abolishing or diminishing the program of Federal support. Certainly none is sufficient to trigger a stampede into a scheme which would apparently abandon tax support of higher education and approach total support by student fees. This would run contrary to three centuries of American experience and progress in higher education and head backward toward the seventeenth century!

The present overconcentration of Federal grant moneys in large and prestigious universities can be corrected. Indeed, the overt policy of the present national administration is to the effect that we shall develop many additional centers of graduate studies and research, geographically widely distributed.

The incubus of useless red tape can at least be persistently attacked, though perhaps it would be a sanguine prophet who would predict that it can eventually be reduced to rational dimensions. The same can be said of the 10-year running battle of the "indirect costs"—one can hope that rationality and fairness will ultimately prevail.

---

[1] Proposed by Kingman Brewster, Jr., president of Yale University, in the Harry Camp Memorial Lectures delivered at Stanford University, May 7-9-11, 1967, and briefly reported in the *New York Times* in July, 1967. Accompanying the brief outline of the proposal is a convincing discourse on the indispensability of academic freedom and university autonomy. A critique of the proposal in some detail is the subject of another chapter in this volume.

The fragmentation of the "project grant" system, threatening as it does the integrity of the universities and creating an arrogant caste of "grant swingers" including a swarm of "influence men" encamped in Washington and selling their services, already shows signs of ultimately losing its hegemony. Some of the agencies, notably the National Science Foundation, are now making some "institutional grants"—bloc grants *to the institution,* not to projects—to be allocated by the institutional administration at its own discretion. The possible future expansion of the "institutional grant" plan may do much to allay the intolerable conditions created by the burgeoning of "project grants" in recent years.

To recapitulate: Tax support, from both state and Federal sources, will continue to increase substantially for many years. This is a prediction, not a wish. An increasing degree of rationality and simplicity will creep into the incredibly complex channeling of support from Federal sources. Gradually the categorization will become less minute. Gradually bloc grants to the state or to the institutions, or both, will supplement and finally largely supplant the bedlam of categorical support, and rescue the responsibility of the states and the autonomy of the universities. This may be spread over many years; but ultimately the supreme error of making the universities "branch plants" of either the state or Federal governments will be avoided. Understanding of the relation between freedom and creativity grows; and comprehension spreads that a university without freedom and integrity is no university, but a treadmill of busy work for mediocrities.

A quantitative glimpse of some major portions of the program of Federal support for higher education current in the middle Sixties is appropriate here. It is supplied by a report of the National Science Foundation.[2] It deals with all obligations by eight major Federal agencies made to all institutions of higher education over a period of four years—1963-66, showing trends manifested during that period. The average rate of growth was 16 per cent per year, so that a doubling occurred within four years. The eight agencies: the Department of Agriculture; the Atomic Energy Commission; the Department of Defense; the bureaus of the Department of Health, Education,

---

[2] National Science Foundation, *Federal Support for Universities and Colleges: Fiscal Years 1963-66.* Washington: Government Printing Office, 1967, 70¢.

and Welfare; the National Aeronautics and Space Administration; and the National Science Foundation. Two-thirds of the total for 1966 was obligated by two bureaus within HEW—the Public Health Service ($940 million) and the Office of Education ($945 million).

The number of institutions on the receiving end rose from about 840 in 1963 to 2,050 in 1966; but the top 100 universities received 70 per cent of the total in 1966. They had received 85 per cent in 1963. In 1966 the top 25 institutions each got $25 million or more, as in Table 12.

Table 12. Federal obligations to 25 institutions by eight major Federal agencies, fiscal year 1966 (figures in thousands of dollars).

Rank	Institutions	Sums Obligated	Rank	Institutions	Sums Obligated
(1)	(2)	(3)	(4)	(5)	(6)
1	U. of Michigan	$66,265	14	New York U.	$37,688
2	Mass. Inst. Technol.	63,232	15	Pennsylvania State U.	37,659
3	Stanford U.	60,621	16	U. of Minnesota	35,935
4	Columbia U.	60,041	17	U. of Washington	35,575
5	U. of Illinois	58,491	18	Cornell U.	35,324
6	Harvard U.	54,008	19	Johns Hopkins U.	31,994
7	U. Cal., Los Angeles	51,298	20	Yale U.	29,830
8	U. of Cal., Berkeley	50,315	21	Washington U. (Mo.)	27,265
9	U. of Chicago	45,286	22	U. of Missouri	26,644
10	Ohio State U.	39,025	23	Indiana U.	26,397
11	U. of Pennsylvania	38,908	24	Purdue U.	26,157
12	U. of Wisconsin	38,756	25	U. of Florida	25,202
13	U. of Texas	38,208			

Source: *The Chronicle of Higher Education*, Vol. 2, No. 2, p. 3 (September 27, 1967).

It will be noted that 14 of the 25 institutions were *state* universities, and 11 private institutions. In 1966 about the same ratio prevailed among the top 100—58 were public and 42 private. The University of Alaska, ranking one hundredth, received more than $7 million. The distribution of the institutions ranking from twenty-sixth through one hundredth, within a few class-intervals, appears in Table 13.

Tables 12 and 13 relate only to the top 100 institutions in the list of 2,050 which received at least some support from some of the eight major Federal agencies. These 100 got 70 per cent of the

Table 13. Seventy-five institutions distributed by selected class-intervals according to the sums obligated to them by eight major Federal agencies, fiscal year 1966.

Class-Intervals	Numbers of Institutions
(1)	(2)
Millions of dollars	
$20 to $25..	14
$15 to $20..	23
$10 to $15..	16
$ 7 to $10..	22

Source: *Ibid.* (Table 12).

money. Thus 30 per cent of it went in generally much smaller amounts to a total of 1,950 colleges and universities. One of the most imaginative and potentially creative programs, aimed more at the upgrading of undergraduate education than at the accomplishment of epochal scientific discoveries, is the National Science Foundation's program of small grants for research in science in undergraduate liberal arts colleges.

With only a few thousand dollars of support, the alert professor of physics, chemistry, or another science in a small and perhaps isolated college is enabled to pursue his research interests and engage the laboratory assistance of a few of his most enthusiastic senior students, thus fostering and strengthening the spirit and attitude of research in the undergraduate college—regarded as a supremely desirable aim.

As calendar 1967 drew toward a close, various plans whereby the nation's private colleges and universities could become the beneficiaries of tax support were urged with increasing importunity. The proposed Federal "Educational Opportunity Bank" has already been discussed in Chapter 14 herein.

The mood among private college partisans is illustrated by quotations from the news media during that year. For example, Byron Trippett of the Colorado Association of Independent Colleges and Universities was reported as saying the crucial question that fathers ask is "What can Colorado College offer my boy for a tuition of

$1,700 that the University of Colorado can't offer for $300?"[3] And almost as though in direct response, though not in precisely the same context, President Kingman Brewster, Jr., of Yale was quoted as declaring "We have to convince the donor we have something to offer. I am sure support will depend on the ability of the institution to excite."[4] The private college can indeed make a strong appeal to the preferences of many persons—the appeal of distinctiveness, of special quality, of family tradition, of religious sentiments, and other characteristics that exert a powerful pull.

Rather similar to Brewster's expression was that of President John A. Howard of Rockford College when he said at the annual meeting of the Association of College Admissions Counselors: "At some point the government is going to ask itself, 'Why should we invest taxpayers' money in a college which charges the student $2,400 a year when there are so many places that charge the student only half that amount?'" He concluded that the only wise course of action for the private colleges would be to make their educational programs "so sound and so useful and so convincingly worthy" that they would be chosen over public institutions by students, teachers, and sources of funds.[5]

Apparently ignoring all this, Chancellor Peter Sammartino of Fairleigh Dickinson University was reported as saying "Why on earth should a student pay $1,200, $1,500, or $2,000 at a private college, when the public institution is charging nothing or a very nominal amount?" He urged a campaign to persuade state legislatures to finance "tuition grants" of $500 to $1,000 or more per year to all students ranking in the upper half of their high school graduating classes.[6]

President Howard R. Bowen of the University of Iowa was said to have described as "essentially unsound" any proposed plan of student loans (such as the "educational opportunity bank") that would involve the "further escalation of tuition fees." He said he leaned toward the view that higher education should be free; but concluded that "Substantial differences in tuition fees between private

[3] *Time*, Vol. 89, No. 25, p. 79 (June 23, 1967).
[4] *Ibid.*
[5] *The Chronicle of Higher Education*, Vol. 2, No. 3, p. 5 (October 12, 1967).
[6] *Ibid.*, p. 1.

and public institutions are practically feasible, socially justifiable, and economically necessary. So long as low-tuition public institutions provide an alternative to students of modest means, no one can claim to be seriously damaged if he pays more to attend a private institution."[7]

Meanwhile in September, 1967, a further proposal for Federal support of higher education emanated from the University of Wisconsin, under the names of Professors William H. Young (Political Science) and Robert Taylor (Journalism). The essence of the proposal was that the Federal government should begin immediately a program of support to all reputable institutions of higher education—private and public alike—amounting to at least one-fourth of their annual educational and general operating expenses. It would be computed on a per-student-per-year basis, varying according to the lower division undergraduate, upper division undergraduate, and graduate and professional levels of instruction. Within those levels, allocations per student would be the same for all institutions.

It was estimated that the minimum cost of such a program would be about $2.2 billion in 1968, rising to $3.9 billion by 1975.

Says the report at one point: "Extensive scholarship, loan, and work-study programs have not solved the problem. A roll-back in fees and tuitions is an obvious solution, since the proportion of students from low-income families is greatest in low-cost institutions. Thus a major part of any effective federal funding program to advance the nation through higher education must be provision for tuition reduction and expansion of low-cost commuter institutions."[8]

And at another point: "Most of the institutional support should be in addition to existing expenditures, if it is to place a floor under quality and a ceiling on the burden borne by the student. Tuition reduction must be encouraged."[9]

While repeatedly mentioning a "roll-back of fees" and "tuition reduction," the report makes no suggestion as to how this result can be assured. Nor does it mention any prohibition of discriminatory

---

[7] *Ibid.,* p. 5.

[8] William H. Young and Robert Taylor, *An Opportunity for a Major American Advance Through Higher Education.* Madison: The University of Wisconsin, September, 1967, p. 7, 32 pp. litho.

[9] *Ibid.,* p. 11.

policies regarding admissions and student aids, based on race, religion, national origin, or clerical or faculty ancestry, all quite commonly practiced by many private colleges.

The proposal is, indeed, a bid for "bloc grants" by the Federal government to the institutions, by-passing the states, and actually containing no guarantees against continuance of rising fees and of discriminatory practices which would be unlawful in a public institution. The suggested use of Federal tax funds without these safeguards raises grave questions. How many and which private colleges would be ineligible because of the First Amendment prohibition of any "law respecting an establishment of religion, or prohibiting the free exercise thereof"? As a practical matter, the sponsors of this proposal believe the Congress will not enact a bill of this nature unless it includes provision for support to private colleges as well as public; therefore they ignore the philosophical questions involved and plump for a simple scheme of Federal support for all colleges, knowing that the public institutions will get two-thirds of it anyway. Two-thirds of a loaf is better than none. This may be practical political compromise, but it leaves something to be said about the safeguards just mentioned. However, since politics is "the art of the possible," we may have here the sketchy beginning of a long-overdue escape from exclusive "categorical aids" to higher education from the Federal government.

Similar in some respects to the foregoing Young and Taylor book is a suggestion publicized briefly in December, 1967, by Joseph P. McMurray, president of Queens College of the City University of New York.[10] Says he, "I should like to recommend a plan that is calculated to bring $6 billion a year to institutions of higher learning. This plan calls for the Federal government to levy a completely new tax, a one per cent value added tax, from which the entire proceeds would go to higher education." A "value added tax," he says, "taxes the difference between a firm's receipts from sales and its purchases of materials, equipment, and services," and is sometimes called a "gross margin tax." He grants that it is "similar to a broad levy on retail sales," and asserts several arguments in its favor, concluding that its proceeds, if allocated on an enrollment basis, would more than equal

---

[10] Joseph P. McMurray, "Plan for Financing Higher Education," *School and Society* 95: 489-490 (December 9, 1967).

New York State's current total annual appropriations for annual operating expenses of public higher education and for student aid in all types of institutions.

This proposal will bear some skepticism: (1) Any "earmarked" tax is generally not viewed with favor by students of government; (2) appropriations out of the general fund of the Federal government would in the long run probably provide a more secure basis; and (3) it probably would be politically impossible to obtain enactment in Congress of a Federal tax resembling a general sales tax (which is now in use in all but 6 of the 50 states and would be strongly opposed at the Federal level by organized labor and other powerful interests).

Conceding that it is desirable that some scheme of general Federal support to higher education should be initiated as promptly as possible, to mitigate the manifest and manifold shortcomings of the categorical schemes which have been in virtually exclusive command of the field up to now, it seems supremely essential that any plan of general support must embody safeguards such as the following:

1. Any institution forfeits its eligibility if its support from state, private, and all other sources except student fees is not continued at least up to current and recent levels, and kept rising at a reasonable rate.

2. Institutional eligibility should be conditioned upon at least a fractional reduction of current student fees, so that for the first few years at least half of the new support from Federal funds would operate as a "tuition reduction supplement," enabling the institution to roll back its fees substantially without loss of operating income.[11] (Allocated on a *pro rata* enrollment basis, only $1 billion a year, as half of an initial Federal appropriation of $2 billion, would amount to about $150 per year per student and would in general enable the fees at public institutions to be immediately reduced by perhaps 30 per cent to 60 per cent, except for out-of-state students. Fees at the private institutions could immediately go down about 6 per

---

[11] Where future tuition fees are pledged for the redemption of outstanding bonds for capital outlay, the new Federal funds in lieu of student fees would be used for that purpose, unless re-funding or other guarantee of payment of such bonds could be obtained from the state concerned. See Chapter 4, *supra*.

cent to about 30 per cent or more, depending on their current levels. Any institution now tuition-free, or enabled to become so by the $150 per student, would nevertheless be entitled to its per-student allotment of $300, the same as any other eligible institution. Over time, public institutions would become tuition-free, at least for students resident in the state. Private institutions would reduce their fees somewhat, but not become tuition-free.)

All institutions, private and public, would receive some new Federal support—free from the harassments and dangers of categorical aid, and in addition to what they are now getting from Federal and other sources except student fees. To the private institutions, especially the wealthier ones, the new support would bear a relatively small ratio to their total operating budgets, and (especially the high-fee ones) even smaller changes in their fee-structures. The public institutions would gradually but expeditiously become free of tuition charges. *All institutions* would be getting some new Federal support, pro rata according to their enrollments. Those of lowest annual current expenditures (and presumably lowest educational quality) would get proportionally a greater lift than those now spending more (and presumably higher quality); but the plan would not "build up the lowest and tear down the best," because it is necessarily assumed that the huge system of selective Federal grants for research and other services will not be dismantled or even substantially reduced for a long time to come. Instead, the new plan would operate to countervail, to some extent, the present situation under which it is complained that "the rich get richer and the poor get poorer" —to say nothing of countervailing the imbalance among academic fields, and other flaws in the present picture.

3. Concurrent with the new plan of direct appropriations from Federal government to universities and colleges, there should be some form of general Federal aid to the states, such as Walter Heller's tax-rebate proposal, and the proposed Federal income tax credit against state income taxes paid. This would negate the accusation of pejorative treatment of the states, but would not contribute directly to the upbuilding of state-

house and statewide educational bureaucracies, as categorical aids to the states do.

An event of early 1968 was a major address in Minneapolis by Alan Pifer, president of Carnegie Corporation of New York, speaking to the annual meeting of the Association of American Colleges.[12] Called "Toward a Coherent Set of National Policies for Higher Education," the speech dealt chiefly with Federal financing of higher education and with national policy-making for higher education, with the speaker declaring the two to be inseparable. In many quarters this coupling is regarded as unnecessary and unfortunate. But Pifer insisted that "the Government will simply not be able to maintain the fiction that its role is purely that of supplementary financier. Its large appropriations will have to be based on policies, and these policies will inevitably have an influence on the nature of higher education."

As against this view, it might be said that the Federal government needs only one major policy for higher education: *that it shall be generously financed and accessible in some form to every high school graduate, without discrimination as to race, religion, sex, age, or economic deprivation, and with maximum freedom of choice and breadth of opportunity in educational and occupational options.*

Pifer would have Federal policy-making for higher education go into much greater detail; and he took occasion to mention briefly some six "random examples":

1. "A minimum standard of free education through the fourteenth grade";
2. "The equalization of opportunity for access to higher education beyond the junior college stage";
3. "The creation of a list of designated 'national universities' which would receive preferential treatment in the support of their research laboratories and libraries and other facilities for advanced study and research";
4. "A national imperative to establish vastly strengthened higher educational facilities in our great cities";
5. "The development of higher educational facilities at selected

---

[12] The full text of this address was published in *The Chronicle of Higher Education*, Vol. 2, No. 1, pp. 4 and 5 (January 29, 1968).

universities to assist economic and social development in the
poorer and technologically less-advanced nations of the world";
6. "The improvement of the academic quality of our colleges
and universities."

For the detailed formulation of these and other policies Pifer
proposed the creation of a "focal point, or center, for higher education
close to the summit of the federal government where it can influence
all federal action that impinges on higher educational institutions."
Turning to "the dangers in the new era," he notes the possibility
of a decline in institutional autonomy and institutional initiative and
concedes that "to some degree this may happen." As to the possible
problem of rapid drying-up of state and local governmental support
and of private gifts as Federal support increases, he suggests the usual
initial safeguards, but then advances what he says is "a heretical
thought"—"I would guess that the financing of higher education will,
like the support of agriculture, more and more come to be regarded
as almost exclusively a federal responsibility, freeing state and local
funds for other pressing purposes and freeing private funds either for
special uses in higher education, such as experimentation or the provision of unusual amenities, or for other fields, such as the arts and
recreation. This, however, will lie a long way in the future, perhaps
around the year 2000."

As to the respective interests of the private and public sectors,
he says this is a side issue, "and those who allow themselves to be
diverted by it are going to miss the main issue and their chance
to have a say in its resolution."

He seems to foretell the vanishing of the distinctive concept of
the private college: "It is conceivable that, over a long period, private
higher education as we have known it in the past will gradually
disappear and we will end up with a system in which some institutions
historically have their roots in the governmental sector and some in
the private sector, but all are, in a general sense of the word, public
institutions, responsive to the public need and articulated with each
other in a national policy framework."

Cogently defending this position before his audience, of whom a
majority were private college administrators, Pifer noted that "Many
of you believe that the preservation of academic freedom, the
maintenance of high academic standards, and the capacity for experi-

mentation in *all* of our colleges and universities, both public and private, is safeguarded by the very existence of private institutions." This, he said, may to some degree all have been true in the past; "but it would be a difficult claim to make today and, I believe, it will be a ridiculous one to make tomorrow." Finally, "What we should be worrying about is how all our institutions, whatever the nature of their control, can preserve academic freedom, high academic standards and an experimental turn of mind in the face of their inevitable heavy financial dependence on the federal government."

This thoughtful statement raises in many minds a question: If we were to have a new Federal agency for policy-distillation in higher education, would it not be of the utmost importance that this agency limit itself to the highest levels of generality, leaving all the vast and varied task of formulating and implementing policies below that highest summit to the state governors and legislatures, the governing boards of colleges and universities, the faculties and students and constituencies, and the national voluntary associations in the field? Is not this the means of preserving and augmenting institutional and individual autonomy and initiative? Is it not unnecessary to concede that these essentials must in part be lost "in the new era"?

Pifer's comments on Federal financing of higher education were succinct: "The time has now come for the federal government to make general, non-categorical support grants to all institutions while at the same time continuing its research support, aid to students, construction grants and loans, and other forms of categorical assistance."

There appears to be a general consensus in regard to Federal aid which seems to focus on two things:

"One, there must be something in it for everyone, that is for every type of institution, large or small, public or private, undergraduate, graduate, or professional;

"Two, we have reached a new stage in the evolution of American higher education where it cannot continue to prosper without general, across-the-board support from the federal government; that is, support simply to meet normal operating expenses."

He buttresses these deductions with statements that all other sources of institutional income, though increasing somewhat, are not keeping pace with the growth of expenditures. These are in general incontrovertible, except one which needs to be seriously questioned: Speaking of the cities and the states, he lumps the two together, and says, "Their resources are derived in major part from tax systems that have virtually reached the limit of productivity." This may be true of the cities, but certainly not of the states. It would be an error to underestimate or "write off" the unused revenue potentials of the states (see Chapters 23-25, *supra*). This is important. The splendid growth of state support of higher education ought not to be minimized, discouraged, or retarded.

The Association of American Universities, composed of 42 institutions in the United States and Canada that maintain the leading graduate schools, issued a position paper in June, 1968, prepared by a committee of five university presidents,[13] and advocating Federal support for annual general operating expenses of all accredited colleges and universities in addition to an increasing volume of categorical subsidies.

The statement declared that in the absence of this new source of substantial funds, serious deterioration of higher education would be inevitable; and would mean "fewer faculty to teach more students, reduced library acquisitions and cultural programs, curtailed opportunities for the disadvantaged, slowed movement into new fields, less competent and productive research, loss of faculty, delayed maintenance, and adherence to the *status quo* instead of vigorous movement into new aspects of education or public service—in short, slow stifling of higher education as a vital, creative, productive force in American life."

Intentionally timed so as to alert candidates for the Presidency and for Congress in the elections of November, 1968, the manifesto was designed to inform the general public, as well as national and local political leaders, about the higher educational task of the nation.

---

[13] The committee was made up of the following: Robert F. Goheen, Princeton, Chairman; William C. Friday, North Carolina; Fred H. Harrington, Wisconsin; G. Alexander Heard, Vanderbilt (Chancellor); and Nathan M. Pusey, Harvard.

Chapter 30

HIGHER EDUCATION AND ECONOMIC GROWTH

"IN THE UNITED STATES," says Walter W. Heller, "less than half of the increase in output can be explained by increases in the stock of tangible capital and man-hours worked." He goes on: "Possibly as much as one-half of the residual—i.e., of the growth not accounted for by increased inputs of capital, land, and labor—can be explained by increased productivity brought about by higher levels of education for greater proportions of our population."[1]

In the same address he concluded: "Maximum employment and production do not only depend upon capital equipment, agricultural and natural resources, and man-hours—the traditional interests of economists—but also on the education of the total population and the skills of its labor force. Programs and policies that maximize the human resources in our nation are a major concern of national economic policy."

In support of this view he also quoted from the economic message

---

[1] Walter W. Heller, "Education and Economic Policy." Address to Washington Conference of the Organization for Economic Cooperation and Development, October 16-21, 1961.

253

of President John F. Kennedy, entitled *A Program to Restore Momentum to the American Economy*:

"Another fundamental ingredient of a program to accelerate long-run economic growth is vigorous improvement in the quality of the nation's human resources. Modern machines and advanced technology are not enough, unless they are used by a labor force that is educated, skilled, and in good health. This is one important reason why, in the legislative programs that I will submit in the days to come, I will emphasize so strongly programs to raise the productivity of our growing population, by strengthening education, health, research, and training activities."

The British economist, Alfred Marshall, had written years ago: "The wisdom of expending public and private funds on education is not to be measured by its direct fruits alone. It will be profitable as a mere investment, to give the masses of the people much greater opportunities than they can generally avail themselves of. For by this means many, who would have died unknown, are enabled to get the start needed for bringing out their latent abilities. And the economic value of one great industrial genius is sufficient to cover the educational expenses of a whole town; for one new idea, such as Bessemer's chief invention, adds as much to England's productive power as the labour of a hundred thousand men. Less direct, but not less in importance, is the aid given to production by medical discoveries such as those of Jenner or Pasteur, which increase our health and working power."

Much more recently, distinguished American economists, including Edward F. Denison,[2] John Kenneth Galbraith,[3] and Theodore W. Schultz,[4] among others, have become convinced from their researches that education as an addition to the value and productivity of human resources has been a very large factor in the economic growth of the United States, and that in the future it merits a great deal heavier investment.

---

[2] Edward F. Denison, *The Sources of Economic Growth in the United States,* Supplementary Paper No. 13, C.E.D., January, 1962.

[3] John Kenneth Galbraith, *The Affluent Society.* Boston: Houghton Mifflin, 1958, 368 pp.

[4] Theodore W. Schultz, *The Economic Value of Education.* New York: Columbia University Press, 1963.

In Britain, where the current status as well as the prospects of expansion for higher education are distinctly less optimistic and ambitious than with us, the Lord Robbins Committee noted that the aggregate provision for higher education in 1962-63 amounted to 0.8 per cent of the gross national product and recommended that it become 1.9 per cent of the GNP by 1980.[5] This more than twofold increase within about 17 years would make our own projected doubling of the percentage between 1966 and 1977 seem not more than mildly sanguine. Our percentages would be 1.25 per cent to 2.5 per cent, over a period of a dozen years.

Increases in industrial productivity now depend to a great extent upon the availability of manpower having appropriate qualifications for the jobs which need to be filled. Shifting occupational patterns point toward increasing demands for higher general educational attainment. Unskilled jobs for the uneducated tend to disappear. Streetcleaners on foot with broom and pushcart have receded into history. Manual elevator-operators are following. The farm worker, for whom a strong back was once the main qualification, now tends to be a skilled mechanic and operator of huge tractors, mechanical harvesters of grain or cotton, and other power machinery, as well as a skilled caretaker of valuable livestock.

Huge power-driven earth-moving machines, concrete-mixers, and cranes are now essential in the construction of roads and buildings, doing the work once done by great gangs of men with picks and shovels, hod-carriers, and other workers whose assets were almost solely strong muscles and physical endurance.

A poignant feature of the current unemployment among young persons is that most of them simply do not possess the minimum education which available jobs require. Only a generation ago it was possible for many a young man to look forward confidently to a career in which he would earn a living for himself and his family by ordinary muscular labor with hand tools. There was always demand for labor by strong men with hand tools in agriculture, lumbering, the construction industry, and many other occupations. That condition is

[5]Lord Robbins Committee Report, *Higher Education*, p. 207. London: Her Majesty's Stationery Office, 1963.

already gone. It is no longer realistic for any man to hope to support a family by unskilled muscular work alone.

Farm workers have declined to 7 per cent of the labor force; manufacturing industries no longer employ large numbers of muscle-men as they proceed farther and farther with automation. Mechanization of coal-mining has created permanent large-scale unemployment in that industry. In an increasingly urbanized society the varied "service occupations" employ increasing numbers of workers; the managerial, supervisory, professional, and sales personnel categories are making the greatest gains in numbers, as the variety of goods and services available to consumers increases, and as family purchasing-power grows. It has been estimated that by 1975 *half* of all employed workers will be in these latter classifications: professional, managerial, supervisory, and sales—for all of which high levels of education are either an essential or an important advantage.

Rapidly into the picture is coming a stratum of the work-force of maximum importance in increasing and maintaining the productivity of the whole complex. These are the "middle-level" or "technician-level" workers who are distinctly better-educated than the skilled labor stratum, but less-educated than the professional, scientific, and managerial levels. These are persons educated to the point of two years or four years beyond high school, including preparation for a large variety of "semiprofessions" or "subprofessions" now increasingly needed.

The top-level fully professional engineer will be most productive if he has at his disposal a team of lesser-grade semiprofessionals—junior engineers, draftsmen, surveyors, and others—, depending on his specialty. The physician or surgeon needs a cadre of nurses, physical therapists, medical technologists, X-ray operators, medical secretaries, and others to enable him to give the largest service. The dentist needs dental assistants and dental hygienists. The scientist needs laboratory technicians and junior assistants. The teaching profession at all levels can become much more productive when it has a sufficient supply of teachers' aides in various specialties, as well as clerical and secretarial assistants. All these occupations are now critically undermanned. They have come to be based on two to four years of college education because, although a certain modicum of intensive technical training is essential in each, yet by and large a college level of *general* education is equally necessary to the best service in such pursuits.

Viewed from the standpoint of a county, city, or metropolitan area rather than nationally, the connection between a college or university and economic growth is equally clear.

The presence of a college attracts people, dollars, and industries. Once the idea prevailed that industries looking for plant locations were heavily influenced by the absence of income taxes or low property taxes or special tax favors offered by the state or city. Today this factor is often outweighed by the presence of a university or technological college to provide scientist-colleagues and consultants for the company's scientists and engineers, or a community college to provide part-time education for its technician-level employees, or an outstanding system of public elementary and secondary schools for the children of its employees at all levels. Education and economic growth tend to form an upward spiral, locally as well as statewide and nationally.

Chapter 31

HIGHER EDUCATION AND THE PROGRESS OF CIVILIZATION

ECONOMISTS, while struggling with the problems of pinpointing the contributions of education to economic growth, and with the "manpower" aspects of education and the needs for vocational and technical training, pause occasionally to rise above those concepts and at least acknowledge the presence of outcomes of formal schooling that are of an entirely different order—the growth of a humane civilization, the elevating of the quality of individual human lives, and the enlightenment of the whole society thereby. These benefits are imponderable in the sense that their value "can not be deduced in a mechanical way from any known set of figures." Nevertheless, they may well be, in the long run, the most important of all results of higher education.

The aspiration for a just and humane society is of great antiquity. It has been, in various forms, expressed again and again since the Code of Hammurabi. It is voiced quite clearly, if in somewhat archaic terminology, in the clause of the Massachusetts Constitution of 1780 in which special mention is made of Harvard University, enjoining future "legislatures and magistrates" to "countenance and inculcate the principles of humanity and general benevolence, public and private charity, industry and frugality, honesty and punctuality in their dealings, sincerity, good humor, and all social affections and generous sentiments, among the people."

This selfsame clause had already directed the "legislatures and magistrates" to "encourage private societies and public institutions, rewards and immunities, for the promotion of agriculture, arts, sciences, commerce, trades, manufactures, and a natural history of the country"; and the whole was prefaced by proclaiming "wisdom and knowledge, as well as virtue, diffused generally among the body of the people," to be "necessary for the preservation of their rights and liberties"; and that "these depend on spreading the opportunities and advantages of education in the various parts of the country, and among the different orders of the people."

In more modern phrases, we would, while subscribing fully to all that was written there, perhaps add that we would foster among people of all ages appreciation of the fine arts, music, the drama, and literature; physical fitness and mental health; and the passion for justice and equality before the law, not excluding care to diminish the prevalence of bigotry, prejudice, superstition, and harsh intolerance based on race, religion, sex, or economic underprivilege.

All the foregoing types of results hoped for from higher education have relatively little to do with marshaling a nation's "manpower" in the sense of any exact fitting of educational experience to particular occupations or specific jobs. They simply transcend the notion of precise measurement of "manpower" requirements, which if overemphasized can become not merely ludicrous but subversive of individual freedoms. The day must not come when the educational and occupational preferences of persons are fully subordinated to some Delphic "manpower" authority which, speaking through the swirling steam of economic statistics, dictates ex cathedra how many young persons shall prepare for each profession and vocation.

Some literal-minded economists and others speak of "waste" if an engineer with four years of training fills a post for which only two years are the minimum requirement. Some affect alarm at the fact that many well-educated engineers do not practice their profession at all, as though in such a case the whole course of engineering education were "wasted." This is absurd on its face. A devastating response to it is found in the words of a Norwegian contributor to the studious review of Sweden by the Organization for Economic Development:

"The delegate from Norway suggested that one of the primary aims of any education system was in some sense 'over-qualification'— the steady increase in the net percentage of the population whose education has gone further than the minimum point necessary to earn a living. Some of the best scientific work has been done by persons who were neither best nor most accurately qualified for their work, so that a leavening influence on society of 'over-qualified' and 'mis-qualified' persons was often tempered by considerable practical advantage."

Certainly the United States suffers no net loss because thousands of well-educated lawyers do not practice law, and many never had any such intention; nor because literally millions of persons educated for the profession of teaching do not practice it, and in many cases never intended to use it for anything other than a short-term stopgap during a certain stage of their lives. It is far better to have this leaven of millions of educated persons in the population than to have the same persons at lower levels of education.

This is only a way of saying liberal or general education and vocational, professional, or specialized education can not be mutually exclusive and ought never to be thought of as such. A grasp of this fundamental concept will do much to prevent one from becoming too engrossed in the symmetrical but chimerical picture of every individual precisely trained for his exact niche in life, and no more; and with the wildly erroneous thought that anything other than this is economically wasteful.

There are frightening implications in that thought: Who is to predetermine each one's exact niche in life? Is it to be done by "experts" armed with batteries of tests stemming from Binet's original work, and is individual predilection to be denied or ignored? Or is account to be taken of the judgments of a succession of teachers, mostly capable, observant, and sympathetic? Do either or both of the techniques, imperfect as they admittedly are, justify smothering or diverting individual choice? This query is most serious. It seeps beneath and undermines the whole structure of "national manpower management," and forces the conclusion that there is a more significant aspect of education—its general function as an elevator of civilization.

In this view, education has in our time come to play some part of the role formerly thought of as belonging almost exclusively to religion—the function of diminishing man's iniquities and uplifting him toward fulfillment of his highest potentialities. Important as this role of religion continues to be, there are questions of ethics and morals, individual and social, that do not necessarily depend solely upon religion—surely not upon any particular sectarian beliefs, for an answer. In the last analysis they depend upon conscience; and both education and religion may contribute to its refinement—and this is true of strictly secular education, when it is characterized by the free and honest search for truth.

Anyone who has lived through the generation just past, or who has some inklings of the history of the past two centuries, knows that the ethical and moral ideals of man have advanced to higher levels and are now on the upward march. More widespread than ever before is the realization that the progress of a great nation will not be forwarded by one class placing its foot upon the prostrate neck of another class—whether the underdog be condemned because of race, sex, religion, poverty, physical handicap, ignorance, unemployment, lack of social éclat, or any misfortune. We shall rise together—not by the fortunate's trampling down the less fortunate; not by the "haves" oppressing the "have nots."

The growth and spread and implementation of this concept come, of course, in part from religion; in part from theology, law, medicine, teaching, social service—all these are in some sense the products of higher education. Do not omit the liberal disciplines of history, political science, sociology, and anthropology; nor economics, business, and statistics. The point is that if these and their sister professions and disciplines, all nurtured in universities and colleges, are expanding the frontiers of knowledge and carrying forward the search for truth, one can easily believe that the aggregate outcomes will far transcend, even in narrow economic terms, the dollar-measured "economies" that might conceivably flow from a frozen fitting of education to exactly computed manpower needs in a planned economy. If this nation boldly advances its ideals of fairness and justice, so as to liberate in greater degree the potentialities of all its people, the consequences in added economic growth, industrial power, and intellectual and moral excellence will be unprecedented.

Chapter 32

TWENTY APOTHEGMS IN FINANCING HIGHER EDUCATION

In any field of knowledge which is long the subject of study and of devoted practice, there accumulates a number of short, pithy sayings—some half-humorous, others of differing character. They may be designated as adages, maxims, aphorisms, or epigrams.

The tendency of such bywords is to hit the nail on the head with a very unwieldy mallet, and thus to be true and useful in some circumstances, but misguided or deceptive in others. Their wide currency argues against ignoring them; and some examination of each may often be instructive, and on occasion amusing.

For those reasons, observe briefly a score of apothegms appertaining to the financial support of higher education in the United States.

1. Let each become all he is capable of being.

The motto on the seal of the State University of New York sets forth in nine words an ideal. But New York State has difficulty in deciding whether the ideal should be implemented by making public higher education tuition-free, accessible to all; or by providing state scholarships mainly used to pay tuition fees in private colleges. Pres-

ently it is doing both, on a large and growing scale. Tuition is free
to regular full-time undergraduates in the City University of New
York, embracing four major five-year colleges and seven two-year
colleges in the nation's largest city. At the same time the state is
spending in the fiscal year 1967 some $72 million for scholarships.

The president of the Constitutional Convention of 1967 led in
advocacy of a provision requiring all public universities and colleges
to be tuition-free, while another faction demanded removal of an
existing prohibition of the appropriation of tax funds to any denominational institution.

In 1964 the Educational Policies Commission (a national voluntary
body) was more explicit. It recommended unequivocally that every
high school graduate should have opportunity for at least two years
of tuition-free education beyond high school, with emphasis on intellectual growth.

2. *Put the colleges where the people are.*

"Going away to college" is expensive for the student and his
family. For large numbers it is prohibitively costly. From one-third
to one-half of the expense of a year in college can be saved if the
student can attend a college nearby while living at home. This is a
main reason for the prairie-fire spread of local public junior colleges,
and for the growth of urban universities and colleges.

While the "streetcar college" (now the "motorcar college") may
not offer all the amenities and opportunities afforded by the traditional residential institution, it is far better than no college at all;
and it is susceptible of much improvement as the idea matures. Without doubt the "commuters' colleges" of all types will enroll increasing
proportions of the nation's students in higher education.

The prim residential colleges, located originally in many cases
"far from the temptations of the wicked city," themselves tend to
become "suitcase colleges," deserted over long week-ends. We can
not escape from urbanism and megalopolitanism.

"Put the colleges where the people are" also is applicable in
sparsely populated and economically depressed remote areas, where a
college may catalyze economic growth and mitigate educational underprivilege, to the advantage of the whole state and nation.

3. *A private college can do many things a public college cannot.*

True, and important, and too-little emphasized. Teaching specific denominational religious discipline; maintaining a traditional religious tone and atmosphere in all activities academic and nonacademic; openly favoring the children of clergymen or faculty children in the award of scholarships and other student aids; selective admissions overtly based on race, religion, sex, economic class, or other factors of privilege—all these are among the policies which private colleges can and do practice, and they are lawful unless expressly forbidden in the college charter.

None of these is lawful for public colleges, except perhaps selectivity in admissions, and some states require that all holders of an accredited high school diploma, if residents of the state, must be admitted to the maximum limit of the existing facilities. Most assuredly it is illegal for a public college or university to discriminate in admissions or student aids on grounds of religion, race, or the circumstance of being the child of a faculty member.

4. *It is hard to sell education for a good price when a competitor down the street is giving it away.*

This is the half-facetious plaint of many presidents of private colleges, and an oblique dig at the low-fee or tuition-free public colleges and universities. Its tendency is callously to narrow and restrict the availability of opportunity for education beyond high school. The statement is inept and pointless for two very important reasons: (1) Education is primarily a service to the society, not merely a consumers' good to be bought and sold for what the market will bear. (2) The facilities and opportunities offered by private institutions are not and ought not to be the *same* as those offered by public institutions. Their differences and their individual character constitute one of the principal reasons for their continued existence. Let the private institutions exploit fully their ability to do what the public institutions can not do. This assures a market for their services.

5. *No college ever has enough money.*

Persons concerned intimately with the operation of colleges almost invariably are so introvertive and self-critical, so conscious of the institution's shortcomings and its needs, that they feel keenly that its service is severely limited by lack of additional financial resources. This is to say they almost automatically have visions of what the college would do if it had more money.

Thus our homely epigram becomes an oblique way of saying every college is aware of some of its own immediate shortfalls, and anxious to overcome them. This is universally true, from the smallest college to the largest university. Generally it is not because governing boards and administrators are greedy empire-builders, bent on self-aggrandizement; but because they are sensitive to the needs and demands of their clientele, and of the state and the nation. Those who are in and of the enterprise know it best. They merit a reasonable confidence.

6. Once endowment, always endowment.

Endowment of a college means a permanent trust fund or funds, of which the principal or corpus must be held inviolate, and only the income expended for the college's purposes.

While it is possible for a donor to establish a trust for a specified limited duration, or to authorize the trustees to expend the principal at their discretion, thus leaving its duration uncertain, most endowment funds are *perpetual*, with no limit on the duration of the trust. No part of the principal of such a perpetual trust can ever lawfully be taken out and used for current expenses or capital outlays for non-income-producing academic buildings. The trustees must *invest* the principal, and expend only the income.

Surpluses from annual operations, or operating funds not needed for immediate expenditure, are also invested and have sometimes been miscalled "temporary endowment" or designated by other phrases containing the word "endowment" which tend to confuse these funds with true endowment funds. This is the origin of the useful and sound apothegm, "Once endowment, always endowment." Funds are not to be lightly transferred to or from endowment at will.

7. Creditors never take endowment.

Although the relative importance of endowment funds and endowment income in colleges and universities has considerably declined since the 1930's, the inviolable character of a perpetual trust fund has in no wise changed. If anything, the courts of equity are growing more solicitous about the inception and operation of charitable trusts.

Thus, if a college having endowment funds becomes insolvent on account of mismanagement or for other reasons, its creditors may lay claim to its campus, physical plant, and movable assets if necessary to discharge its obligations; but creditors are never under any circumstances entitled to the principal of endowment funds or property.

After a college has permanently ceased to operate, with no likelihood of resumption, its endowment funds are under the protection of the court of equity, which will usually transfer them to some other college similar in denominational affiliation and deemed most likely to effectuate, as nearly as possible, the charitable intents of the donors.

8. *A trustee of a private college should give, get, or get out.*

So blunt a statement is close to the reality, though many would prefer to sugar-coat it. It does not say a trustee should be ignorant of or indifferent to educational or philosophical issues, and concerned only with money. It merely makes plain that he should not usually be inattentive or impotent in the financial support of the college.

Henry M. Wriston made a similar statement in a somewhat more moderate vein when he said he expected from a trustee "work, wealth, and wisdom; preferably all three, but at least two of the three."[1]

Such is the niche carved for a member of the governing board of a nonprofit charitable corporation in Anglo-American society, largely dominated by free-enterprise private capitalism.

9. *He who pays the piper calls the tune.*

A pernicious proverb. If a voice in the management of a college were assumed to be a perquisite of every private donor, academic freedom and the institution's integrity would always be in jeopardy. It could be "bought." An appellate court has said, "Neither the donors of a fund devoted exclusively to charitable purposes, nor contributors to such a fund, have such an interest in the fund as

---

[1] Henry M. Wriston, *Academic Procession.* New York: Columbia University Press, 1959, p. 44, 222 pp.

to entitle them to . . . interfere with, or direct, the management of the fund by the trustees."[2]

No one would want to believe the great private universities have their policies dictated either by the wealthy benefactors from whom they receive many millions of dollars in gifts, or by the Federal government from which some of them now receive half or more of their annual operating expenses, in the form of grants and contracts.

In connection with Federal tax support of public or private education at any level, the false canard that "federal aid must necessarily mean federal control," stems in part from this insensitive and undiscriminating adage.

10. *Overcentralization produces apoplexy at the apex and paralysis at the periphery.*

This somewhat sardonic maxim has for some years been prominent in the management policies of military and industrial organizations, and in large business and governmental bureaucracies.

This is why in military tactics and strategy the initiative of small-unit commanders and of individual soldiers is stressed; why in business, industry, and government a leading principle is that branch managers and department heads should be given as much autonomy as possible; and that no employee should be regarded as an automaton.

In higher education these principles are doubly deserving of emphasis, because the paramount purpose is to stimulate the development of individual thoughtfulness and initiative. Decisions seldom need to be instantaneous, as they sometimes must be in military or industrial situations. Most of them can and should be results of an ongoing consensus in which each individual has some satisfaction in his own independence and his own contribution.

11. *Uniformity is the enemy of the human spirit; against this we must keep our vision keen and our weapons sharp.*

This is a widely needed warning against the overstructuring and routinizing of instruction, research, and administration in colleges

---

[2] Judge Coleman in *Coffee* v. *William Marsh Rice University* (Tex. Civ. App.), 387 S.W. 2d 132 (1965). See also *Amundson* v. *Kletzing-McLaughlin Memorial Foundation College*, 247 Iowa 91, 73 N.W. 2d 114 (1955).

and universities. From the viewpoint of finance and financial management, it warns against the allocation of resources within a state or within an institution on the basis of rigid and oversimplified formulas such as fixed teacher-student ratios, fixed sums for operation per student per year, fixed sums per semester credit hour, and similar simplistic simulations.

The foregoing, as well as norms for the cost of structures per square foot of floor space, for the utilization of square feet of floorspace per student per day and per week, have a limited usefulness; but their value is severely restricted and they can be used with devastating effects if employed without full knowledge and sensitive awareness of their limitations. Colleges are never alike, and their diversity is a prime virtue.

12. *Formulas make decision easy, but rob it of wisdom.*

Allocation of appropriated funds to institutions of higher education on an arithmetically predetermined basis involving numbers of students, teacher-student ratios, types and levels of instruction, seems deceptively simple and just. The temptation is to make decisions on the basis of mathematical calculations alone and thus obviate the necessity of any actual reasoning or judgment. Such formulas seem to promise "how to make decisions without really trying."

Formulas may have a very closely limited usefulness, but the great danger is in adhering to them with stubborn rigidity.

Every year brings needs for innovations not embraced in the formula; therefore even a newly devised formula should never be used as a substitute for thought (though it often is!). This year's formula will be out of date next year. Any formula needs constant revision, especially in a field undergoing rapid change, as is true of higher education now.

No magic formula can excuse an abdication of reason by responsible public officers. The formula fad is a menace to progress.

13. *Morale can not be forced; it can only be fostered.*

High morale is the phrase applicable to people who are happy and confident in their work, pleased with their surroundings and their associates, industrious and persevering, and generally hopeful of discoveries or other advances that will make matters even better.

Low morale characterizes people who are dispirited, unsatisfied with their current work and location, indifferent to the opportunities before them, and who feel disaffected and alienated from their associates, and without much hope for the immediate future.

In all kinds of work, and especially in the work of learning, morale is all-important. In a college or a state system of higher education, the morale of students, faculty, and administrators can be built by providing for maximum freedom in educational and vocational choices, decentralization and flexibility of administration, and care for the *espirit de corps* of each individual. It can not be enforced or maintained by centralized authoritarian management, with orders moving downward from a remote center.

14. *Money spent for higher education is not an unrecoverable cost, but a productive investment for the whole society.*

Education and economic growth form an upward spiral, each pushing the other upward. Everywhere it is manifest that education beyond high school makes better producers and better consumers, raises personal incomes, and stimulates business and industry. They in turn require higher and higher levels of educational attainment by their prospective employees, managers, and directors.

Employees in industry have a right to insist that plants shall be located in places accessible to good public elementary and secondary school facilities for their children, and a junior college or a four-year college. Managers and employees in engineering and scientific jobs find great advantages in proximity to a full-fledged university having a graduate school. This is why "research parks" near large universities are tenanted by manufacturing plants of "growth industries" and by research divisions of great industrial corporations.

15. *Property taxes can become confiscatory for farm owners, and for home owners having small fixed incomes.*

It is the nature of agricultural industry that it requires a heavy investment in land, buildings, and machinery in relation to each individual in the labor force and in relation to its income-producing capacity.

Often a farm owner-operator has difficulty in earning a profit sufficient to pay a moderate return on his large investment and to cover depreciation and maintenance. His personal compensation for his own labor and management skill is often small—sometimes less than that of a factory laborer. He may even incur losses in his annual operations. Ad valorem taxes at high rates on his property over a period of years can ruin him. Farmers continue to incur this hazard chiefly because they enjoy the independence and self-reliance of the farm way of life; but their numbers have greatly declined.

Widows with young children and elderly retired couples who own valuable family homes often find it impossible to hold and maintain these properties, paying for repairs and maintenance, insurance, and taxes on the value of the properties, because their personal earning-power is small and inflation diminishes the purchasing-power of their fixed incomes from pensions or modest investments in bonds.

16. *Income is a better measure of taxpaying ability than property ownership.*

A century and more ago, when most of the wealth of the nation was in the form of farms and homes, when public services were simple and few and largely financed by local taxing subdivisions, and when money was scarce and wages and salaries small, ownership of property was a reasonably good index of ability to pay taxes.

Now much of the nation's wealth is in the form of incorporeal property—stocks and bonds issued by vast corporations which own and operate huge productive and distributive industries and gigantic systems of transport and communication. Salaries and wages at all levels are beyond the dreams of earlier generations. Public services have been multiplied and expanded, and inflation maximizes their costs. Most of the states have had to adopt general sales taxes and income taxes (not practicable for local levy and administration) to produce large revenues. Each of these taxes is in some sense adjusted to the current getting and spending of large numbers of people, which is "where the action is" today. Nearly all the states have had to abandon wholly the use of property taxes for state-level purposes.

More than half the large annual revenue of the Federal government comes from the Federal income tax.

17. *In the modern economy, exercise of the taxing power necessarily tends to move upward to the larger governmental units.*

Neither rural townships nor agricultural or urban counties, nor towns or large cities, are able to obtain local revenues sufficient to support their own essential public services. The same is true of local school districts, sanitary districts, and other *ad hoc* local authorities. The day of the self-sufficient, self-supporting local civil subdivision is past. These units must depend almost wholly on local property taxes, because the newer and more productive types of taxes can not be administered economically and efficiently in a unit smaller than the state.

So it is that the 50 states now collect as much revenue at the state level as all the thousands of local subdivisions; and the Federal government, chiefly through personal and corporate income taxes, collects nearly twice as much as all the states and local subdivisions combined. Thus there must be state aid to cities, counties, and school districts, and Federal aid to the states and their subdivisions. Careful separation of control from support is necessary to avoid drifting toward a congested unitary national government.

18. *Any state revenue system should be diversified.*

As the three-level system of government has developed to date, the 50 states have available to them a variety of revenue sources. They have given up the property tax for state-level purposes; but they are using general and selective sales taxes, personal and corporate income taxes, sumptuary taxes on tobacco products and beverages, severance taxes, succession taxes, and various license charges. The Federal government credits Federal estate taxpayers with 80 per cent of their payments under state succession taxes. If this principle were extended to apply to state and Federal income taxes, the tax resources of the states could thereby be considerably strengthened.

A state revenue system should be diversified for two important reasons: (1) it will thus be less likely to be suddenly weakened by unforeseen drastic economic changes and will have more stability and predictability than a system depending too heavily on one or two types of sources could have; and (2) it will be more just and equitable because the incidence of taxes of progressive tendency will in some degree countervail the effects of taxes of regressive tendency, and the imperfections of one type may be counterbalanced by the characteristics of another type of tax.

19. *Any state revenue system is always susceptible of being made more equitable and more productive.*

Invariably true, because of the rapidity and continuity of economic changes in our time. Even if a given state tax pattern were perfect today, it would have imperfections within a year or two, because it would begin to become out of harmony with the distribution of income levels, the occupational patterns, or other factors influencing taxpaying ability. This means it would become less equitable and less productive than would be desirable.

Unremitting study and almost constant revamping are necessary—much more so in our day than in earlier years when the pace of technology was slower and the ways of life were materially simpler and more stable. We now require a great many more public services at increasing expense to the taxpayers. We have the resources, but we can not expect to utilize them if we cling to outdated revenue systems.

20. *State tax support of higher education is not a question of resources, but of policy.*

Put the proposition in other words: Is the real "gut question" whether the 50 states and the United States can *afford* universal higher education, or whether they *want* it?

It is very difficult to doubt that the most affluent nation in all history, in the unprecedented "economy of abundance," can afford to invest twice or four times the current sums being put into higher education. Currently the aggregate operating cost may be a little more than is spent annually for cigarettes, but much less than what is spent for alcoholic beverages. Without proposing any sumptuary laws, one could plead for a more appropriate balance. Even the poorest

state can and will greatly increase its annual investment in higher
education. One-sixth of the 1967 national defense budget would be
sufficient to double the annual investment in higher education from
all sources. The *resources* are here, and the *policy* is developing
rapidly.

Consider the words of the Robbins Report in Great Britain,
where the total of economic capacity is far less than in the United
States. After urging a huge expansion of tax-supported higher education, the report says:

"The costs of the plan we have put forward are considerable.
They involve an increase in the percentage of the national income
devoted to higher education. They may involve increases in taxation,
though whether this will be so depends upon the extent of other
commitments, upon financial policy in general, and upon the increase
of productivity. But we are convinced that no economic consideration
need hinder their adoption if we as a nation desire the educational
changes they will make possible. Whether we have them or not, is a
question of choice. It is not a question of any technical or economic
ability to achieve them."[3]

---

[3]Lord Robbins Committee Report, *Higher Education,* p. 216. London: Her
Majesty's Stationery Office, 1963.

Chapter 33

EPILOGUE

THE EFFORT HERE is to find and examine *principles* applicable to the support of higher education in the United States in the final third of the twentieth century. The emphasis is on broad ideas, not on technical details.

Hence this book is a subjective essay dealing with comprehensive concepts. It is not a heavily-documented encyclopedic textbook. It is not a statistical reference work. It does not record norms for unit costs of instruction, space-utilization, or any of a thousand other minutiae which become outdated with each passing year. Nor is it a "cookbook" technical manual of accounting or of any of the related processes in college business management.

It does not dwell upon catch phrases such as "proliferation of courses" in a time of the most explosive expansion of knowledge in all history. It does not extol the virtues of "educational hardware," though the author anticipates that electronic aids to storage, retrieval, and transmission of knowledge will enrich the educational process, but only in ways supplementary to the intellectual labors of students and teachers, not in lieu thereof; nor by any means reducing its costs, at least in the foreseeable future. It does not countenance a return to the Lancastrian system of one teacher per one thousand students, nor expouse any other faddish panacea.

This essay is addressed to all who have an interest in the financing of higher education—and they are many millions. It is not especially or exclusively for scholars, administrators, or business officers, nor for advanced students of institutional management. It is not itself a research report, nor a compendium of abstracts of scattered and fragmentary scientific or pseudo-scientific projects. It does not purport to be "objective" in the sense that it tests any hypothesis by exact mathematically quantifiable methods; or that the author has kept himself and his biases out of it. Rather would the author wish it known that it is the result of his observations, careful thought, familiarity with the literature of the field, and best judgment.

"Subjective"? Of course; for far from keeping himself out of it, the author has put his own cogitation into it, without apology. He makes no pretense of having reached "findings" by mathematical or mechanical manipulation of data ("hard" or "soft"), other than the simple inferences implicit in the essay. He conceives his function as interpretative and tendentious in an area involving great issues not susceptible of resolution by other means. Not only is complete "objectivity" in the approach to such issues impossible, but a too-zealous adherence to it can stymie decision and produce blindness to public needs. Though mathematics may merge with symbolic logic, it is incapable of answering philosophical questions, or questions involving imponderable human values in the realm of ethics, morality, law, or public policy.

What are some of the conclusions of the thesis here?

1. Universal education beyond the high school, with perhaps 80 to 95 per cent of high school graduates going on with further schooling, is inevitable in the United States.

2. Public higher education free of tuition charges and accessible to all is the paramount basic goal.

3. A flourishing nonprofit private sector, occupying a proportionally smaller part of the total field than hitherto, will continue to co-exist with public higher education.

4. Institutions in the private sector will be free to establish their own tuition fees and other charges, and to discriminate

in admissions and in the award of student aids, within the terms of their charters.

5. Institutions in the public sector, though retaining the function of classifying and assigning their own students, will do so with increasing care to preserve maximum freedom of individual preference in educational and vocational choices; and it will be unlawful for them to discriminate on grounds of sex, race, religion, or other irrelevancies in the award of student financial aids.

6. State and Federal systems of scholarships, fellowships, loans, and other student aids have hitherto been in large part forms of indirect public support of private institutions; have had a strong tendency to encourage raising of student fees; and have almost wholly failed to reach the economically underprivileged and the student who is "average" in academic promise. Their tendency to cause raising of fees actually is a narrowing of educational opportunity *in toto*, counter to the aim of broadening such opportunity. A notable exception is the Permanent G.I. Bill of 1966; and some of the provisions of the Economic Opportunity Act, and the "Educational Opportunity Grant" provisions of the Higher Education Act of 1965 seem promising. State and Federal student aids merit continuation on a controlled and experimental basis, as partial supplements to a system based mainly on the principle of public higher education—accessible to all and tuition-free, not as a central element.

7. For public universities and colleges, there is no substitute for free tuition. Student financial aids applicable to expenses of books, maintenance, or necessary travel are useful supplements to the free-tuition norm; and for private institutions, as an indirect channel of limited tax aid which also extends the freedom of choice of beneficiary students and their parents.

8. Schemes of graduated tuition fees according to family income may be of interest and perhaps practicable within the private sector, but wholly inappropriate for public institutions.

9. Tax credits against tuition fee payments, as proposed in recent bills before Congress, are unlikely to be approved because (1) they would absorb $1½ billion of Federal revenue annual-

ly—a sum sufficient to make all public universities and colleges tuition-free; (2) they would be of negligible help in any case (a maximum of $375 per year); and (3) they would not benefit at all the families whose incomes are so low, or their dependents so numerous, that they pay no Federal income tax, or only trivial amounts.

10. All student loan schemes in operation up to 1968 were discriminatory against women students, for the simple and all-pervasive reason that the resulting debt constituted a "negative dowry" rightly distasteful to all young women. This is an extremely serious drawback. Another grave shortcoming is the undeniable tendency to distort the student's educational and occupational choices in order to facilitate payment of the indebtedness.

11. The Zacharias Panel proposal of 40-year or lifetime student loans from the Federal government to be repaid through the Internal Revenue Service in the form of a fixed percentage of annual income might be a bonanza for the private sector, but is unthinkable for public institutions. It would charge almost the whole cost of higher education to the students; would cause fees to rise inordinately, even in public universities and colleges, and would probably diminish or destroy the tax support of public higher education which has developed over a full century of progress.

12. State and Federal tax support of public higher education can and will be multiplied severalfold within the present century. The most damaging single error made by orthodox economists has been their gross underestimation of the ability and desire of the 50 states to support and upgrade education beyond the high school. We are on the threshold of universal higher education, largely tax-supported. The whole society pays, and the whole society gains. Individual talents are developed. Great gains are forthcoming in technology, public health, the social sciences, the humanities, the arts, the quality of our lives.

BIBLIOGRAPHY

Highlights in the History of College Finance

Joyal, Arnold E., Chm., Technical Committee on Costs. *The Costs of Higher Education in California 1960-1975.* Berkeley: University of California President's Office, 1960. 124 pp.

Rudolph, Frederick. "Who Paid the Bills? An Inquiry into the Nature of Nineteenth Century College Finance." *Harvard Educational Review* 31: 144-157 (Spring 1961).

Financing Capital Improvements: Academic Facilities

Collins, George. "College Construction: 1966-70." *College Management* 2: 57-78 (July 1967).

Financing Income-producing "Nonacademic" Buildings

Binning, Dennis W. "College Operating Practices Analysis, Part I: Feeding and Housing Operations." *College and University Business* 43: 66-73 (September 1967).

Garrigan, Richard. "You Can Accurately Predict Land Acquisition Costs." *College and University Business* 43: 35-36 (August 1967).

Financing Annual Operations

Fund for the Advancement of Education. *California and Western Conference Cost and Statistical Study for the Year 1954-55.* New York: The Ford Foundation, 1962. 129 pp.

National Federation of College and University Business Officers' Associations (now superseded by the National Association of College and University Business Officers). *The Sixty College Study: A Second Look: 1957-58* and *A Study of Income and Expenditures in Sixty Colleges, 1953-54.*

National Science Foundation (Publication No. 67-15). *Systems for Measuring and Reporting the Resources and Activities of Colleges and Universities.* Washington: Government Printing Office, 1967. 444 pp.

A Primer of College Accounting

Scheps, Clarence. *Accounting for Colleges and Universities.* Baton Rouge: Louisiana State University Press, 1949. 391 pp.

Smith, Donovan E. (Ed.). *California and Western Conference Cost and Statistical Study.* Berkeley: University of California Printing Department, 1960. 129 pp.

Virginia State Council of Higher Education. *A Forum on the Theory and Practice of College Accounting.* Richmond, Virginia, August 1966. 24 pp.

Accounting and Management

Benezet, Louis T. "Half-Way to Where? or the Quantity-Quality Muddle in College Education." *NEA Journal* 53: 57-58 (April 1964).

Bowker, Albert H. "Quantity and Quality in Higher Education." *American Statistical Association Journal* 60: 1-15 (March 1965).

Doctorate Production in U.S. Universities, 1920-62. Washington: National Academy of Sciences, 1964. 215 pp.

Hungate, Thad L. *Management in Higher Education.* New York: Bureau of Publications, Teachers College, Columbia University, 1964. 348 pp.

Kintzer, Frederick C. "Structuring the Annual Report." *Junior College Journal* 35: 17-19 (September 1964).

Long, Durward. "Faculty Responsibility and the Executive Conquest of Academe." *School and Society* 94: 89-92 (February 19, 1966).

Medlyn, William H. *Potential Doctorate Productivity in Selected Colleges and Universities-1965.* American Association of Colleges for Teacher Education, 1965. 22 pp.

Rourke, Francis E. and Glenn E. Brooks. "The Managerial Revolution in Higher Education." *Administrative Science Quarterly* 9: 154-181 (September 1964).

Scheuerman, J. C. "What's Wrong with Business Management in Public Colleges?" *College and University Business* 40: 43-45 (May 1966).

Wescoe, W. Clarke. "Expansion and Excellence: A Choice in Higher Education?" *State Government* 37: 221-227 (Autumn 1964).

Williams, Harry. *Planning for Effective Resource Allocation in Universities.* Washington: American Council on Education, 1966. 78 pp.

The Meaning of "Efficiency" in Higher Education

Brown, Ray E. "Facts Are Good Friends but They Are No Substitute for Judgment." *College and University Business* 36: 61-63 (June 1964)

Committee on Government and Higher Education, (Milton S. Eisenhower, Chairman). *The Efficiency of Freedom.* Baltimore: Johns Hopkins Press, 1959. 44 pp.

Pike, Walter L. "What You Can Learn from Unit Costs." *College and University Business* 37: 39-41 (July 1964).

Ruml, Beardsley and Donald H. Morrison. *Memo to a College Trustee.* New York: McGraw-Hill, 1959. 94 pp.

Thompson, Daniel C. "Problems of Faculty Morale." *Journal of Negro Education* 29: 37-46 (Winter 1960).

Williams, Robert L. *The Administration of Academic Affairs in Higher Education.* Ann Arbor: University of Michigan Press, 1965. 182 pp.

Endowment Funds and Endowment Income

Bates, George E. "Difficulties in Investment Policies," pp. 214-218, in Seymour Harris (Ed.), *Higher Education in the United States: the Economic Problems.* Cambridge: Harvard University Press, 1960. 225 pp.

Blackwell, Thomas E. "Changing Needs Create Endowment Conflicts." *College and University Business* 43: 22 (August 1967).

Cain, J. Harvey. "Recent Trends in Endowment," pp. 242-244, in Seymour Harris (Ed.), *Higher Education in the United States: The Economic Problems.* Cambridge: Harvard University Press, 1960. 255 pp.

Tripp, H. W. "How to Get More Dollars from Your Endowment." *College Management* 2: 12-21 (August 1967)

Underhill, Robert M. "Special Problems in Public Institutions," pp. 245-247, in Seymour Harris (Ed.), *Higher Education in the United States: The Economic Problems.* Cambridge: Harvard University Press, 1960. 255 pp.

How Much Should the Students Pay?

— Chambers, M. M. "Higher Education: Who Should Pay?" *Vital Speeches of the Day* 32: 447-448 (May 1, 1966). Reprinted in Glenn R. Capp, *The Great Society: A Sourcebook of Speeches.* Belmont, California: Dickenson Publishing Co., 1967. 195 pp.

Emens, John R. "Education Begets Education: The G.I. Bill Twenty Years Later." *American Education* 1: 11-13 (September 1965).

Hollis, Ernest V. *Costs of Attending College.* U.S. Office of Education Bulletin 1957, No. 9. Washington: Government Printing Office, 1962. (Reprint) 91 pp.

National Association of State Universities and Land-Grant Colleges, and Association of State Colleges and Universities. *Recommendations for National Action Concerning Higher Education.* Washington, January 1967. 37 pp.

Ostar, Allan W. and Laura Godofsky. "The Geography of Higher Education." *American Federationist* 72: 21-24 (October 1965).

Taylor, Hobart, Jr. "Higher Education and Equal Opportunity." *Educational Record* 45: 385-388 (Fall 1964).

West, Elmer D., Robert L. Farrell, and Martha F. Blakeslee. "Trends in College Costs—and in Family Income." *College and University Journal* 3: 37-43 (Summer 1964).

Wolfman, Bernard. "Tax Deductions and Credits for Tuition Payments." *AAUP Bulletin* 49: 380-382 (December 1963).

Support from Private Donors

Desmond, Richard L. *Higher Education and Tax-Motivated Giving: The Federal Tax History of Life Income and Annuity Gifts.* Washington: American College Public Relations Association, 1967. 89 pp.

Giving, U.S.A.: Facts About Philanthropy. New York: American Association of Fund-Raising Counsel, Inc., 1966. 60 pp.

Margin for Excellence: The Role of Voluntary Support in Public Higher Education. Washington: Office of Institutional Research, National Association of State Universities and Land-Grant Colleges, 1966. 16 pp.

Seymour, Harold J. *Designs for Fund-Raising: Principles, Patterns, Techniques.* New York: McGraw-Hill, 1966. 210 pp.

Toll, Maynard J. "Tax Problems in Connection with Contributions to Colleges." Los Angeles: *Fourteenth Tax Institute,* University of Southern California, 1962, pp. 859-887.

Venman, William C. *Gift Annuity Agreements for Colleges.* Ann Arbor: University of Michigan, Center for the Study of Higher Education, 1962. 33 pp.

Voluntary Support for Public Higher Education 1964-65. New York: G. A. Brakeley & Company, Incorporated, 1966. 13 pp. (Fourth in a series that began with 1957-58.)

Voluntary Support of Education 1965-66. New York: Council for Financial Aid to Education, 1967.

Alumni as a Source of Support

Hickerson, Loren. "Developing the Alumni Resource at Public Colleges and Universities." Washington: Association of State Colleges and Universities, 1966. 12 pp.

Taylor, Bernard P. "Basics of Annual Alumni Giving" and "Developing a Deferred Giving Program," *CASC Newsletter* 9: 8-10 (November 1964).

The Philanthropic Foundations

Andrews, F. Emerson. *The Foundation Directory* (2nd edit.). New York: Russell Sage Foundation, 1963.

Andrews, F. Emerson (Ed.). *Foundations: Twenty Viewpoints.* New York: Russell Sage Foundation, 1965. 108 pp.

Andrews, Richard H., Robert J. Wert, and Jeanne Brewer. "Three Views of Foundation Giving." Number 9 in the *Educational Fund-Raising Manual.* Washington: American Alumni Council, 1958. 12 pp.

Bremner, Robert H. *American Philanthropy.* Chicago: University of Chicago Press, 1960. 230 pp.

Broce, Thomas. "When Colleges Approach Foundations." *CASC Newsletter* 9: 10-11 (February 1965).

Curti, Merle and Roderick Nash. *Philanthropy in the Shaping of American Higher Education.* New Brunswick, New Jersey: Rutgers University Press, 1965. 340 pp.

Heald, Henry T. "In Common Cause: Foundations and Higher Education." *College and University Journal* 3: 7-10 (Winter 1964).

Karst, Kenneth L. "The Tax Exemption of Donor-Controlled Foundations." *Ohio State Law Journal* 25: 183-221 (Spring 1964).

Morison, Robert S. "Foundations and Universities." *Doedalus* 93: 1109-1141 (Fall 1964).

Morrisett, Lloyd N. "Appraising a Partnership: How Does a Foundation Give Away Its Money?" *College and University Journal* 3: 3-6 (Winter 1964).

Nelson, Robert E. "Foundations and the Small Colleges." *CASC Newsletter* 9: 11-12 (November 1964).

Sears, Jesse B. *Philanthropy in the History of American Higher Education.* Washington: Government Printing Office, 1922.

Taft, J. Richard. *Understanding Foundations.* New York: McGraw-Hill, 1967. 205 pp.

Wallace, Burt. "Struck by Ford Lightning." *Saturday Review.* pp. 86-87, 102-103 (April 16, 1966).

Walsh, John. "Foundations: Regulation of Tax-Exempt Organizations." *Science* 145: 559-561 (August 7, 1964).

Weaver, Warren and others. *U. S. Philanthropic Foundations: Their History, Structure, Management and Record.* New York: Harper and Row, 1967. 512 pp.

Contributions from Religious Organizations

Pattillo, Manning M. and Donald M. Mackenzie. *Church-Sponsored Higher Education in the United States:* Report of the Danforth Commission. Washington: American Council on Education, 1966. 309 pp.

Pattillo, Manning M. and Donald M. Mackenzie. *Eight Hundred Colleges Face the Future.* St. Louis: The Danforth Foundation, 1965. 74 pp.

Wicke, Myron F. *The Church-Related College.* New York: Center for Applied Research in Education, 1964. 116 pp.

Gifts from Business and Industrial Corporations

Eells, Richard. *Corporation Giving in a Free Society.* New York: Harpers, 1956. 210 pp.

Hawes, Gene R. *Why Businesses Sponsor Scholarship Programs.* Princeton, New Jersey: College Entrance Examination Board, 1965. 41 pp.

Holder, Jack J., Jr. *Corporate Support Programs to Institutions of Higher Learning.* Danville, Illinois: The Interstate, 1967. 161 pp.

Morton, Benjamin L. *State and Regional Cooperative Fund-Raising Associations of Private Colleges.* Ann Arbor: University of Michigan doctoral dissertation, 1963. 211 pp.

Pitchell, Robert J. *Corporate Tax Support of Public Institutions of Higher*

Education. Bloomington, Indiana: Institute of Public Administration, Indiana University, 1966. 90 pp.

Pollard, John A. (Ed.). *Aid-to-Education Programs of Some Leading Business Concerns.* New York: Council for Financial Aid to Education, Inc., 1959. 128 pp.

Shapiro, Leo J. *Company Giving.* Chicago: Survey Press, 1961. 136 pp.

Sheetz, John W. "Selected Programs of Corporate Solicitation." Number 12 in a series constituting the *Educational Fund-Raising Manual.* Washington: American Alumni Council, 1959, 20 pp. 25¢.

Stevens, James W. "How Corporations Decide Where to Give." *College and University Business* 37: 37-40 (December 1964).

Community Support from Private Sources

Chambers, M. M. "Something Could Be Added to the Self-Surveys." *North Central Association Quarterly* 33: 281-284 (April 1959).

Foegen, J. H. "With Dollars and Diplomas a College Boosts Its Community." *American School and University* 39: 45-46 (March 1967).

Le May, G. H. L. "The University in a Diverse Community." *Universities Quarterly* (England) 21: 243-253 (March 1967).

Self-financing: Trustees, Faculty, Students, Parents, Friends

Farmerie, S. A. "Characteristics and Functions of Trustees Serving Pennsylvania Liberal Arts Colleges." *Journal of Educational Research* 59: 374-376 (April 1966).

Hawes, Gene R. "Academic Philanthropy: The Art of Getting." *Saturday Review.* pp. 65-67, 77-78 (December 16, 1967).

Reavis, C. A. "Ten Positive Commandments for Trustees." *Liberal Education* 53: 223-228 (May 1967).

Reinert, Paul C. "Lay Leadership for Catholic Universities." *Phi Delta Kappan* 48: 518-519 (June 1967).

Support from Local Taxing Subdivisions

Bird, Frederick L. *The General Property Tax: Findings of the 1957 Census of Governments.* Chicago: Public Administration Service, 1960. 83 pp.

Fernbach, Frank. "The Financial Crisis of State and Local Governments." *American Federationist* 72: 7-14 (October 1965).

Netzer, Dick. *Economics of the Property Tax*. Washington: The Brookings Institution, 1966. 326 pp.

State Tax Support

Carovano, J. Martin, "Financing Public Higher Education, 1969-1970." *National Tax Journal* 19: 125-137 (June 1966).

Miller, James L., Jr. *Budgeting for Higher Education: The Use of Formulas and Cost Analysis*. Ann Arbor: University of Michigan, Institute of Public Administration, 1965. 228 pp.

Quindry, Kenneth E. *Revenue Potentials in Southern States*. Atlanta: Southern Regional Education Board, 1962. 54 pp.

Stubblebine, William Craig. "Institutional Elements in the Financing of Education." *Southern Economic Journal* 32: 15-34 (Supplement, July 1965).

Eight Years of Progress

Chambers, M. M. *Appropriations of State Tax Funds for Operating Expenses of Higher Education, 1967-68*. Washington: Office of Institutional Research, National Association of State Universities and Land-Grant Colleges, 1967. 30 pp. mimeo.

Drews, Theodore H. and Sheila Martin. *Appropriations to Higher Education in Fifty States for the Years 1956-57, 1963-64 and 1964-65*. Ann Arbor: University of Michigan Office of Institutional Research, 1965. 55 pp.

Mushkin, Selma J. and Eugene P. McLoone. *Public Spending for Higher Education in 1970*. Chicago: Council of State Governments, 1965. 68 pp. litho.

Williams, Robert L. *The Preparation of Requests for Legislative Appropriations for Operations in Midwestern State Universities*. Chicago: Council of State Governments, 1966. 41 pp.

State Revenue Systems

Ecker-Racz, L. L. "State Taxes for the 1970's." *State Government* 39: 14-19 (Winter 1966).

Maxwell, James A. *Financing State and Local Government*. Washington: The Brookings Institution, 1965. 276 pp.

National Education Association, Committee on Educational Finance. *State Taxes in 1966.* CEF Report, No. 14, April 1967. 20 pp.

Quindry, Kenneth E. *Revenue Potentials in Southern States.* Atlanta: Southern Regional Education Board, 1962. 54 pp.

"The Search for State Revenues." *NEA Research Bulletin* 44: 61-63 (May 1966).

"State Taxes in 1966." *NEA Research Bulletin* 45: 60-64 (May 1967).

U.S. Department of Commerce, Bureau of the Census. *State Tax Collections in 1966.* Series GF—No. 8. Washington, D.C.: Government Printing Office, November 1966. 40 pp.

Statewide "Coordination" in Public Higher Education

Brumbaugh, A. J. *State-wide Planning and Coordination.* Atlanta: Southern Regional Education Board, 1963. 50 pp.

Chambers, M. M. *Freedom and Repression in Higher Education.* Bloomington, Indiana: Bloomcraft Press, Inc., 1965. 126 pp. (Out of print.)

Chambers, M. M. *Voluntary Statewide Coordination in Public Higher Education.* Ann Arbor: University of Michigan, 1961. 83 pp. (Out of print.)

Conant, James B. *Shaping Educational Policy.* New York: McGraw-Hill, 1964. 139 pp.

Egner, Anton J. "How Big Can a Campus Get?" *College and University Business* 37: 57-61 (November 1964).

Glenny, Lyman A. *Autonomy of Public Colleges: The Challenge of Coordination.* New York: McGraw-Hill, 1959. 325 pp.

Illinois Board of Higher Education. *A Provisional Master Plan for Higher Education in Illinois.* Springfield: 600 State House, March 1964. 65 pp.

McConnell, T. R. *A General Pattern for American Public Higher Education.* New York: McGraw-Hill, 1962. 198 pp.

Millett, John D. "State Planning for Higher Education." *Educational Record* 46: 223-230 (Summer 1965).

ten Hoor, Martin. "The Administration of Public Higher Education in a Democracy." *Association of American Colleges Bulletin* 32: 202-215 (May 1946).

Walsh, John. "California: The Master Plan." *Science* 144: 34-35 (April 3, 1964).

Walsh, John. "Ohio Takes Plunge into State-Wide Planning." *Science* 145: 253-255, 305 (July 17, 1964).

Williams, Robert L. *Legal Bases of Coordinating Boards of Higher Education in Thirty-Nine States.* Chicago: Council of State Governments, 1967. 129 pp.

The Campus Under Statehouse Control

Chambers, M. M. *Freedom and Repression in Higher Education.* Bloomington, Indiana: Bloomcraft Press, Inc., 1965. 126 pp. (Out of print.)

Committee on Government and Higher Education. *The Efficiency of Freedom.* Baltimore: Johns Hopkins Press, 1959. 44 pp.

Melloan, George. "States and Universities: Legislative Control over College Planning Is Debated." *Wall Street Journal.* p. 8, Monday, August 10, 1964.

Moos, Malcolm and Francis E. Rourke. *The Campus and the State.* Baltimore: Johns Hopkins Press, 1959. 414 pp.

Interinstitutional and Interstate Cooperation

Anderson, Wayne W. *Cooperation Within American Higher Education.* Washington: Association of American Colleges, 1964. 74 pp.

Blocker, Clyde E. "Cooperation Between Two-Year and Four-Year Colleges." *School and Society* 94: 218-222 (April 16-30, 1966).

Brickman, William W. "Historical Background of International Cooperation Among Universities." *School and Society* 94: 227-234 (April 16-30, 1966).

Cadbury, William E., Jr. "Cooperative Relations Involving the Liberal Arts Colleges." *School and Society* 94: 213-217 (April 16-30, 1966).

Cartter, Allan M., James B. Conant, and James E. Allen, Jr. "The Compact for Education: Panacea or Pestilence?" *Educational Record* 47: 77-115 (Winter 1966).

Fraser, Stewart E. "Some Aspects of University Cooperation in International Education." *School and Society* 94: 234-244 (April 16-30, 1966).

Holy, Thomas C. "The Coordinating Council for Higher Education in California." *Journal of Higher Education* 35: 313-321 (June 1964).

Johnson, Eldon L. "College Federations." *Journal of Higher Education* 37: 1-9 (January 1966).

Johnson, Eldon L. "Consortia in Higher Education." *Educational Record* 48: 341-348 (Fall 1967).

Lunsford, Terry L. *Graduate Education and the West.* Boulder: Western Interstate Commission for Higher Education, 1963.

McGrath, Earl J. (Ed.). *Cooperative Long-Range Planning in Liberal Arts Colleges.* New York: Teachers College, Columbia University, 1964. 108 pp.

Moore, Raymond S. *A Guide to Higher Education Consortiums: 1965-66.* Washington: Government Printing Office (OE 50051), 1967. 175 pp.

Salwak, Stanley F. "The Need for Cooperation and the C.I.C. Response." *Educational Record* 45: 308-316 (Summer 1964).

Thackrey, Russell I. "National Organization in Higher Education." pp. 75-89 in *Autonomy and Interdependence: Emerging Systems in Higher Education.* Washington: American Council on Education, 1964. 89 pp.

Wells, Herman B "A Case Study in Interinstitutional Cooperation." *Educational Record* 48: 355-362 (Fall 1967).

The Federal Involvement

Arnold, Christian K. "Federal Support of Basic Research in Institutions of Higher Learning: A Critique." *Educational Record* 45: 199-203 (Spring 1964).

Babbidge, Homer D., Jr. and Robert M. Rosenzweig. *The Federal Interest in Higher Education.* New York: McGraw-Hill, 1962. 214 pp.

Chase, John L. "The Numbers Game in Graduate Education." *Journal of Higher Education* 35: 138-143 (March 1964).

Clegg, Ambrose A., Jr. "Church Groups and Federal Aid to Education, 1933-1939." *History of Education Quarterly* 4: 137-154 (September 1964).

Dobbins, Charles G. (Ed.). *Higher Education and the Federal Government: Programs and Problems.* Washington: American Council on Education, 1963. 126 pp.

Educational Policies Commission. *Educational Responsibilities of the Federal Government.* Washington: National Education Association, 1964. 40 pp.

Green, Edith (Chm., Subcommittee on Education), Committee on Education and Labor, House of Representatives, 88th Cong., 1st Sess. *The Federal Government and Education.* Washington: Government Printing Office, 1963. 176 pp.

Greenberg, D. S. "The Grant System: Flaws in Practices of Federal Agencies." *Science* 145: 795-798 (August 21, 1964).

Greenberg, D. S. "Questions and Answers with Grant Swinger." *Science* 151: 1201 (March 11, 1966).

Greenberg, Daniel S. "The Scientific Pork-Barrel." *Harper's Magazine* 232: 90-92 (January 1966).

Harrington, Fred Harvey. "The Federal Government and the Future of Higher Education." *Current Issues in Higher Education, 1963:* 22-28 (1963). Washington: Association for Higher Education. 302 pp.

Hunter, Willard. "Federal Aid: More Than Grants." *College and University Journal* 3: 3-7 (Summer 1964).

Hutchins, Robert M. "Science, Scientists, and Politics." *Journal of General Education* 16: 197-202 (October 1964).

Hutchinson, Eric. "Politics and Higher Education." *Science* 146: 1139-1142 (November 27, 1964).

Johnson, Walter and Francis J. Colligan. *The Fulbright Program: A History.* Chicago: University of Chicago Press, 1965. 380 pp.

Keeney, Barnaby C. "Proposal for a National Foundation for the Humanities." *School and Society* 93: 211-218 (April 3, 1965).

Keppel, Francis. "Education and the States." *AAUW Journal* 58: 111-113 (March 1965).

Kidd, Charles V. *American Universities and Federal Research.* Cambridge, Mass.: Harvard University Press, 1959. 272 pp.

Knight, Douglas M. (Ed.). *The Federal Government and Higher Education.* Englewood Cliffs, New Jersey: Prentice-Hall, Inc., 1960. 203 pp.

Little, J. Kenneth. *A Survey of Federal Programs in Higher Education.* U.S.O.E. Bulletin, 1963, No. 5. Washington: Government Printing Office, 1962. 56 pp.

Macy, John W., Jr. "The Scientist in the Federal Service." *Science* 148: 51-54 (April 2, 1965).

Marmaduke, Arthur S. "Can We Live with Federal Funds?" *College Board Review* 59: 7-10 (Spring 1966).

Marsh, Paul E. and Ross A. Gortner. *Federal Aid to Science Education: Two Programs.* Syracuse: Syracuse University Press, 1963. 97 pp.

McCamy, James L. *Science and Public Administration.* Tuscaloosa: University of Alabama Press, 1960. 218 pp.

Moore, Raymond S. and David W. Field. "The Higher Education Facilities Act." *The Phi Delta Kappan* 46: 277-279 (February 1965).

Morgenthau, Hans J. "Modern Science and Political Power." *Columbia Law Review* 64: 1386-1409 (December 1964).

National Science Foundation. *Federal Funds for Research, Development, and Other Scientific Activities.* Washington: Government Printing Office, 1964. 180 pp.

Orlans, Harold. *The Effects of Federal Programs on Higher Education: A Study of 36 Universities and Colleges.* Washington: The Brookings Institution, 1962. 361 pp.

Orlans, Harold. "Federal Expenditures and the Quality of Education." *Science* 142: 1626 (December 27, 1963).

Orlans, Harold. "Some Current Problems of Government Science Policy." *Science* 149: 37-40 (July 2, 1965).

Page, Howard E. "Lessons of the National Science Foundation Science Development Program." *Educational Record* 47: 50-56 (Winter 1966).

Quattlebaum, Charles A. *Federal Legislation Concerning Education and Training: Enactments of 1963 and Issues of 1964.* Washington: Government Printing Office, 1964. 156 pp.

Rivlin, Alice M. *The Role of the Federal Government in Financing Higher Education.* Washington: The Brookings Institution, 1961. 179 pp.

Rosenzweig, Robert M. "Universities and the Foreign-Assistance Program." *Journal of Higher Education* 35: 359-366 (October, 1964).

Rossi, Peter H. "Researchers, Scholars and Policy Makers: The Politics of Large Scale Research." *Daedalus* 93: 1142-1161 (Fall 1964).

Sasscer, Harrison (Ed.). *New Prospects for Achievement: Federal Programs for Colleges and Universities.* Washington: American Council on Education, 1963.

Shirley, John W. "Problems Involved in Cooperation Between Universities and Government Agencies." *School and Society* 94: 222-226 (April 1966).

Snow, C. P. *Science and Government.* The Godkin Lectures, 1961. Cambridge: Harvard University Press, 1960. 88 pp.

Snow, C. R. "Government, Science, and Public Policy." *Science* 151-153 (February 11, 1966).

Tiedt, Sidney W. *The Role of the Federal Government in Education.* New York: Oxford University Press, 1966. 265 pp.

Weiss, Paul. "Science in the University." *Daedalus* 93: 1184-1218 (Fall 1964).

Wolfle, Dael (Ed.). *Symposium on Basic Research.* Washington: American Association for the Advancement of Science, 1959. 308 pp.

Higher Education and Economic Growth

Anderson, C. Arnold and Mary Jean Bowman (Eds.). *Education and Economic Development.* Chicago: Aldine Publishing Co., 1965. 436 pp.

Becker, Gary S. *Human Capital: A Theoretical and Empirical Analysis, with Special Reference to Education.* New York: Columbia University Press, 1964. 187 pp.

Benson, Charles S. *The Cheerful Prospect.* Boston: Houghton Mifflin, 1965. 134 pp.

Bowen, William G. *Economic Aspects of Education:* "Assessing the Economic Contribution of Education," "University Finance in Britain and the U.S.," and "British University Salaries." Princeton, New Jersey: Industrial Relations Section of Princeton University, 1964. 128 pp.

Cockcroft, Sir John, A. H. Halsey, and Ingvar Svennilson. *Higher Education and the Demand of Scientific Manpower in the United States.* Paris: Organization for Economic Cooperation and Development, 1963. 102 pp. (McGraw-Hill).

Daniere, Andre. *Higher Education in the American Economy.* New York: Random House, 1964. 206 pp.

Denison, Edward F. *Sources of Economic Growth in the United States and the Alternatives Before Us.* New York: Committee on Economic Development, 1962. 297 pp.

Harbison, Frederick and Charles A. Myers. *Education, Manpower, and Economic Growth: Strategies of Human Resource Development.* New York: McGraw-Hill, 1964.

Harris, Seymour E. (Ed.). *Economic Aspects of Higher Education.* O.E.C.D. Study Group in the Economics of Education. New York: McGraw-Hill, 1964. 252 pp.

Heller, Walter W. "Education and Economic Policy." *College and University Journal* 35-39 (Summer 1962).

Henry, David D. *What Priority for Education?* Urbana: University of Illinois Press, 1961. 92 pp.

Hirsch, Werner Z. and Morton J. Marcus. "Some Benefit-Cost Considerations of Universal Junior College Education." *National Tax Journal* 19: 48-57 (March 1966).

Kraushaar, John L. "How Much of an Asset Is a College?" *College and University Business* 36: 43-45 (February 1964).

Miller, H. P. "Lifetime Income and Economic Growth." *American Economic Review* 55: 834-844 (September 1965).

Robbins, Lord Lionel. Committee Report. *Higher Education.* London: Her Majesty's Stationery Office, 1963. 335 pp.

Schultz, Theodore W. *The Economic Value of Education.* New York: Columbia University Press, 1963. 92 pp.

Wiseman, Jack. "Cost-Benefit Analysis in Education." *Southern Economic Journal* 32: 1-12 (Supplement, July 1965).

INDEX